Julia Atnipp

THE STAR OF
TEXAS
COOKBOOK

THE STAR
OF TEXAS
COOKBOOK

*The Junior League
of Houston, Inc.*

FOREWORD

This is the original STAR OF TEXAS COOKBOOK now in a striking new cover to celebrate its 10th anniversary. First published in 1983, more than 50,000 copies have been sold through The Junior League of Houston, Inc. Now this nationally-known cookbook is also available in bookstores and specialty shops.

THE STAR OF TEXAS COOKBOOK owes its success to the dedicated efforts of the Junior League of Houston members.

In addition, THE HOUSTON JUNIOR LEAGUE COOKBOOK commemorates its 25th anniversary this year, with more than 100,000 copies sold since 1968. The sale of both of these cookbooks contributes to the charitable endeavors of The Junior League of Houston, Inc.

The Junior League of Houston, Inc.   May 1992

THE JUNIOR LEAGUE OF HOUSTON, INC. IS AN ORGANIZATION OF WOMEN COMMITTED TO PROMOTING VOLUNTARISM AND TO IMPROVING THE COMMUNITY THROUGH THE EFFECTIVE ACTION AND LEADERSHIP OF TRAINED VOLUNTEERS. ITS PURPOSE IS EXCLUSIVELY EDUCATIONAL AND CHARITABLE.

Additional copies of either book may be purchased by addressing:

The Junior League of Houston, Inc.
Post Office Box 22252
Houston, Texas 77227
ATTN: Cookbooks

or

For your convenience, credit card orders are accepted:

MASTERCARD or VISA

(Specify Mastercard or Visa and include cardholder's name,
mailing address, card number, expiration date and signature.)

Credit card telephone orders accepted:
1-713-627-COOK

Cover design courtesy of Panhandle-Eastern Corporation
"Star" fabric courtesy of Schumacher
Cover photography by J. Michael Martinez, Temple Webber Photography

Illustrated by Mona Mark
DESIGN BY M FRANKLIN-PLYMPTON

Library of Congress Cataloging in Publication Data
Main entry under title:

The Star of Texas cookbook.

I. Cookery. I. The Junior League of Houston, Inc.
TX715.S7846   1983   641.5

ISBN 0-963242-1-1-3 (PREVIOUSLY ISBN 0-385-18167-1)
Library of Congress Catalog Card Number: 82-45328

Printed in the USA by
WIMMER BROTHERS
A Wimmer Company
Memphis • Dallas

A HOUSTON COOKBOOK

CHAIRMAN
Betty Walker Cochran

CO-CHAIRMAN
Rebecca Brown Rogers

RECIPE CHAIRMEN
Jan Havens Greer
Sue Harrington Price

Carol Crump Holcomb, Typist
Christian Inkley Manuel, Copy Editor
Deborah Detering Pannill, Financial Advisor
Linda Leigh Sylvan, Manuscript Copy Editor

SECTION CHAIRMEN

Jane White Braden
Donna Temple Brown
Dorothy Peek Currie
Carol Lovelady Dehan
Margaret White Guerriero
deSha Norwood Gunter

Susan Ray Mayfield
Mary Martin McGurl
Dale Porter Miller
Carol Ann Weber Paddock
Mary Hannah Smith
Shirley Cooper Wozencraft

TESTING COMMITTEE

Sue Ledbetter Bell
Wende Morehouse Bell
Karen Diehl Benner
Sidney Walsh Brown
Susan Judd Brown
Janet Carroll Cartwright
Alice Picton Craig
Jenny Adams Crain
Betty Lou Lamaster Crittenden
Elizabeth Safford Elliott
Gay Gooch Estes
Katherine Riggs Grella
Catherine Coburn Hannah
Lydia Caffery Hilliard
Sharon Miller Kempner
Mary K. Pederson Kyger
Anne Layman Martin
Sally Wall McCollum
Emily Ann Finch McKay

Sue Henderson McMurrey
Kathleen Dies Munger
Linda Lackey Murphy
Laurie Salvatori O'Connell
Beverly Means Ogilvie
Sharon Laessig Protzmann
Betsy Calhoun Reichert
Barbara Wheeler Reid
Peggy Ratcliffe Roe
Sallie Davis Schwall
Sandra Stuart Sells
Binky Peters Stephenson
Leslie Fulton Taylor
Marilyn Dubach Taylor
Ray Taggart Thomson
Ann Gordon Trammell
Catherine Houston Umstattd
Julia Picton Wallace
Renee Paris Wright

The Junior League of Houston, Inc. would like to thank
Mr. Lenoir M. Josey for contributing "A Guide to Wine Selection."

Chapter Introductions by Sandy Sheehy

CONTENTS

INTRODUCTION
Houston's Hospitable Heritage

Houston is, at the same time, the most bustling, worldly, world-class city in the Lone Star State and the most quintessentially Texan. This is where the gracious South, the expansive Great Plains, and the rugged Southwest come together. It is also where the frontier meets the Space Age.

With the fourth-largest population and the third-largest port in the country, Houston still incorporates all the ethnic influences, the pioneer energy, and the bigger-than-life legends that make Texas what it is. In fact, here in Houston, the legends are still being made, and the original national and ethnic groups that built the city in its youth are being joined by vital newcomers.

Houston began as a dream—a flamboyant real estate promotion. In August 1836, fourteen years after the Mexican government opened up the territory to American settlers, two New York speculators, John K. Allen and Augustus C. Allen, paddled a pirogue from Galveston Bay up Buffalo Bayou. They were looking for a site to build a trading center where the crops produced by the Texicans could be loaded onto paddlewheelers and shipped to Galveston and thence to New Orleans and the rest of the civilized world.

Four months earlier, Texas had won its independence from Mexico, and the ambitious Allen brothers reckoned that the location might make a good capital for the new republic. Augustus disembarked on a grassy bank and sketched a town plan, using his broad-brimmed hat for a drawing board. Within ten days, the Allens had purchased two leagues of land from the Austin family for six thousand dollars, part cash, part promissory note.

They convinced the new Republic of Texas to move the capital to their paper town, which they'd named after Sam Houston, first President of the Republic of Texas.

The Allens erected a capitol building, then leased it to the government for five thousand dollars a year. Downtown lots sold for five thousand dollars as well—almost the price of the city. By 1837, what had been a muddy, swampy, desolate plain infested with mosquitoes and alligators was a thriving community of twelve hundred. Responding to ads placed by the Allens in eastern newspapers, immigrants flocked to the area. They rode in on horseback from Tennessee, Arkansas, Missouri, and Mississippi. They came by boat from Maryland, Pennsylvania, and the Carolinas, entering through the port of Galveston fifty-five miles to the southeast on the Gulf of Mexico. And they sailed over directly from Europe—from England, Ireland, Germany, Eastern Europe, the Mediterranean countries, and Scandinavia.

Although the capital was moved to Austin in 1839 and the republic joined the United States in 1845, Houston continued to boom. Most of the Mexicans who were there before independence stayed on. Southern farmers brought their slaves, and freed Blacks came West in search of jobs. Cotton warehouses blossomed along the bayou, and paddlewheelers 170 feet long ferried to and from Galveston.

In those days, hospitality was a necessity. People had to cooperate to survive, and the very vastness of the country they sought to tame drew them closer together. Newcomers camped out in churches and in City Hall; Houstonians opened their doors to strangers who stopped in the bustling little city to buy seed and farm implements before continuing inland. Quilting bees and barn raisings, hunting parties and church socials were high points of frontier existence. The music, the gossip, the politicking, and especially the lavish food and drink made the settlers and their guests temporarily forget the hardships of their existence.

Today, almost a century and a half later, the traditions of a state that was once an independent republic and the optimism of a city that started as a speculative dream underlie the Space Center, the oil refineries, the busy freeways, and the futuristic office towers. It's as if the frontier is still with us but in economic, scientific, and social form. People like oil wildcatter Glen McCarthy, astronaut Dr. Anna Fischer, and heart surgeon Dr. Denton Cooley are as much frontiersmen in their own ways as Sam Houston and Stephen F. Austin were in theirs.

Nothing reflects this rich and ongoing heritage better than our food, both the food of the modern, cosmopolitan city and the food brought by the early settlers—beef barbecue, venison chili, Cajun gumbo, Mexican enchiladas, spicy pinto beans, and jalapeño cornbread. It's food meant to be savored and meant to be shared. Join us. And enjoy.

CHAPTER I

MENUS
Ethnic Celebrations

Over the decades, most of the ethnic groups who make up Houston have become assimilated into the whole, establishing businesses, enrolling their children in school, and learning to speak English. But they've generally held onto their food, their religion, their music, and their ways of marking holidays, weddings, and other major events.

Houston is a place of great culinary diversity. Restaurants specializing in elegant French or hearty Southern cooking stand chockablock with those featuring Cuban, Thai, Ethiopian, and Moroccan cuisine. Fundraisers held by churches, synagogues, and student groups give those with adventurous palates opportunities to sample exotic dishes and admire traditional dances and costumes.

In January or February, Houston's Chinese celebrate the Lunar New Year by first paying off all their debts and then holding an elaborate street parade, complete with paper dragons and fireworks. In March, the city is awash in green beer and conviviality in honor of Ireland's St. Patrick. On April 21, everyone—but especially the descendants of the original settlers—relives the decisive victory of Sam Houston over the Mexican forces under Santa Anna at the Battle of San Jacinto.

For Cinco de Mayo (May 5), Houston's Mexican community dons *vaquero* gear and holds a mass fiesta to commemorate the Battle of Puebla, in which Mexico defeated Napoleonic forces in 1862. Local Blacks celebrate Juneteenth (June 19–Emancipation Day) with a jazz festival lasting several days and drawing musicians from all over the country. July brings the Cajun Crawfish Festival in nearby Port Arthur. And October is one long multinational feast: the German Wurstfest, the Czech Festival in neighboring Fort Bend County, the Italian Festival, the Greek Festival and the International Food Fair sponsored by the foreign students at the University of Houston.

For those who can still stand the thought of food after November's hunting parties and the Anglo-American excesses of Thanksgiving, there are the tempting cakes and cookies sold at church and charity bazaars around Christmas.

Several of Houston's ethnic groups have their own ways of celebrating common holidays. The Mexican Christmas season lasts almost a month, beginning December 16 with Posadas—candlelight processions reenacting the

search for the inn—and ending January 6 with the Fiesta de los Tres Reyes
—the Feast of the Three Kings. These solemn religious pageants are followed by parties at which everyone drinks cinnamon-flavored chocolate
and blindfolded children take turns swinging at papier-mâché *piñatas*
stuffed with candy and toys. For the Greeks, Easter is the most important
holiday. After a midnight procession and services at the Greek Orthodox
Church, they sit down to a sumptuous breakfast to celebrate the end of
Lent. The lavish spread includes *tsoureki*—a sweet bread topped with eggs
dyed red to symbolize the blood of Christ.

Many of the descendants of Houston's original Anglo, Irish, and German
settlers celebrate Christmas, the Fourth of July, and other major holidays
on their ranches, inviting their city-bound friends to camp out in the
bunkhouse or spread sleeping bags on the floor. These parties usually last
for days and feature whole barbecued steers, hearty predawn hunt breakfasts, and eye-watering chili concocted from whatever game was bagged
that week, seasoned with plenty of peppers and liberal doses of tequila.

Elements of Houston's diverse cuisine show up in less ambitious enter-
taining as well. Houston hosts and hostesses are quick to press chefs, bar-
tenders, and friends for recipes, then add their own touches and bring them
out for everything from chili cookoffs to lawn parties to elegant little after-
the-symphony suppers. The bills of fare at these parties are as eclectic as
the city itself, and the menus that follow accurately reflect Houston's culinary complexity. The Miller Theatre Gourmet Picnic is as authentically
Houstonian as Tex-Mex Tradition or Under the Gun, the Azalea Spring
Brunch as local as the Southern Comfort Dinner. To make these feasts
truly Houstonian, serve them with an outgoing attitude and the conviction
that any occasion that brings good friends—old and new—together is an occasion well worth celebrating.

A GUIDE TO WINE SELECTION

"What wine should I drink with . . . ?" is probably the most frequently asked wine question. The answer is simple: drink what *you* like with the dish in question. If you prefer red wine with fish or white wine with red meat, then that is the "right wine" for you. In our do-your-own-thing society, doing your own thing certainly extends to choosing wines—wines you, and hopefully those with you, enjoy the most. The days of the wine steward or knowledgeable wine guest raising his or her eyebrows at your selection may not be totally past, but such behavior is definitely out of style. If you or your guests dislike your choice, you can always open another bottle, try again, and write off the first attempt as an interesting experiment and a good excuse to try a second bottle!

Keeping in mind the above, the following chart can be used as a general guide. It should help a novice begin to determine what he or she prefers while it may provide a knowledgeable wine lover some "food" for thought. But no one should ever lose sight of the major objective—to have fun!

FOOD	SUGGESTED WINE
Caviar	Champagne
Oysters and Clams	Dry French white such as Muscadet, Chablis, Graves, or dry California such as Sauvignon or Fumé Blanc
Hors d'Oeuvre	Champagne, dry white, dry sherry, Sercial Madeira
Soups:	Soups are difficult to match with wine;
Consommé type	Possibly dry or medium sweet sherry or Sercial Madeira
Cream type	Possibly white wine
Heavy vegetable or meat type	Possibly red wine
Fish and Shellfish:	
Meunière, poached or grilled	Light dry white such as French Macon or Saint Véran, semi-dry French such as Vouvray, Italian Soave, or any good French or California white

With sauces	Fuller French dry white such as Meursault, Montrachet region or California Chardonnay
Chicken, Turkey, and Other Domestic Fowl	Preferably light red such as California Cabernet Sauvignon or French Bordeaux or even Burgundy; also full white wines as with shellfish and sauce above
Ham and Pork	Medium-dry white such as Gewürztraminer, Vouvray, Chenin Blanc, rosé, or a red as with turkey and chicken above
Veal	Red Bordeaux or California Cabernet Sauvignon
Lamb	Fine California Cabernet Sauvignon or red Bordeaux
Beef	Full-bodied red Bordeaux (especially Pomerol or Saint-Emilion), red Burgundy, or a full-bodied California Cabernet or Italian red
Game	The most full-bodied red wines such as Italian Barolo, French Burgundy or Rhône, or a full-bodied California Zinfandel
Stews	Côtes-du-Rhône, Beaujolais, lesser California Cabernet, Zinfandel, or Gamay
Mexican Food	Beer, margaritas, or an inexpensive wine
Italian Food	Italian wines or California Italian-style wines such as Barbera
Cheese	Red wine with just enough body to match the type of cheese

Dessert   California and German late harvest
                        wines, French Sauternes, sweet Loire
                        wines, or Champagne sweeter than Brut

After Dinner   Madeira (especially Boal or Malmsey),
                        port, sweet sherry, or dessert wines as
                        above

SERVING NOTE ON WINE TEMPERATURE: Champagne should be served iced
(50° F. or below), white and rosé wine served well chilled (50°–55° F.),
the finest dessert wines and Beaujolais served chilled (60° F.) and red wines
served at room temperature (65°–70° F.). The colder the wine the less
bouquet and flavor it will show. Hence, the warmer the wine the "bigger"
it will seem, but its imperfections will also be "bigger" and more obvious.
Thus, generally speaking, the better the wine the warmer it can and should
be served; however, it should not be served warmer than the limits stated
above.

MENUS

The recipe for each item marked with an asterisk in
the menus that follow can be found by consulting the Index.

MEXICAN MENUS

El Rancho Grande Barbecue
*Santa Rosa Pie
*Lolita's Fajitas or *Barbecued Ca-
    brito
*Divine Chili Relleno Casserole or
    *Tomatoes a Queso
*Mexican Red Beans
  Green Salad
*Cissy's Cinnamon Ice Cream
*Margaritas or Beer

Tex-Mex Tradition
*Blender Picante with Tostados
*Guacamole
*Cheese Enchiladas
*Chalupas
*Spanish Rice
*Mexican Red Beans
*Flan
*Book Club Sangria or Beer

Teenage Amigos

*Chili con Queso with Tostados
*Mother's Chili con Carne
*Arlene's Green Turkey Burritos
    or *Chalupas
*Guacamole
*Fritole
*Best Ever Pralines

Celebrácion

Avocado Soup
*Red Snapper Veracruz
*Green Rice
Marinated Asparagus or Green
    Salad
*Cold Kahlua Soufflé with *Choco-
    late Sauce
*Las Vegas Piña Colada

Fiesta

*Shrimp and Scallop Ceviche
*Chicken Breasts with Chilies or
    *Chicken Portuguese
*Spanish Rice
*Molded Gazpacho
*Lemon Pecan Slices
*Margaritas

Under the Gun
(An Easy Supper)

*Bay City Jalapeño Pie
*Jackie's Tortilla Soup
Green Salad or Sliced Tomato
    with *Guacamole
Sherbet

Mexican Border Barbecue Feast

*Mexican Meatballs
*Cream Cheese Layered with
    Shrimp and Guacamole
*Shrimp and Scallop Ceviche
Tostados
*Barbecued Cabrito
*Lolita's Fajitas
Venison Sausage or Smoked Link
    Sausage
*Green Rice
*Tomatoes a Queso
Green Salad or Molded Avocado
    Salad
Flour Tortillas
*Blender Picante
*Cold Kahlua Soufflé with *Choco-
    late Sauce
*Boo's Puerto Rican Flan

South-of-the-Border Luncheon

*Gazpacho
*Enchiladas Verdes or *Longneck
    Jalapeño Quiche
Green Salad
Tostados
*Summerhouse Fantastic Fudge
    Pudding

BARBECUES AND PICNICS

Saturday Night Special
*Texas Crabgrass
*Texas Sirloin and One-Shot Steak
  Sauce
*Jalapeño Potatoes
  Green Salad with *Sweet and
  Sour Dressing
*Mother's Sally Lunn Bread
*Peppermint Ice Cream

Elegant Dinner
*Hot Crabmeat Appetizer
*Barbecue Butterfly Lamb
*Fresh Mint Jelly
*Wild Rice en Consommé
*Escalloped Celery
*Spinach-Mushroom Salad
*Pears in Chocolate Sabayon

Galveston Bay Sailing Picnic
*Smoked Salmon Mousse
*Four Seasons' Watercress Vichyssoise
*Cold Pasta and Chicken Salad
*Dilled Carrots
*Lemon Pecan Slices

Seafood Barbecue
*Curried Chicken Canapés or
  *Holland Rusk Appetizer
*Whole Grilled Fish
*Cauliflower with Avocado Sauce
  or *Tomatoes and Artichokes
  au Gratin
  Green Salad
*Sour Cream Lemon Pie

Miller Theatre Gourmet Picnic
*Smoked Salmon-Stuffed Eggs
*Cold Carrot Soup with Basil
*Marinated Beef
*Oriental Drumsticks
*Piquant Pea Salad or *Green Vegetable Salad
*Pecan Tarts

Trail Ride Picnic
  Raw Vegetables with *Dill Dip
*Gazpacho
*Jalapeño Fried Chicken
*Rice and Artichoke Salad
*Fudge Cake

BRUNCHES AND LUNCHEONS

Azalea Spring Brunch
*Cold Tomato Soup with *Parmesan Rounds
*Salmon and Fresh Mushroom Quiche
*Green Greek Salad
*Peach Sherbet or *Lotus Ice Cream
*Super Crunch Cookies

Buffalo Bayou Brunch
*Shrimp and Scallop Ceviche or *Cold Crab Soup
*Spinach Quiche Kinkaid
Romaine and Mushroom Salad
Fresh Berries with *Dancy's Grand Marnier Sauce

Super Bowl Luncheon
*Cuban Black Bean Soup
Green Salad with *Cream Bordelaise Salad Dressing
*Savory Cheese Loaf
*Apple Crumb Pie

Fall Football Luncheon
*Duck Stew
Green Salad with Oil and Vinegar Dressing
*Muenster Bread
*Cranberry Ice Cream

Live Oak Luncheon
(On the Patio)
*Fluff's Chutney Chicken Salad
Cold Marinated Broccoli
*Lemon Muffins
*Amaretto Mousse

Lone Star Luncheon
(A Formal Affair)
*Artichoke Heart Mousse with Curried Mayonnaise
*Filled Soufflé Roll with *Salmon/Dill Filling
Avocado and Grapefruit Salad
Fresh Strawberries with Raspberry Sauce

Luncheon on the Terrace
*Bloody Mary Mix
*Fresh Mushroom Bisque
*Cobb Salad or *Paella Salad
*Herb Bread
*Chocolate Angel Food Cake

DINNERS AND SUPPERS

Joint Venture Dinner
(A Kitchen Party)
*Fried Cheese Squares with To-
    mato Sauce or *Artichoke Frit-
    ters
*Szechwan Shrimp Appetizer
*Vegetable Pasta Supper
*Wilted Spinach Salad
*Macaroon Dessert

Space City Gourmet
(A Quick and Easy Elegant
Dinner)
*Baked Brie
*Shrimp Stroganoff or *Venison
    Sauté with Sauce Quest
 Steamed Rice
*Snowpeas and Mushrooms
*Chef Waldo's Popovers
*Easy Chocolate Pie

After the Alley Theatre Buffet
*Stuffed Mushrooms
*Eggs à la Abney
*Foies de Volailles aux Champign-
    ons Frais
 Toasted English Muffins
 Green Salad
*Velvet Mint

Blue Norther Special
(A Dinner from the Freezer)
*Cheese Pockets or *Spanakopetes
*Chicken in a Packet
*Zucchini Casserole
*Frozen Brandy Alexander Pie

Lone Star Legacy
(A Formal Dinner)
*Oyster and Artichoke Soup
*McVea's Oven-Roasting Method
    for Beef Tenderloin or Stand-
    ing Rib Roast
*Rice Pilaf or *Mushroom Strudel
 Peas
*Caesar Salad
*Bavarian Crème

Big Thicket Dinner
*Salmon-Cucumber Mousse
 Flank Steak with *Helms Mari-
    nade
*Stuffed Zucchini
 Escalloped Potatoes
 Green Salad with *Tarragon
    Roquefort Dressing
*Peaches and Cream Dessert Soup

Symphony Supper
*Artichoke Fritters
*Veal Vermouth
*Cold Stuffed Zucchini
*Frozen Caramel Soufflé or
    *Brandy Freeze

A Do-Ahead Dinner
*Marinated Shrimp
*Burgundy Brisket
*Corn Casserole
*Tomatoes, Deviled and Broiled
*Seven Layer Salad
*Texas Gold Bars

International Dinner
*Crab Cream Cheese Dip
*Brazilian Chicken
*Carrots in a Ring with Peas
*Green Greek Salad
*Easy Dinner Rolls
*Raspberry Cheese Pie

Boomtown Bonanza
*Bull's-Eye
*Oyster Curry
 Steamed Rice
 Green Vegetable
*Spinach Salad with Chutney
 Dressing
*Coconut Pound Cake with Ice
 Cream

Birthday Dinner
*Crab Appetizers
*Stuffed Pork Roast
*Rice Ring filled with Mushrooms
*Cranberry Conserve
 Bibb Lettuce with *Cream Salad
 Dressing
*Almond Macaroon Cake with Ice
 Cream

After Jones Hall Supper
*Caviar Cake
*Mushroom-Stuffed Eggs with
 Mornay Sauce
*Marinated Tomatoes or Asparagus
*Semester Muffins
*Cappuccino or *Easy Coffee
 Mousse

Southern Comfort Dinner
*Shrimp Rémoulade Mold
*New Year's Ham
*Apple and Pear Chutney
*Cheese Grits or *Lana's Yams or
 *Stuffed Acorn Squash
 Spinach or *Greens
*Riz Biscuits
*Texas Pecan Balls

Seafood Dinner
*Escargot Provençale
*Fish Fillets with Basil Sauce
*Carrots and Zucchini
*Rich and Charlie's Salad
*Easy Dinner Rolls
*Eileen's Buttermilk-Coconut
 Cream Pie

Out of This World Dinner
*Oriental Crab
*Veal Casserole
 Wild Rice
*Herbed Green Beans
*Angel Pie

GAME DINNERS

Heritage Game Dinner

*Wild Game Pâté
*Doves Chasseur or *Pheasant à la Crème
*Wild Rice en Consommé
*Nutcracker Avocado-Grapefruit Salad
*Frosty Green Grapes

The Hunter's Grilled Game Dinner

*Curried Chutney Spread
*Grilled Duck Breasts or *Mexican Mallards
 Angel Hair Pasta with Garlic Butter
*Orange-Almond Salad
*Chocolate Intemperance or *Cranberry Ice Cream

Celebration Dinner

*Mushrooms Paprika
*Quail in Orange Sauce
*Rice Oriental
 Green Vegetable
*Wilted Spinach Salad
*Chocolate Mousse Cake

Company Game Dinner

*Cricket's Marinated Shrimp
*Wild Duck Breasts with Green Peppercorn Sauce
 Wild Rice
*Carrots Parmesan
*Spinach Salad with Chutney Dressing
*L'Orange de Menthe

Game Barbecue

*Venison Chili con Queso
*Antichukas
*Charcoal Dove
*Green Rice or *Skillet Rice Dressing
*Molded Gazpacho with *Guacamole
*Frozen Caramel Soufflé or *English Toffee Ice Cream

Quail Game Dinner

*Clam-Stuffed Mushrooms
*Grilled Quail with Tarragon
*Robert's Avocado Pilaf
*Molded Fresh Cranberry Salad
*Praline Cheesecake

BAY-BEACH WEEKEND

Seawall Supper
*Curried Chutney Spread or
  *Stuffed Mushrooms
*Scampi alla Guiglio or *Sally's
  Shrimp
 Tossed Green Salad
 French Bread
*Fresh Blueberry Pie

Beach Eye-Opener
*Orange Julius Delight
*Crustless Quiche Lorraine
 Sliced Fresh Fruit
*Morning Meeting Roll or *Ber-
  nice's Cinnamon Rolls

Picnic on the Pier
*Cold Stuffed Zucchini
*Mother's Bayhouse Crab Salad
  (Red Bluff)
*Parmesan Rounds or Bread Sticks
*Clyde Tea
*Lemon Drop Cookies

Bay Area Buffet
*Brother's Rum Lovely
*Crunchy Sour Cream Spread
*Butterfly Leg of Lamb
*Fresh Mint Jelly
 Brown Rice or *Green Beans Su-
  preme
*Caesar Salad
*Cheesecake Father Sarducci

Laffite's Retreat
(A Sunday Brunch)
 Brandy Milk Punch
*Eggs Parmesan
 Canadian Bacon
 Toasted English Muffins
*Spiced Orange Jelly

HILL COUNTRY WEEKEND

Family Reunion Dinner

*Salmon Cheese Ball
*Vicksburg Stuffed Ham
*Apple and Pear Chutney
 Steamed Asparagus
*Seven Layer Salad
*Rene's Chess Pie

Country Breakfast

*Buffet Cheese Dish
 Venison Sausage
*Apple Goody or *Cowboy Coffee
 Cake

River Luncheon

*Zucchini Soup or *Cauliflower
 Soup
*Beef Vinaigrette
 Sliced Tomatoes

Good Friends Barbecue Dinner

*Barbecue Beef Ribs or Brisket in
 *Mop Sauce
*Bacon and Corn Spoonbread
*Overnight Salad or *Nine-Day
 Slaw
*No-Cook Pickles
*Country-Crust Bread
*Peppermint Ice Cream

Goodbye Brunch

*Bloody Mary Mix
*Country-Style Eggs
 Fried Tomato Slices or Broiled
 Tomatoes
*Country-Crust Bread, toasted
*Microwave Strawberry Jam

CHAPTER II

APPETIZERS
The Heights and the West End

Houston's altitude is about fifty feet above sea level—lower along the bayou. And the thick, grayish gumbo soil is slow to absorb water after a hard rain. During wet weather, Houstonians have often wondered whether they lived on a plain or in a swamp, and the lush conditions so good for livestock are also ideal for mosquitoes.

When floods and yellow fever epidemics hit, as they did all too frequently, early settlers retreated to the land north of Buffalo Bayou, a section they called the Heights. It was only twenty-five feet higher than the rest of town, but that was enough. As the city expanded, this pleasant wooded area three miles northwest of Allen's Landing began to look like a promising place to live. In 1892, the Nebraska-based Omaha and South Texas Land Company began developing the Heights, selling homesites to longtime Houstonians and newcomers alike. Today, modest late Victorian cottages and two-story gingerbread houses with cupolas line wide streets shaded by live oaks. The Heights still looks and feels like a small town, even though it's surrounded by a big city.

The Heights Civic Association works to maintain the neighborhood's charm and character, giving it cohesion and erecting gingerbread bus shelters to go with the architecture. Over on Washington Avenue, a cultural renaissance is taking place. The old Heights State Bank has become a jazz club. Piano bars, good little restaurants, and trendy art galleries stand next to thrift stores and pawn shops where you can still find some good antiques among the junk. Rather than tear things down and build anew, most developers are recycling the old buildings, restoring the pressed-tin ceilings and hardwood floors.

The Heights and the area immediately next to it, called the West End, were the first stop for many of the foreign immigrants who flocked to Houston during the late nineteenth and early twentieth centuries. Today the area is still the first place many immigrants stop. Mexicans, Germans, Poles, Blacks, and Vietnamese rub shoulders with young people who've just moved down from Michigan and are buying up the cottages as "handyman's specials." Salvadorans, Laotians, and Nigerians all seem to have a place there, and the neighborhood is proud of its polyglot personality. It's like a good selection of hors d'oeuvre—a sampling of flavors, a little of everything. Part of the fun is the variety.

The appetizer recipes that follow are like that—a cultural jumble. They work well alone or in hodgepodge. Some—like Texas Crabgrass, Bull's-Eye, and Green-Chili Pie—have western overtones. Others—like Escargots Provençale, Fettucini Roberto, Szechwan Shrimp, Curried Chicken Canapés, Spanakopetes, and Swiss Fondue—are as varied as the people who live in the Heights and the West End.

ANTIPASTO

2 heads cauliflower, separated
   into florets
3 green peppers, cut in strips
2 bags carrots, cut in strips
1 pound button mushrooms
1 bunch broccoli, florets only
1 ½ cups salad or olive oil

3 cups tarragon vinegar
½ to ¾ cup sugar
3 cloves garlic, minced
1 tablespoon prepared mustard
1 tablespoon salt
2 teaspoons tarragon leaves
Pepper to taste

Mix all ingredients. Chill at least 12 hours, turning frequently. Drain well before serving.

Serves 25

ARTICHOKE FRITTERS

2 cans (8 ½ ounces each)
   artichoke hearts
1 egg
½ cup milk
½ cup Bisquick mix
¼ cup flour
1 ½ teaspoons double-acting
   baking powder

1 teaspoon salt
½ teaspoon garlic powder
¼ cup finely chopped onion
1 tablespoon chopped parsley
Oil for frying

Drain artichokes, cut into quarters, and set aside. Combine egg and milk. Stir in dry ingredients, onion, and parsley. Dip artichokes in batter. Fry in at least 2 inches of oil at 350 degrees F. for 6 to 8 minutes each. Drain on paper towels. Sprinkle with extra salt and serve.

Yield: 32 fritters

ARTICHOKE HEART MOUSSE
WITH CURRIED MAYONNAISE

1 envelope unflavored gelatin
3 tablespoons cold water
2 cans (8½ ounces each)
 artichoke hearts
Juice of ½ lemon

1½ cups mayonnaise
1 cup sour cream
½ teaspoon salt
½ teaspoon white pepper
1 teaspoon curry powder

In a small bowl, sprinkle gelatin over water and let soften. Stir over simmering water until dissolved. Cool. Drain artichoke hearts and chop. Sprinkle lemon juice over them. Combine artichokes, gelatin, ½ cup of the mayonnaise, sour cream, salt, and pepper in a food processor. Mix well. Pour into a lightly oiled 1-quart mold. Chill for at least 6 hours. Unmold and serve with curried mayonnaise made from 1 teaspoon curry powder blended into 1 cup mayonnaise.

Yield: 1 quart

ARTICHOKE SQUARES

2 jars (6 ounces each) marinated
 artichokes
1 small onion, chopped
1 small clove garlic, chopped
2 tablespoons butter
4 eggs

¼ cup bread crumbs
Dash of Tabasco
¼ teaspoon oregano
Salt and pepper to taste
2 cups shredded Cheddar or
 Parmesan cheese

Preheat oven to 325 degrees F. Drain juice from 1 of the jars of artichokes into a skillet. Discard the juice from the second jar. Chop artichokes and set aside. Sauté onion and garlic in butter in skillet until tender. Beat eggs. Add bread crumbs, seasonings, onion mixture, and cheese. Stir in artichokes and mix well. Bake in an ungreased 8-inch square pan for 30 minutes. Cut into squares and serve hot.

Yield: 36 squares

AVOCADO SPREAD

1 package (8 ounces) cream
  cheese, softened
1 package Good Seasons Italian
  salad dressing
1 tablespoon mayonnaise

Juice of ½ lemon
1 avocado, chopped
1 tomato, chopped
Dash of Tabasco

Mix all ingredients. Refrigerate until ready to use. Serve with crackers.

Yield: Approximately 2 cups

BAKED BRIE

This is also delicious for dessert, served with fruit.

1 small Brie cheese (8 ounces)
1 cup slivered almonds

Preheat oven to 350 degrees F. Place cheese in an ovenproof serving dish. Sprinkle almonds over top and sides. Push slightly into cheese and bake for 20 to 25 minutes or until cheese is soft and almonds browned. Serve with crackers.

Serves 4

BLACK CAVIAR APPETIZER

1 package (8 ounces) cream
  cheese, softened
1 tablespoon grated onion
1 tablespoon Worcestershire
  sauce

2 drops Tabasco
2 tablespoons mayonnaise
1 tablespoon lemon juice
1 jar (4 ounces) black caviar

Combine all ingredients except caviar. Blend thoroughly and form into a mound on serving plate. Spread with caviar. Serve with melba toast rounds.

Serves 6 to 8

BULL'S-EYE

This is an especially pretty appetizer. It looks like a red, yellow, black, and white target!

2 packages (8 ounces each)
  cream cheese
½ cup sour cream
Juice of 1 lemon
1 jar (2 ounces) red caviar
2 egg yolks, hard-cooked and
  crumbled

1 jar (4 ounces) black caviar,
  drained
1 bunch green onions, white
  parts only, finely chopped

Blend cream cheese, sour cream, and lemon juice until smooth. Spread over bottom of flat round dish. Spread red caviar in small solid circle on center of cream cheese. This forms the "bull's-eye" of the "target." Sprinkle egg yolks in a circle around caviar. Continue forming concentric circles with black caviar and then onions. Chill, and serve with crackers.

Serves 12

CAVIAR CAKE

6 hard-cooked eggs, chopped
3 tablespoons mayonnaise
½ onion, minced
1 package (8 ounces) cream
  cheese
⅔ cup sour cream

1 jar (4 ounces) Romanoff
  Icelandic lumpfish caviar,
  drained
Lemon wedge
Parsley for garnish

Combine chopped eggs and mayonnaise and press into small springform pan. Chill. Spread onion over egg layer. Blend cream cheese and sour cream until smooth. Spread over onion layer. Chill at least 6 hours or overnight if possible. Unmold. Spread caviar over top. Squeeze lemon wedge over caviar. Surround with parsley and serve with crackers or melba toast.

Serves 10 to 12

CHEESE POCKETS

2 packages (8 ounces each)
   cream cheese
5 eggs, beaten

8 ounces Parmesan cheese
1 pound phyllo pastry
2 cups butter, melted

Preheat oven to 375 degrees F. Mix together cream cheese, eggs, and Parmesan cheese. Place sheet of phyllo on work surface and brush with butter. Lay another sheet on top and brush with butter. Repeat so that there are 4 sheets. Cut into 3-inch squares. Put 1 teaspoon filling on pastry square. Fold into a pocket and seal the edges with melted butter. Repeat the process with remaining phyllo. Bake for 15 minutes and serve. These freeze well. Brush with melted butter before freezing. Bake frozen for 20 to 25 minutes or until golden.

Yield: 100 to 120

CURRIED CHICKEN CANAPÉS

1 cup minced cooked chicken
1 cup mayonnaise
¾ cup grated Monterey Jack
   cheese
¼ cup chopped parsley
⅓ cup finely minced almonds
4 green onions, finely chopped
2 teaspoons fresh lemon juice

1½ teaspoons curry powder or
   to taste
Dash of Tabasco
Salt and freshly ground pepper
   to taste
60 to 72 thinly sliced bread
   rounds (about 1½ inches in
   diameter)

Preheat oven to 500 degrees F. Combine all ingredients except bread rounds and blend well. Refrigerate until ready to use. Spread 1 teaspoon chicken mixture on each round. Bake on a cookie sheet for 5 to 8 minutes or until lightly browned and sizzling. This also is good with crab or shrimp.

Yield: 5 to 6 dozen

CURRIED CHICKEN TRIANGLES

¼ cup minced onions
¼ cup minced fresh mushrooms
1½ cups unsalted butter
2 cups finely minced cooked
   chicken
½ cup chopped pecans
2 tablespoons chopped parsley
1 tablespoon crumbled dried
   tarragon

½ teaspoon salt
½ teaspoon white pepper
1 teaspoon curry powder
1 cup thick Béchamel sauce
Cream
1 box phyllo pastry, defrosted
   according to directions

Preheat oven to 375 degrees F. Sauté onions and mushrooms in 2 tablespoons of the butter until moisture has evaporated. In a large bowl, combine remaining ingredients except phyllo and butter. Add onions and mushrooms and mix thoroughly. If filling seems too dry, add some cream. Melt remaining butter. Unwrap phyllo dough and work quickly. Cut 8 dough leaves lengthwise into 6 strips (2½ × 18 inches). Cover strips with a damp towel and work with one at a time. Brush first strip with melted butter. Place a spoonful of filling at one end. Fold corner over to form a triangle. Continue folding into triangles as you would fold a flag. When strip is folded, brush lightly with melted butter to seal the ends. Place on a cookie sheet and brush with melted butter. Repeat with remaining strips. Bake for 20 minutes or until golden brown. These can be frozen before baking. Brush with melted butter before freezing. Remove from freezer and bake for about 30 minutes or until done. This can also be made into one large strudel and served as a luncheon entree.

Yield: 48 Triangles

CRAB APPETIZERS

8 ounces fresh lump crab meat,
   drained and picked
½ cup mayonnaise

2 tablespoons tiny capers
1 tablespoon lemon juice
2 tablespoons melted butter

Preheat oven to 350 degrees F. Toss crab meat lightly with mayonnaise, capers, and lemon juice. Spoon into individual baking shells or ramekins. Brush with melted butter. Bake for 10 minutes. Place under broiler for 2 to 3 minutes until browned on top.

Serves 6 to 8

CRAB CREAM CHEESE DIP

1 pound fresh lump crab meat
1 tablespoon lemon juice
1 package (8 ounces) cream
  cheese

1 cup sour cream
½ cup mayonnaise
1 bottle (12 ounces) chili sauce
2 teaspoons Worcestershire

Pick shell from crab; wash and drain well. Toss gently with lemon juice. Soften cream cheese and add sour cream and mayonnaise. Combine chili sauce and Worcestershire. Place cream-cheese mixture in a serving dish. Top with crab meat. Pour chili sauce over all. Chill. Serve with crackers.

Serves 8 to 10

HOT CRAB MEAT APPETIZER

1 package (8 ounces) cream
  cheese, softened
6 to 8 ounces fresh crab meat,
  drained and picked
2 tablespoons minced green
  onions

1 tablespoon milk
1½ tablespoons creamy
  horseradish
¼ teaspoon salt
Dash of pepper
½ cup sliced almonds, toasted

Preheat oven to 275 degrees F. Combine all ingredients except almonds. Blend well. Spread in ovenproof dish and top with almonds. Bake until hot. Serve with Triscuits.

Serves 6

ORIENTAL CRAB

1 can (8 ounces) sliced water
  chestnuts, drained
½ cup mayonnaise
2 whole green onions, sliced
2 tablespoons soy sauce

1 pound lump crab meat, drained
  and picked
Fresh chopped parsley for
  garnish

Combine water chestnuts, mayonnaise, onions, and soy sauce in advance.

Store in refrigerator. Just before serving, gently toss in crab. Sprinkle chopped parsley on top. Serve with crackers.

Serves 8

TEXAS CRABGRASS

1 package frozen chopped
  spinach
1 medium onion, finely chopped
½ cup butter
8 ounces fresh or frozen cooked
  crab meat, flaked

¾ cup freshly grated Parmesan
  cheese
¼ cup dry sherry or sauterne

Cook and drain spinach. Sauté onion in butter. Add remaining ingredients and heat thoroughly. Serve in a chafing dish with crackers.

Serves 10

CURRIED CHUTNEY SPREAD

2 packages (8 ounces each)
  cream cheese
½ cup Major Grey's chutney

½ cup chopped almonds, toasted
1 teaspoon curry powder
½ teaspoon dry mustard

Bring cream cheese to room temperature. Mix all ingredients until well blended. Pack in crock and chill. Serve with crackers or use to stuff dates or celery.

Yield: Approximately 3 cups

DILLED CARROTS

3 pounds carrots
¾ cup finely grated onion
4 tablespoons chopped parsley
1½ cups Italian dressing

1½ teaspoons pepper
3 tablespoons dillweed
¾ teaspoon salt

Cut carrots into strips and refrigerate in cold water. Twenty-four hours before serving, combine remaining ingredients and add carrots. Refrigerate, stirring three times or more. Drain to serve.

Serves 20

CRUNCHY SOUR CREAM SPREAD

1 cup sour cream
¼ cup finely chopped bell
   pepper
¼ cup finely chopped celery
2 tablespoons chopped onion
2 tablespoons chopped
   pimiento-stuffed green olives
1 teaspoon lemon juice

½ teaspoon Worcestershire
   sauce
Paprika
Salt and pepper to taste
2 to 3 drops Tabasco
12 Cheese Ritz crackers,
   crumbled

Combine all ingredients except crackers. Line a small mold or bowl with plastic wrap. Spread ⅓ of sour cream mixture into bowl. Sprinkle with ⅓ of crackers. Repeat layers. Top with remaining sour cream mixture and refrigerate overnight. Turn out onto serving plate. Remove plastic wrap and top with remaining cracker crumbs. Serve with Ritz crackers.

Serves 4 to 6

DILL DIP

2 cups mayonnaise
2 cups sour cream
3 tablespoons minced dried onion
2 tablespoons parsley flakes

3 teaspoons dillweed
3 teaspoons Beau Monde
   seasoning

Combine all ingredients. Refrigerate overnight. Best served with fresh raw vegetables.

Yield: 4 cups

ESCARGOTS PROVENÇALE

24 large snails
½ cup white wine
4 tomatoes, cut in wedges, or 1
   can (15 ounces), drained
8 tablespoons butter

1 cup minced onions
4 teaspoons minced garlic
4 slices (1 inch thick) French
   bread, toasted

Cook snails in wine over medium heat for 10 minutes; drain. While snails are cooking, sauté tomatoes in 6 tablespoons of the butter for 10 minutes. Add half of the onions and 3 teaspoons of the garlic to tomatoes and simmer for 3 minutes more. Add the remaining 2 tablespoons butter to skillet containing snails. Sauté snails for 3 minutes. Add remaining onion and garlic and cook for 1 minute more. Place toasted bread on four warmed plates. Spoon half the tomato sauce evenly over bread, place 6 snails on each slice, and cover with remaining sauce. Serve immediately.

Serves 4

FETTUCINI ROBERTO

1 tablespoon oil
5 tablespoons butter
8 ounces fresh mushrooms, sliced
1 cup julienne strips ham
1 cup cooked fresh or frozen
   green peas
8 ounces spinach fettucini
   noodles

8 ounces egg fettucini noodles
½ cup finely grated Parmesan
   cheese
½ cup finely grated Swiss cheese
1 pint (or more) heavy cream,
   warmed
Salt and freshly ground pepper
   to taste

In the oil and 1 tablespoon of the butter, sauté mushrooms briefly over high heat. Reduce heat, add ham and peas, and keep warm. Boil noodles until just tender. Drain and return to the pot over low heat. Add the remaining 4 tablespoons butter and the cheeses. Toss with noodles, while adding enough warm cream to reach desired consistency. Add the mushroom mixture, salt, and pepper. Serve immediately.

Serves 6 to 8 as main course

FRIED CHEESE SQUARES WITH TOMATO SAUCE

¼ cup unsalted butter
6 tablespoons plus extra flour
1½ cups milk
2 cups grated Gruyère cheese
1 cup freshly grated Parmesan
    cheese

½ teaspoon salt
½ teaspoon white pepper
3 egg yolks, lightly beaten
2 eggs, whipped
1 cup bread crumbs
Tomato Sauce (below)

Melt butter over low heat and stir in 6 tablespoons flour. Remove pan from heat and slowly add milk, stirring constantly. Return to heat and cook, stirring constantly, until thickened to the consistency of thick mashed potatoes. Add cheeses and seasonings. Mixture will be rubbery. Remove from heat and beat in egg yolks. Pour into a 9-inch square or an 8 × 10-inch pan lined with wax paper. Cool and refrigerate overnight. Cut into squares and coat with flour. Dip in whipped eggs and roll in bread crumbs. Set on wax paper and let dry. Fry in deep fat at 390 degrees F. Serve with Tomato Sauce.

Yield: 64 squares

TOMATO SAUCE

6 small green onions or 3 large
    green onions
4 cloves garlic, minced
1 tablespoon olive oil
1 can (28 ounces) stewed
    tomatoes or 2 pounds fresh
    tomatoes, peeled, seeded, and
    chopped

½ cup fresh chopped parsley
2 bay leaves
1 teaspoon oregano
½ teaspoon salt
¼ teaspoon pepper

Lightly sauté onions and garlic in oil. Purée all other ingredients in blender or food processor and add to onions. Cook to desired thickness.

Yield: 3 to 3½ cups

JADA'S VEGETABLE DIP

1 cup mayonnaise
2 teaspoons tarragon vinegar
Dash pepper
½ teaspoon salt
⅛ teaspoon thyme

¼ teaspoon curry powder
2 teaspoons chili sauce
1 teaspoon prepared horseradish
2 teaspoons chopped chives
2 tablespoons grated onion

Mix all together. Serve with raw vegetables or chips.

Yield: 1½ cups

FRIED WON TONS
WITH SWEET AND SOUR SAUCE

Oil
1 package won ton wrappers
1 cup plus 2 tablespoons water
⅓ cup cider vinegar
½ cup brown sugar

⅛ teaspoon salt
¼ teaspoon soy sauce
1 tablespoon ketchup
2 tablespoons cornstarch
2 tablespoons water

In Dutch oven or deep-fat fryer, heat oil until very hot. Drop wrappers, one at a time, into hot oil. When they begin to brown (about 2 minutes), remove and drain. Combine water, vinegar, brown sugar, salt, soy sauce, and ketchup. Bring to a fast boil. Combine cornstarch and water and add to mixture. Continue cooking, stirring constantly, until mixture thickens. Serve with fried won ton wrappers for dipping.

Serves 6 to 10

HOLLAND RUSK APPETIZER

Lettuce
Holland Rusks
Cream cheese
Caviar
Tomato slices

Artichoke hearts
Russian dressing
Crumbled bacon
Hard-cooked egg

To make individual salads, arrange a bed of lettuce on a salad plate. Spread a Holland Rusk with cream cheese and caviar. Cover with tomato slices and an artichoke heart. Pour Russian dressing over top and sprinkle with crumbled bacon and chopped egg. Serve immediately to prevent rusk from getting soggy.

GREEN-CHILI PIE

1 can (4 ounces) green chilies	½ to ¾ onion, chopped
10 ounces Cheddar cheese, grated	6 eggs, beaten
	¼ teaspoon salt

Preheat oven to 350 degrees F. Spray a 9-inch pie pan with Pam. Seed, wash, and quarter green chilies. Line pie pan with chilies. Mix cheese and onions and sprinkle over chilies. Combine eggs and salt and pour over cheese. Bake for 40 to 45 minutes. Remove from oven and serve warm or cold. Cheese will puff up and brown while in the oven but will fall when removed.

Serves 6 to 8

MARINATED BEEF

1 large onion	Freshly ground pepper
¼ cup celery	Salt to taste
3 cloves garlic	2 pounds raw fillet of beef,
⅓ cup olive oil	trimmed of all fat and sliced
1¼ cups dry red wine	paper thin
1½ cups strong beef stock	
1 tablespoon chopped parsley plus extra for garnish	

Combine onion, celery, and garlic in food processor and chop very fine. Sauté in olive oil until golden. Add wine and beef stock, and cook over high heat for 5 minutes. Add 1 tablespoon parsley, pepper, and salt. Spoon some of hot liquid into deep 2-quart casserole. Add single layer of beef. Continue to add layers of liquid and beef until all is used up. Cover and refrigerate for 24 to 48 hours. (After 3 days, the meat gets too soft.) When ready to serve, drain and arrange beef on a platter and cover with freshly chopped parsley, or roll up a slice of beef, skewer with a toothpick and dip in chopped parsley.

Serves 20

MEXICAN MEATBALLS

1 pound finely ground lean beef
1 cup Italian-seasoned bread
  crumbs
1 egg, beaten
¾ cup half-and-half
1 small onion, minced

1 tablespoon butter
2 ½ tablespoons chopped chili
  chipotle
½ teaspoon crushed oregano
Salt to taste
Butter and oil for frying

Combine all ingredients and mix thoroughly. Shape into 1-inch balls. Heat butter and oil in a heavy skillet. Sauté meatballs until browned. Serve from a chafing dish with toothpicks. These freeze well. Thaw and reheat in a covered pan or microwave oven.

Yield: 80 to 90 meatballs

MOREDADDY'S PIMIENTO CHEESE

A spicy version of an old favorite.

1¼ pounds sharp Cheddar
  cheese, grated
2 jars (4 ounces each) diced
  pimientos, drained

1 jar (8 ounces) Pace Picante
  sauce
Freshly ground pepper
3 tablespoons mayonnaise

Combine cheese, pimientos, and picante sauce. Add pepper to taste. Add mayonnaise and blend thoroughly. Store in refrigerator. This is quite hot; use less picante sauce for a milder mixture.

Yield: 1 quart

CLAM-STUFFED MUSHROOMS

24 large mushrooms
⅓ cup melted butter or
　margarine
1 can (8 ounces) minced clams,
　drained and rinsed
3 tablespoons sliced green onions
　(white part only)

1 tablespoon chopped parsley
¼ teaspoon salt
⅛ teaspoon pepper
1 clove garlic, minced
¾ cup mayonnaise
½ teaspoon prepared mustard

Preheat oven to 350 degrees F. Remove mushroom stems, leaving caps intact. Set aside. Chop stems and sauté in butter for 10 minutes. Add clams, onions, parsley, salt, pepper, and garlic. Sauté for 5 minutes. Stuff mushroom caps with clam mixture and place in lightly greased baking dish. Chill. Combine mayonnaise and mustard, and place a dollop on each mushroom. Bake for 10 to 15 minutes. Serve hot.

Serves 12

STUFFED MUSHROOMS

1 package (3 ounces) cream
　cheese with chives

6 strips crumbled bacon
16 to 20 fresh mushrooms

Preheat oven to 350 degrees F. Mix cream cheese and bacon. Remove stems from mushrooms and stuff with cheese mixture. Bake for 15 minutes, then broil to brown. Serve hot.

Serves 8 to 10

OLIVE ENGLISH MUFFINS

1 package English muffins
1 cup chopped ripe olives
1½ cups grated sharp Cheddar
　cheese

½ cup chopped green onions
½ cup Hellmann's mayonnaise
½ teaspoon curry powder

Split muffins and set aside. Combine remaining ingredients and mix well. Spread mixture on muffins and cut into quarters. Broil until bubbly. Serve piping hot. These freeze well.

Yield: 48 quarters

MUSHROOMS PAPRIKA

1 pound fresh mushrooms, sliced
2 tablespoons finely chopped onion
1 teaspoon paprika
¼ cup butter
¼ teaspoon salt or to taste
Dash of cayenne
2 tablespoons flour

¼ cup white wine
1 cup sour cream
Pickapeppa sauce to taste (optional)
Tabasco to taste (optional)
Pepper to taste (optional)
6 puff pastry shells

Sauté mushrooms, onions, and paprika in butter until tender. Season with salt and cayenne. Stir in flour, and cook for 1 minute. Add wine, then sour cream. Bring almost to a boil but do not allow to boil or sour cream will curdle. Taste and add seasonings as desired. Serve in puff shells or in a chafing dish with toasted melba rounds.

Serves 6

ORIENTAL DRUMSTICKS

1 cup soy sauce
2 tablespoons freshly ground ginger
2 cloves garlic, minced
2 teaspoons sugar

¼ cup pale dry sherry
24 chicken wings (first joint only)

Combine all ingredients and marinate chicken overnight. Preheat oven broiler. Drain chicken and arrange in a large, shallow baking dish. Broil on the middle rack of the oven for 20 minutes on each side. Serve hot or cold.

Serves 4 to 6

SALMON CHEESE BALL

2 cups canned salmon (1
  pound), drained and picked
1 package (8 ounces) cream
  cheese
1 tablespoon minced onion

¼ teaspoon salt
1 tablespoon lemon juice
1 teaspoon horseradish
Parsley or chopped nuts for
  garnish

Mix together salmon, cream cheese, onion, salt, lemon juice and horse-radish. Shape into ball and roll in parsley or chopped nuts. Refrigerate. Serve at room temperature with crackers.

Yield: one 5-inch ball

SMOKED SALMON MOUSSE

This makes a wonderful gift when packed in decorative crocks or molds.

1 pound smoked salmon
¼ cup lemon juice
1 cup butter, melted
1 cup sour cream

Salt and pepper to taste
Capers and lemon wedges for
  garnish

Purée salmon in blender or food processor. Add lemon juice. With machine on, add butter, a little at a time. Remove mixture to mixing bowl. Gently fold in sour cream. Season to taste with salt and pepper. Pack into serving dish or crock. Garnish with capers and lemon wedges. Serve with plain crackers.

Serves 16 to 18

SMOKED SALMON-STUFFED EGGS

4 hard-cooked eggs
½ cup mashed smoked salmon

3 tablespoons mayonnaise
Capers and dillweed for garnish

Cut eggs in half lengthwise. Remove and mash yolks. Combine yolks with salmon and mayonnaise. Fill egg whites with mounds of stuffing and garnish with capers and dillweed.

Serves 4 to 6

CREAM CHEESE LAYERED WITH SHRIMP AND GUACAMOLE

1 8-ounce package cream cheese,
  softened
2 tablespoons mayonnaise
Worcestershire sauce to taste
1 clove garlic, minced
1 tin (6 ounces) frozen Calavo
  Avocado dip, thawed

½ cup Pace Picante sauce
1 can (8 ounces) baby shrimp,
  drained
2 green onions, finely chopped

Cream together cheese, mayonnaise, Worcestershire sauce, and garlic. Spread mixture on a rimmed plate. Cover and refrigerate. Just before serving, frost chilled cheese with avocado dip; then frost with a layer of Picante Sauce; top with shrimp. Sprinkle with green onions and serve with tortilla chips. Be sure to scoop through all layers.

Serves 6 to 8

CRICKET'S MARINATED SHRIMP

1 pound cleaned undercooked
  shrimp
1 medium onion, thinly sliced
1 lemon, thinly sliced
½ cup white vinegar
¼ cup water
2 teaspoons salt or to taste
1 teaspoon sugar

½ teaspoon dry mustard
¼ teaspoon ginger
½ teaspoon whole black pepper
1 bay leaf
Dash of Tabasco
¼ cup lemon juice
½ cup salad oil

Combine all ingredients and marinate for at least 24 hours. Turn at least twice. This will keep for two days in the refrigerator if tightly covered. (For 3 pounds of shrimp, use 1½ times the amount of marinade; for 9 pounds, use 4 times the amount.)

Each pound serves 3 to 4

MARINATED SHRIMP

5 pounds raw medium shrimp
2 bottles (8 ounces each) Kraft
  Catalina dressing
5 bay leaves
1 tablespoon celery seed
2 bottles (3 ounces each) capers,
  undrained

8 whole cloves
20 small (boiling) onions, sliced
  into rings
2 bottles (10 ounces each)
  Durkee Famous Dressing

Season one gallon of water with some or all of the following: salt, black pepper, red pepper, a whole onion, a stalk of celery, a little fresh lemon juice and peel. Boil for 10 minutes. Drop in shrimp and turn off heat. Let stand for 5 minutes. Drain shrimp and run under cold water to stop cooking. Shell and devein. Combine remaining ingredients and add cooked shrimp. Refrigerate mixture overnight. Before serving, add salt and pepper to taste. Serve with crackers as an hors d'oeuvre or use to fill half an avocado or papaya.

Serves 20

SZECHWAN SHRIMP APPETIZER

3 green onions
1 clove garlic, minced and
  crushed
2 teaspoons minced fresh ginger
1 tablespoon ketchup
1 tablespoon chili sauce
2 tablespoons sherry

1 tablespoon soy sauce
1 teaspoon sugar
2 tablespoons oil
1 pound cleaned raw shrimp
½ teaspoon salt
½ teaspoon crushed red pepper

Mince white parts of green onions. Mince green parts separately and set aside. Mix together white parts of the green onions, garlic, ginger, ketchup, chili sauce, sherry, soy sauce, and sugar. Heat oil in a wok or heavy skillet. Add shrimp, and stir-fry until color just begins to change. Stir in onion mixture. Add salt and pepper and continue cooking for 1 to 2 minutes more. Garnish with minced green parts of onions. Serve with toothpicks.

Serves 4 to 6

SHRIMP RÉMOULADE MOLD

1 envelope of gelatin
Juice of 1 lemon
2½ pounds shrimp, cooked,
  chopped
1 stalk celery, finely chopped
6 hard-cooked eggs, chopped
½ onion, grated
½ cup mayonnaise

½ jar (5 ounces) prepared
  horseradish
½ jar (5¼ ounces) Zatarain's
  mustard
Worcestershire sauce to taste
Tabasco to taste
Lawry's Seasoned Salt, and
  pepper to taste

Soften gelatin in lemon juice and combine with all remaining ingredients. Mix well. Pour into mold and chill until firm. Serve with melba rounds or crackers, or serve on lettuce as a luncheon salad.

Serves 4 for lunch or
10 as an appetizer

SWISS FONDUE

2 cups white wine
1 pound Emmentaler cheese, cubed
  or shredded
1 pound Gruyère cheese, cubed
  or shredded
4 cloves garlic, minced

Salt to taste
White pepper to taste
5 teaspoons cornstarch
¼ cup Kirsch
1 loaf French bread, cut into
  bite-size pieces

Bring wine almost to a boil. Melt cheeses and add garlic, salt, pepper, and wine, stirring constantly. Combine cornstarch and Kirsch and add to cheese. Cook over medium heat 2 minutes more or until cheese is completely melted and smooth. When ready to serve, pour into a chafing dish or fondue pot. Serve with fondue forks and pieces of bread. Stir often to keep from separating. Adjust temperature as needed. For variety, serve with apple chunks.

Serves 15

SPANAKOPETES

PASTRY:

1 package (8 ounces) cream
   cheese, softened
1 cup butter, softened
2 cups sifted flour

FILLING:

1 onion, finely chopped
3 tablespoons olive oil
1 package (10 ounces) frozen
   chopped spinach, thawed

Salt to taste
¼ pound feta cheese, crumbled
½ cup cottage cheese, drained
1 egg, beaten

PASTRY: With a fork, combine cheese and butter. Cut in flour. Work dough with hands until it holds together. Make a ball; wrap and chill overnight. On floured surface, roll dough to ¼ inch thickness. Cut into 2-inch circles.

FILLING: Sauté onion in oil until soft. Drain thawed spinach well and add to onions with salt. Cook over low heat until tender. Remove and drain. Let cool. Mix cheeses and add egg. Stir into spinach mixture and mix well.

ASSEMBLY: Preheat oven to 425 degrees F. Place a dab of filling on each pastry circle. Moisten edges and fold over. Press edges with fork. Prick pastries. Bake on a cookie sheet for 15 minutes or until golden. These freeze well.

Yield: 5 to 6 dozen

CHAPTER III

BEVERAGES

Downtown

Rising up from the south bank of Buffalo Bayou, the shimmering glass office towers of Downtown Houston seem to embody the city's energy and optimism about the future. Progressive developers have given a free hand to such world-famous architects as Philip Johnson and I. M. Pei. The result is a cluster of glass and polished stone, with angles and parapets catching the sun.

Oil companies, drilling and construction contractors, banks, law firms, and shipping brokers own the towers or lease space in them. On the top floors are private clubs with thick carpets and sweeping views, where big oil and land deals are sealed over a handshake and a glass of bourbon and branchwater.

In the shadow of these monoliths is the old Rice Hotel building, the blocky brick structure which stands on the land once occupied by the capitol of the Republic of Texas. In its heyday, the Rice was the home of the Old Capitol Club, called the Old Cap by its members, who insisted that the club's bar was the same one that had adorned the capitol in the days of the Republic. It was the kind of place where the bartender began mixing your favorite drink as soon as you appeared at the door.

Two blocks over, on Market Square, quiet little wine bars and restaurants inhabit some of the oldest buildings still standing in town. At lunch hour and after work, lawyers stroll over from the courthouse and curious reporters from the city's daily papers mingle with young executives, city officials, and administrators for the opera, the symphony, and the Alley Theatre. It's the best place in town to find out what's going on. As the evening wears on, theater- and concertgoers drop by for before-and-after refreshment, and some of the lunch spots turn into jazz clubs.

Houston's Downtown pace picks up again early. This is a city that runs on business breakfasts—strong coffee with everything from biscuits and gravy to croissants at 6:30 or 7:00 in the morning. There's a feeling here that 9:00 A.M. might be too late. After all, people in Aberdeen, London, Abu Dhabi, and other centers of the energy industry are already well through the day. Besides, it's important to get started before calls start coming in from New York and Caracas.

Despite its fast pace and high energy, Houston is still a city where business is often done on a social basis. And most of these interactions are accompanied by a beverage—chicory coffee, imported beer, shots of tequila, or tall glasses of Artesia, the Lone Star State's own mineral water. The recipes that follow include some of the more elaborate concoctions designed to turn a business occasion into a social one and a social occasion into a memorable experience. From regional Margaritas, Book Club Sangria, and Ramos Gin Fizz to tempting Velvet Mint and Pineapple Frappé to festive Perked Wassail, Jay's Eggnog, and Christmas Coffee, they're all worth a toast. Cheers!

PERKED WASSAIL

This makes your house smell divine.

¾ cup sugar
1 quart apple cider or juice
2 cups cranberry juice
1 cup orange juice

¾ cup lemon juice
1 teaspoon whole allspice
1 teaspoon whole cloves
3 cinnamon sticks

Combine sugar and juices in an automatic percolator. Place the spices in the percolator basket. Allow to go through the perk cycle. Serve hot. If you do not have a percolator, you can simmer ingredients in a saucepan. Strain and serve.

Yield: 16 cups

BANANA BERRY SHAKE

1 box (10 ounces) fresh frozen
   strawberries in syrup
1 cup plain yogurt

1 banana
½ cup club soda
¼ cup light corn syrup

Do not allow berries to thaw. Put all ingredients in a blender and blend for 30 seconds or until smooth.

Serves 2

BANANA PUNCH

This is very unusual and makes a big hit at a luau.

3 cups sugar
6 cups water
1 can (46 ounces) unsweetened
  pineapple juice

2 cups orange juice
½ cup lemon juice
5 bananas, mashed
3 quarts ginger ale

Combine the sugar and water and boil for 3 minutes. Let cool. Add all remaining ingredients except ginger ale. Mix well and place in the freezer overnight or until frozen. When ready to serve, soften slightly and add ginger ale. Serve in pineapple or coconut shells.

Serves 40

JAY'S EGGNOG

1 cup whipping cream
6 eggs, separated
¾ cup sugar
1 cup half-and-half

2 cups milk
2 cups bourbon
1 ounce rum
Nutmeg for garnish

Beat separately in this order: whipping cream, egg whites (stiff), and egg yolks. Add the sugar to the yolks and beat. Fold in egg whites, half-and-half, and milk. Slowly pour in bourbon, then rum. Fold in whipped cream and refrigerate. Sprinkle with nutmeg.

Yield: Approximately 5 pints

SPIKED CAPPUCCINO

3 cups strong coffee
3 cups half-and-half
½ cup dark crème de cacao

¼ cup rum
¼ cup brandy

Combine all ingredients and steam in a saucepan. Do not boil. Serve immediately.

Yield: 6 to 8 servings

CHRISTMAS PUNCH

This makes your house smell like Christmas.

4 cups pineapple juice
1 can (12 ounces) apricot juice
　or nectar
2 cups apple cider

1 cup orange juice
6 cinnamon sticks
14 whole cloves

Combine all ingredients and heat long enough to absorb spices. Strain and serve while hot. This is also good cold.

Yield: 8½ cups

CHRISTMAS COFFEE

6½ tablespoons instant coffee
1 stick of cinnamon
¼ cup sugar
7 whole cloves

7 cups hot water
Whipped cream and chocolate
　sprinkles for garnish

Combine first 5 ingredients and bring to a boil. Strain, pour into mugs and top with whipped cream and chocolate sprinkles.

Yield: 7 cups

HOLLINS COFFEE

½ gallon cold strong coffee
2 teaspoons vanilla
1 teaspoon cinnamon

½ gallon chocolate ice cream
½ gallon vanilla ice cream
1 pint heavy cream, whipped

Combine coffee, vanilla, and cinnamon; chill well. When ready to serve, pour coffee into a large punch bowl. Spoon in ice cream in chunks. Fold in whipped cream and serve immediately.

Yield: Approximately 1¼ gallons

RAMOS GIN FIZZ À LA VALENCIA

3 teaspoons lemon juice
2 teaspoons lime juice (Mexican or key limes preferred)
1 heaping tablespoon powdered sugar

6 drops orange flower water
3 ounces gin
2 handfuls crushed ice
1 egg white
½ cup milk

Blend all ingredients in the blender for 10 seconds. Serve in chilled glasses.

Yield: 2 drinks

BRANDY FREEZE

½ gallon coffee ice cream
1½ ounces crème de cacao
1½ ounces Drambuie

1½ ounces Cointreau
8 ounces brandy

Put half the ice cream in a blender. Combine liqueurs and add half the mixture to the blender. Blend well. Repeat with remaining ingredients. Store in the freezer until ready to serve.

Yield: Approximately ½ gallon

PINEAPPLE FRAPPÉ

Try this as a luncheon dessert.

1 can (8 ounces) pineapple slices, drained
1 pint vanilla ice cream

½ teaspoon peppermint extract
1 cup ginger ale

Crush the pineapple slices in a blender. Add the remaining ingredients, and blend on low speed until just combined and smooth. Serve in frosted glasses.

Serves 2 to 4

VELVET MINT

6 large scoops vanilla ice cream
2 tablespoons brandy
3 tablespoons orange liqueur

3 tablespoons green crème de
menthe

Combine ingredients and blend until smooth but not milky.

Serves 4

CHERRY MINT LIMEADE

½ cup fresh mint sprigs
¾ cup sugar
4 cups water

1 cup fresh lime juice
1 tablespoon red maraschino
cherry syrup

Combine mint and ½ cup of the sugar. Crush the mint with a fork. Add 1 cup of the water and set aside for 5 minutes. Strain into a 1½-quart pitcher. Discard the mint leaves. Add the lime juice, cherry syrup, remaining sugar and water. Chill. Fill glasses with ice, a mint sprig, a slice of lime or a cherry. Pour limeade into the glasses.

Yield: Approximately 6 cups

ORANGE JULIUS DELIGHT

Children love this.

⅓ cup frozen orange juice
concentrate
½ cup milk
½ cup water

½ teaspoon vanilla
6 ice cubes
¼ cup sugar (optional)

Combine all ingredients in a blender. Blend until smooth.

Yield: 2 large drinks or 4 small ones

BROTHER'S RUM LOVELY

1 can (6 ounces) frozen
   lemonade concentrate
1 can (6 ounces) frozen limeade
   concentrate

1 can (46 ounces)
   pineapple-grapefruit juice
⅘ quart Bacardi light rum

Mix all ingredients and freeze for 24 hours. This makes a frozen slush that keeps in the freezer, ready to serve, for months.

Yield: 20 servings

LAS VEGAS PIÑA COLADAS

2 cups Coco Lopez
1½ cups Orgeat
   almond-flavored syrup
1¾ cups white rum
1¼ cups orange curaçao

1 can (46 ounces) unsweetened
   pineapple juice
4 cups half-and-half
Dark rum for topping

Mix all ingredients well. At this point, you may store mixture in the refrigerator for several days or freeze it. Fill blender no more than half full of cubed ice, add enough liquid to fill blender. Blend until smooth. Top each drink with a dash of dark rum.

Yield: 1 gallon before adding ice

CRANBERRY TEA PUNCH

1 quart boiling water
6 tea bags
8½ cups cold water
2 cans (6 ounces each) frozen
   lemonade
2 cans (6 ounces each) frozen
   limeade

2 cans (6 ounces each) frozen
   cranberry juice, *or* decrease
   water by 2 to 4 cups and use
   bottles of cranberry juice
2 bottles (23 ounces each)
   ginger ale, chilled

Pour boiling water over the tea bags and steep for 10 to 12 minutes. Add tea to the cold water and juices. Just before serving, add the ginger ale. For a festive touch, freeze additional lemonade in a ring mold with cherries, mint, or whatever seems pretty. Float the frozen ring in the punch.

Yield: 1 gallon

MARGARITAS

3 parts tequila
1 part Triple Sec or Cointreau
1 part fresh lemon juice
1 part fresh lime juice

3 cubes ice, crushed, per ½ cup
    margarita mixture
Salt

Combine all ingredients in a blender. Dip the rim of the glass in the mixture, then salt. Fill with margarita and serve. Optional: The crushed ice may be placed in a glass and the mixture poured on top.

BLOODY MARY MIX

2½ cups tomato juice
1 can (12 ounces) V-8 juice
1 jar (16 ounces) Clamato juice
¾ cup lemon juice
1 tablespoon Worcestershire
    sauce

1 tablespoon salt
¼ teaspoon Tabasco
1 teaspoon celery salt

Mix all ingredients well. Chill. Add more seasoning if needed. Serve as is or add three parts mix to one part vodka.

Yield: Approximately 7 cups

CLYDE TEA

8 tea bags
20 mint sprigs
2 quarts boiling water

1 cup ReaLemon
1 cup sugar
1 cup orange juice

Put tea bags and mint in 2 separate pitchers. Pour 1 quart boiling water over each and let steep for 15 minutes. Remove tea bags, strain the mint and discard. Combine all the ingredients and chill.

Yield: 10 cups

BOOK CLUB SANGRIA

This is best if made one day ahead.

SANGRIA BASE:
1 lime
2 large oranges
2½ lemons

1 quart water
3⅓ cups sugar

SANGRIA:
1 fifth good red burgundy
1 cup sangria base, strained
4 tablespoons brandy
1 lemon, thinly sliced

1 cup fresh pineapple chunks
1 fresh peach, sliced (if available)
1 cup ginger ale, chilled

BASE: Cut fruit in wedges. Slowly boil the lime, 1 orange, and 1½ lemons in the water, adding sugar slowly as it dissolves. Cook about 30 minutes until syrupy, stirring occasionally. Squeeze remaining fruit into the hot liquid and let stand until cool. Refrigerate in closed jars for at least one day before mixing with the wine. This will keep indefinitely in the refrigerator.

SANGRIA: Several hours before serving, or the night before, combine wine, sangria base, and brandy. Chill. When ready to serve, pour the chilled mixture into a large glass pitcher. Add a dozen ice cubes, the fruit, and the ginger ale. Stir with a tall wooden spoon, which is left in the pitcher to hold back the fruit when you pour.

Yield: 8 to 10 glasses

WASSAIL

Cloves
1 orange
1 gallon apple cider
1 cinnamon stick

½ teaspoon nutmeg
½ fifth white wine
1 cup peach brandy
2 cups vermouth

Push cloves into the rind of the orange. Heat the cider to near boiling and add the orange. Allow to cool until just warm. Add the remaining ingredients and steep for 2 hours. Sweeten if desired. Serve warm.

Yield: 24 servings

CHAPTER IV

BREADS
Hermann Park

Houston has a history of philanthropy, and many of its public amenities have resulted from private gifts. One of its most generous citizens was George W. Hermann, the son of Swiss immigrants, who was born in a log cabin near the present site of City Hall on August 6, 1843.

Although he became a successful financier, Hermann remained a bachelor and considered the city his heir. In 1910, four years before his death, he gave the people of Houston 278 acres of woods and meadow at what was then the south edge of town.

Today, Hermann Park is a lush, 545-acre expanse almost in the heart of the growing city. On its north edge are the Contemporary Arts Museum, the Museum of Fine Arts, and a cluster of new high-rise condominiums looking out over the fountains and gardens. To the west are the spreading oaks of Rice University, which grocery and import-export mogul William Marsh Rice founded in 1891. To the south is the Texas Medical Center, with Hermann Hospital—another project of the humbly born philanthropist—as its cornerstone.

The Medical Center is like a town unto itself; some 30,000 people work in its medical and dental schools and nine hospitals. Front-line cancer research at M. D. Anderson, heart research at the University of Texas and Baylor medical schools, environmental issues at the U. T. School of Public Health, and emergency medicine at Ben Taub have focused national attention on the Center. Royalty, business people, and government officials from Latin America, the Middle East, and other parts of the world come there for everything from major surgery to routine checkups.

In the midst of all this activity, Hermann Park is an oasis of fragrant camphor trees and rose gardens, of winding drives and bridle paths, with a statue of General Sam Houston surveying the scene from horseback at one corner and a likeness of George W. Hermann looking out over the greenery at another. The zoo, the Museum of Natural Science, the stables, and the municipal golf course draw visitors throughout the year. During the summer, Miller Outdoor Theatre plays host to the Shakespeare Festival and to free ballet, opera, plays, concerts, and musicals. The members of the Houston Symphony, who normally wear tuxedos or long black dresses to play downtown at Jones Hall, don gingham shirts and bandannas for renditions of "Billy the Kid" and the "Grand Canyon Suite." People bring their children and dogs and spread picnics on the grass while they enjoy the performances.

More than anything else, picnics are what Hermann Park is all about—Miller Theatre picnics, picnics by the reflecting pool with ducks begging for crumbs, picnics on balmy January and February weekends when the Gulf breezes forget that it's supposed to be winter and the buds begin to open on peach trees.

Apart from good companions, a cooler or basket, and something to spread on the ground, the central requirement for a good picnic is bread—crusty French bread or fruited muffins, sandwich bread, or sweet tea loaves. What follows is a sampling of breads to fuel the spirit and fire the imagination—Cowboy Coffee Cake, Cornbread Davis, Morning Meeting Rolls, Strawberry Nut Bread, Herb Bread, Country-Crust Bread, and many more. They're all delicious, and most are as easy to put together as a picnic.

APPLE GOODY

½ cup vegetable oil
1 egg
1 cup sugar
1 cup unsifted flour
½ teaspoon baking soda
½ teaspoon salt

½ teaspoon cinnamon
½ teaspoon vanilla
1 tablespoon dark rum or brandy
2 Granny Smith or pippin
   apples, peeled and cored
⅓ cup chopped nuts

Preheat oven to 350 degrees F. Beat oil with egg until foamy. Stir in sugar, flour, baking soda, salt, cinnamon, vanilla, and rum. Finely chop 1½ apples and add to batter with nuts. Batter will be stiff. Spoon mixture into a greased 9-inch pie pan. Slice remaining ½ apple and press into batter to form a swirl pattern. Bake for 35 to 40 minutes. This can be served warm with ice cream, hard sauce, or eggnog, as a dessert. It is also good cold.

Serves 8

BRUNCH DELIGHT

3 cups granola cereal
1½ cups brown sugar, firmly
   packed
3 teaspoons cinnamon

2 packages (8 ounces each)
   refrigerator biscuits
½ cup butter, melted

Preheat oven to 350 degrees F. Combine granola, brown sugar, and cinnamon in a small bowl and mix well. Separate biscuits and divide each in half. Dip each piece in melted butter and then in cereal mixture. Coat biscuits generously, pressing cereal mixture into dough. Arrange biscuits in overlapping layers in a greased bundt pan. Sprinkle any remaining cereal mixture on top and drizzle with remaining butter. Bake for 30 minutes. Turn out immediately on a plate and serve warm.

Serves 6 to 8

BERNICE'S CINNAMON ROLLS

DOUGH:
2 cups milk
2 packages dry yeast
½ cup sugar
2 teaspoons salt

6 cups flour, sifted
½ cup shortening, melted
2 eggs

FILLING:
1 cup butter, melted
1 cup sugar
1 cup brown sugar

1½ tablespoons cinnamon
3 ounces raisins (optional)

GLAZE:
3½ cups powdered sugar, sifted
4 tablespoons butter, softened

½ teaspoon vanilla
4 tablespoons milk

DOUGH: Heat milk. When lukewarm, add yeast, sugar, and salt; stir until dissolved. Add 1 cup of the flour and stir until smooth. Add shortening and eggs; when well-blended, add 4 more cups of the flour. Again, blend well. Spread remaining cup flour on pastry cloth or bread board and place the dough on top. Knead for 8 to 10 minutes, working in all the flour until the dough is smooth and elastic. Place dough in a greased bowl and flip it over to grease the top. Cover with a cloth and put in a warm place until it is double in size, about 1 hour. Punch down and divide in half. Roll out half the dough to ½-inch-thick rectangle.

FILLING: Brush dough with 3 or more tablespoons melted butter. Combine sugars and cinnamon and sprinkle half evenly on the dough. Add raisins if desired. Roll up jelly-roll fashion and cut in ¾-inch slices. Repeat with other half of dough. Place rolls in greased round cake pans. Brush remaining butter on top. Cover and let rise in a warm place until the dough has doubled. Preheat oven to 350 degrees F. Bake for 12 to 15 minutes or until golden brown. Cool slightly.

GLAZE: Combine ingredients for glaze and mix until smooth. Glaze rolls when they are barely warm.

Yield: 4 dozen

COWBOY COFFEE CAKE

2½ cups all-purpose flour	1 cup coarsely chopped walnuts
1½ cups light brown sugar,	or pecans
firmly packed	¼ heaping teaspoon nutmeg
½ cup plus 2 tablespoons sugar	1 teaspoon baking soda
½ teaspoon salt	1 egg
1½ teaspoons cinnamon	1 cup buttermilk
¾ cup butter, softened	

Preheat oven to 350 degrees F. Butter and flour a 13 × 9 × 2-inch pan. Combine flour, brown sugar, ½ cup of the sugar, salt, and 1 teaspoon of the cinnamon in a mixing bowl. With mixer on low speed, blend in butter until mixture is crumbly. Remove 1½ cups crumb mixture and mix with nuts. Press 1¼ cups nut mixture into bottom of pan. Take ¼ cup of the nut mixture and add the remaining ½ teaspoon cinnamon, nutmeg, and 2 tablespoons sugar. Set aside for topping. Mix the remaining cup of the nut mixture into the remaining crumb mixture and add baking soda, egg, and buttermilk. Mix at medium speed for ½ minute. Pour batter over crumb mixture in pan. Sprinkle with reserved topping. Bake for 40 to 45 minutes. Serve warm or at room temperature. Freezes well.

Yield: 15 to 20 servings

DANISH PUFF

PASTRY:
1 cup flour
½ cup butter
2 tablespoons water

TOPPING:
½ cup butter
1 cup water
1 teaspoon almond flavoring

1 cup all-purpose flour
3 eggs

ICING:
1 cup powered sugar
½ teaspoon almond flavoring

Milk
Slivered almonds

PASTRY: Preheat oven to 350 degrees F. Place flour in a bowl, cut in butter, sprinkle with water, and mix with a fork. Form into a ball and divide in half. Pat into two 12 × 3-inch strips and place about 3 inches apart on an ungreased baking sheet.
TOPPING: Mix butter and water in a saucepan and bring to a boil. Remove from heat and add flavoring. Beat in flour quickly to prevent lumping. When smooth, add eggs, one at a time, beating well after each addition. Divide in half and spread evenly over pastry strips. Bake for 1 hour. Cool and drizzle with icing.
ICING: Mix powdered sugar, almond flavoring, and enough milk to reach spreading consistency. Sprinkle with slivered almonds.

Serves 10 to 12

MORNING MEETING ROLL

Making this is messy, but the results are delicious.

½ cup butter, cut in pieces
1 cup flour
4 ounces cream cheese, cut in
    pieces

1 jar (16 ounces)
    apricot-pineapple jam
1 cup grated coconut
1 cup finely chopped nuts

Preheat oven to 350 degrees F. Blend butter, flour, and cream cheese in the food processor as you would pie dough. Wrap in wax paper and refrigerate. Roll out into an 8 × 12-inch rectangle. Spread with jam and sprinkle with coconut and nuts. Starting with shorter end, roll up like a jelly roll, pinch ends together, and seal seam. Bake on a greased cookie sheet for 40 to 45 minutes. Slice and serve. This may be wrapped in foil and reheated or frozen.

Serves 8 to 10

TAFFY'S CARAMEL PECAN ROLLS

DOUGH:

½ cup butter

½ cup sugar

1 teaspoon salt

½ cup boiling water

1 package dry yeast

½ cup lukewarm water

1 egg, beaten

3 heaping cups Wondra flour

FILLING:

1 teaspoon cinnamon

1 cup sugar

TOPPING:

½ cup butter

1 heaping cup brown sugar

2 tablespoons water

Pecan pieces

DOUGH: Let butter and egg come to room temperature. Cream butter, sugar, and salt. Add the boiling water and stir until all ingredients are melted. Let cool to lukewarm. Soak yeast in the lukewarm water. When dissolved, add to sugar mixture. Add egg and flour and stir until well blended. Place in a buttered bowl, cover with buttered wax paper, and refrigerate overnight.

FILLING: Divide dough in half, and roll each half into a ⅛-inch-thick rectangle. Sprinkle with cinnamon and sugar mixture and roll up jelly-roll fashion. Cut each roll into 1-inch-thick slices, about 14.

TOPPING: Heat butter and brown sugar until melted. Add water, and cook, stirring constantly, until mixture bubbles around the edges. Prepare greased muffin tins by placing 1 tablespoon topping and 10 to 12 pecan pieces in each cup. Top with rolls, cover, and let rise in a cold oven until doubled in bulk, about 2 to 3 hours. Bake in a preheated 350 degree F. oven for 15 minutes or until light golden brown. When done, invert onto a plate. These muffins must be removed from the pans and served while still warm. Do not freeze. Reheat, if necessary, in aluminum foil.

Yield: Approximately 2 to 2½ dozen rolls

ALMOND-LEMON ROLLS

3 cups sugar
½ cup butter or margarine
½ cup light corn syrup
¼ cup lemon juice
3 tablespoons grated fresh lemon
    rind

2 cups almonds, lightly toasted
2 teaspoons nutmeg
Refrigerator Sweet Yeast Dough
    (below)

Preheat oven to 350 degrees F. Combine 1½ cups of the sugar, butter, corn syrup, lemon juice, and grated lemon rind in a saucepan. Bring to a boil, and cook for 4 minutes, stirring constantly. Grease four 9-inch cake pans. Sprinkle almonds into the pans. Pour lemon topping over almonds and set aside. In a small bowl, combine the remaining 1½ cups sugar with nutmeg. Divide Refrigerator Sweet Yeast Dough into four portions. Roll each one into a 9 × 12-inch rectangle. Brush with melted butter to within ½ inch of the edges. Sprinkle ¼ sugar mixture over each rectangle. Starting with the long side, roll tightly, jelly-roll fashion. Pinch seam and ends to seal. Cut into 1½-inch slices and place in prepared pans. Cover rolls and let rise until light and touching, about 30 minutes. Bake in preheated oven for 20 to 25 minutes or until golden brown. Place foil under wire racks. As soon as rolls are done, invert onto wire racks to allow syrup to run through. Serve warm.

Yield: 2 to 3 dozen

FRESH LIME TWISTS

½ cup sugar
Grated rind of 1 large lime
⅛ teaspoon nutmeg
½ Refrigerator Sweet Yeast
    Dough recipe (below)

Melted butter or margarine
1 cup powdered sugar
2 tablespoons lime juice

Preheat oven to 375 degrees F. Combine sugar, grated lime rind, and nutmeg in a small bowl and set aside. Divide Refrigerator Sweet Yeast Dough into 2 portions and roll each portion into a 9 × 16-inch rectangle. Brush with melted butter to within ½ inch of edges. Sprinkle sugar mixture lengthwise over ½ of each piece. Fold in half and pinch edges to seal. Beginning at narrow end, cut into ½-inch strips. Twist each piece twice and place on a greased cookie sheet. Cover with a cloth and let rise until doubled, about 45 minutes. Bake for 12 to 15 minutes. Cool on wire racks. Mix powdered sugar and lime juice. Brush on warm twists.

Yield: 2 to 3 dozen

REFRIGERATOR SWEET YEAST DOUGH

2 packages dry or compressed
    yeast
½ cup warm water
1¾ cups milk
¼ cup sugar

1½ cups butter, softened
½ teaspoon salt
4 eggs, slightly beaten
8 cups unsifted all-purpose flour

Dissolve yeast in warm water. Scald milk; add sugar and ½ cup of the butter, stirring until butter melts. Cool to lukewarm. Stir in yeast and salt. Beat milk mixture into eggs until well blended. Place flour in a very large bowl and add milk mixture. Blend until dough forms a ball. It may be necessary to add a bit more flour to form a workable ball. Place the dough on a floured board and knead for about 5 minutes, kneading in about ¼ cup flour as needed. Knead until dough is smooth and elastic. Let the dough rest for 5 minutes. Roll out into a rectangle about ¼ inch thick, about 12 × 36 inches. Spread ⅓ cup of the butter over the center third of dough, fold the right third of the dough over the buttered section. Spread with another ⅓ cup of the butter. Fold the left third of the dough over the buttered right section. Turn ¼ turn clockwise and again roll into a ½-inch-thick rectangle. Spread the center third of the rectangle with the remaining butter. Bring the sides of the rectangle to meet in the center and fold in half, bringing the edges together. Place in a greased bowl, cover lightly with plastic wrap, and let rise in a warm place until almost doubled in bulk, about 1 hour. After dough rises, punch down, wrap tightly in plastic wrap, and chill for 3 hours or overnight. This dough *must* be well chilled before using. It keeps in the refrigerator for 3 to 4 days.

NICKI'S ENVELOPE PASTRIES

PASTRY:

2 packages dry yeast
¼ cup warm water
2 cups butter, softened
4 cups flour

2 tablespoons sugar
2 eggs, separated
1 cup sour cream
Jam: peach, apricot, or raspberry

GLAZE:

2 cups powdered sugar, sifted
3 tablespoons water

Dissolve yeast in warm water and set aside. With hands, mix butter, flour, sugar, egg yolks, and sour cream. Blend in dissolved yeast. Shape into a log, wrap in wax paper, and refrigerate for several hours or overnight. Preheat oven to 375 degrees F. Divide dough into four equal portions. Roll out each piece to ⅛-inch thickness. Cut into 2½-inch squares. Place ½ to ¾ teaspoon jam in the middle of each square. Brush the edges with egg white to help form a good seal. Bring up the corners and pinch together well or fold over and seal firmly as you would an envelope. Place on a greased cookie sheet and bake for 10 to 12 minutes or until light golden brown. Remove to wire racks and glaze while still warm. Use about 1 teaspoon glaze for each pastry. Freezes well. Dough keeps 2 to 3 days.

Yield: Approximately 100

DATE NUT BREAD

2 cups dates
1½ cups boiling water
2 teaspoons baking soda
½ cup butter
1½ cups sugar

2 eggs, beaten
Pinch of salt
1 teaspoon vanilla
3 cups flour
1 cup chopped nuts

Preheat oven to 325 degrees F. Chop dates and add boiling water and baking soda. Let stand until cool. Add butter, sugar, and eggs. Mix well. Stir in salt, vanilla, flour, and nuts. Pour into greased and floured pans. Bake for 1 hour. Cool. Remove from pans and wrap in foil. Loaves keep well in the refrigerator or freezer. Best if made the day before.

Yield: two medium loaves or
three small loaves

BANANA NUT BREAD

¾ cup butter, softened
1½ cups sugar
1½ cups mashed bananas (4
  medium bananas)
2 eggs, well-beaten
1 teaspoon vanilla

2 cups flour
1 heaping teaspoon baking soda
¾ teaspoon salt
½ cup buttermilk
¾ cup chopped nuts

Preheat oven to 325 degrees F. Cream butter and sugar thoroughly. Blend in bananas, eggs, and vanilla. Sift together flour, baking soda, and salt. Add to banana mixture alternately with buttermilk, mixing thoroughly after each addition. Add nuts and mix. Pour into greased and floured 9 × 5 × 3-inch pan. Bake for 1¼ to 1½ hours. If top becomes brown before bread is done, lower oven temperature to 300 degrees F. and bake until done.

Yield: 1 loaf

BOSTON BROWN BREAD

5 cups flour
1½ cups sugar
5 teaspoons baking soda
2½ teaspoons salt

5 cups buttermilk
⅔ cup molasses
2½ cups raisins
5 cups All-Bran cereal

Preheat oven to 350 degrees F. Sift together flour, sugar, soda, and salt; set aside. In a large bowl, mix buttermilk and molasses. Add raisins and cereal, and mix. Add dry ingredients and mix enough to moisten well. Divide batter into five well-greased 2-pound coffee cans. Cover tightly with foil. Place rack in bottom of a roaster. Place filled cans on rack. Fill the pan with enough water to come one third of the way up the sides of the cans. Cover the roasting pan tightly and place in oven to steam for about 2½ hours. Remove cans from roaster. Run a knife around bread and remove from cans as soon as possible. Cool completely and wrap in foil. Freezes well. This recipe may be halved.

Yield: 5 loaves

GINGERBREAD MUFFINS

This is wonderful served warm for breakfast.

2 teaspoons baking soda
1 cup buttermilk
1 cup sugar
1 cup brown sugar
1 ½ cups shortening
4 eggs

1 cup dark Karo syrup
4 cups flour
3 teaspoons cinnamon
3 teaspoons ginger
2 teaspoons allspice

DAY 1: Dissolve baking soda in buttermilk. Cream sugars and shortening. Add one egg at a time, beating after each addition. Stir in Karo syrup. Sift together flour and spices. Add to sugar mixture alternately with buttermilk, beating after each addition. Refrigerate for at least 24 hours. *Do not stir.* This will keep for several days.

DAY 2: Preheat oven to 350 degrees F. Fill paper-lined muffin tins half full with batter. Bake in preheated oven for 20 to 30 minutes.

Yield: 48 muffins

PUMPKIN BREAD

3 ⅓ cups flour
2 teaspoons baking soda
1 teaspoon nutmeg
3 teaspoons cinnamon
Dash of salt
3 cups sugar

1 cup Crisco oil
⅔ cup water
1 can (16 ounces) pumpkin
4 eggs
1 cup chopped nuts (optional)

Preheat oven to 350 degrees F. Mix together flour, baking soda, nutmeg, cinnamon, and salt. Combine sugar and oil and mix in dry ingredients. Add remaining ingredients, mix, and pour into three 8- or 9-inch loaf pans. Bake for 1 hour or until done.

Yield: 3 loaves

STRAWBERRY NUT BREAD

3 cups flour
1 teaspoon baking soda
1 teaspoon salt
1 tablespoon cinnamon
2 cups sugar
4 eggs

1 ¼ cups vegetable oil
2 packages (10 ounces each)
    frozen sliced strawberries,
    thawed
1 ¼ cups pecans, chopped

Preheat oven to 350 degrees F. Sift together flour, baking soda, salt, cinnamon, and sugar into a large bowl. Add eggs and oil, and mix well. Add thawed strawberries with juice and pecans. Mix well with an electric mixer. Pour into two greased and floured 8 × 4-inch or 9 × 5-inch loaf pans. Bake for 1 hour or until bread tests done. Let stand for 5 minutes, remove from pans, and cool on wire racks. Freezes well.

Yield: 2 loaves

BLUEBERRY MUFFINS

1 ½ cups flour
1 cup sugar
1 ½ teaspoons baking powder
9 tablespoons butter
1 egg

½ cup evaporated milk
½ teaspoon vanilla
1 cup blueberries, fresh, or
    well-drained and rinsed frozen
    berries

Preheat oven to 350 degrees F. Mix flour, sugar, and baking powder in a large bowl. Add 8 tablespoons of the butter and blend until mixture is crumbly. Set aside ½ cup. Add egg, milk, and vanilla to remaining crumb mixture and mix until smooth. Gently fold in blueberries. Spoon into greased or lined muffin tin, filling cups ⅔ full. Mix remaining tablespoon butter, melted, into remaining crumb mixture and sprinkle on top of muffins. Bake for 20 to 30 minutes until light brown. Let muffins cool in tin before removing.

Yield: 12 muffins

LEMON MUFFINS

1 cup butter	1 teaspoon salt
1 cup sugar	½ cup lemon juice
4 eggs, separated	2 teaspoons grated fresh lemon
2 cups flour	peel
2 teaspoons baking powder	

Preheat oven to 375 degrees F. Cream butter and sugar. Add beaten egg yolks and beat until light. Combine flour, baking powder, and salt, and add alternately with lemon juice to sugar mixture. Fold in stiffly beaten egg whites with grated lemon peel. Bake in greased or lined muffin tins for 20 minutes. Bake miniature muffins for 10 to 15 minutes. Serve warm. These do *not* freeze well.

Yield: Approximately 2½ dozen large
or 5 dozen small muffins

SEMESTER MUFFINS

This batter will keep for six weeks if refrigerated in covered jars.

4 cups All-Bran cereal	5 cups flour
2 cups boiling water	5 teaspoons baking soda
1 cup shortening	1 teaspoon salt
2½ cups sugar	2 cups 100% Bran cereal
4 eggs, beaten	2 heaping cups cut-up dates
4 cups buttermilk	

Preheat oven to 400 degrees F. Soak All-Bran cereal in boiling water for a few minutes. In a very large bowl, combine shortening, sugar, eggs and buttermilk. Add soaked All-Bran, flour, baking soda, salt, and 100% Bran. Blend thoroughly. Add dates. Bake in greased or paper-lined muffin tins for 25 minutes.

Yield: 4 quarts mix or 6 dozen regular
muffins or 10 dozen mini-muffins

SOUR CREAM MUFFINS

2 cups self-rising flour
1 cup butter, melted and cooled
1 cup sour cream

Preheat oven to 400 degrees F. Mix ingredients with a fork. Drop into ungreased muffin tins. Bake for 20 to 25 minutes, until brown around sides and top. If using the small muffin tins, reduce cooking time to 15 minutes.

Yield: 12 regular or
24 small muffins

CHEF WALDO'S POPOVERS

2 cups flour   4 eggs
2 cups milk   1 teaspoon salt

Combine all ingredients and stir by hand until reasonably smooth. Pour into six liberally greased Pyrex cups, filling them ⅔ full. Place directly on oven rack in a cold oven. Bake at 400 degrees F. for 40 minutes or until golden brown and completely puffed. Popovers will fall if undercooked. Serve at once. Muffin tins can also be used.

Yield: 6 popovers or 9 to 10
muffin-size popovers

COUNTRY-CRUST BREAD

Excellent for sandwiches or oven toast.

2 packages dry yeast   2 eggs
2 cups warm water   ¼ cup salad oil
½ cup sugar   6 cups flour
1 tablespoon salt   Melted butter

Combine all ingredients except 3 cups of the flour and beat for 5 minutes in mixer. Add remaining flour and mix with dough hook or knead by hand for 10 minutes. Place in greased bowl and let rise for 1 hour. Divide into 2 regular or 3 small greased loaf pans and let rise again for 1 hour. Preheat oven to 350 degrees F. Bake for 30 minutes on lower oven rack. Remove from pans and brush tops with melted butter.

Yield: 2 regular or 3 small loaves

EASY DINNER ROLLS

3 eggs, beaten
1 heaping teaspoon salt
½ cup sugar
½ cup butter, melted

1 cake or package dry yeast
1 cup warm water
4½ cups flour

Combine eggs, salt, sugar, and butter. Dissolve yeast in warm water and add to butter mixture. Using electric mixer, gradually blend in flour. Dough will be gooey. Let rise in a warm place for 4 hours. Cover tightly and refrigerate overnight. Four hours before cooking, roll out the dough to ¼ inch thick and cut out rolls with a biscuit cutter to make Parker House rolls. Dip in melted butter, fold in half, and place in a pan touching each other. Let rise again for 4 hours. Preheat oven to 450 degrees F. Bake for 7 to 12 minutes. If rolls brown too quickly, cover loosely with foil. This dough will keep refrigerated for 3 to 4 days. Rolls may be frozen after they are in the pans but before the second rising. Remove rolls from the freezer 4 to 5 hours before cooking and put them in a warm place to rise. Baking time may be a little longer.

Yield: 50 to 70 rolls

HERB BREAD

¾ cup milk, scalded
2 tablespoons sugar
2 tablespoons shortening
1 egg
1½ teaspoons salt
½ teaspoon nutmeg

1 teaspoon sage
2 teaspoons caraway seeds
1 package dry yeast
¼ cup warm water
3 to 3¾ cups flour

Combine hot milk, sugar, shortening, egg, and seasonings in a large bowl. Cool to lukewarm. Dissolve yeast in warm water and add to lukewarm milk mixture. Stir well. Gradually add flour. Mix with spoon, then with hands. When you have a workable dough, turn out onto a floured board and knead until smooth and elastic, about 8 to 10 minutes. Place in a greased bowl and turn to grease all sides of the dough. Cover lightly with plastic wrap and a cloth. Let rise in a warm place until doubled in bulk, about 1 to 2 hours. Punch down and divide into 2 portions. Shape 2 small loaves and place in greased pans. Let rise again until doubled. Preheat oven to 375 degrees F. Bake for 30 to 40 minutes until well browned. Bread should sound hollow when tapped. After baking, let bread cool for 6 hours. Slice thinly, butter, and wrap in foil. Freeze or refrigerate. To serve, heat unfrozen bread in foil at 350 degrees F. for 25 to 30 minutes until piping hot. Heat frozen bread at 400 degrees F. for 30 to 40 minutes.

Yield: 2 small loaves

FOOD PROCESSOR WHOLE WHEAT BREAD

1 package active dry yeast
1 cup warm water (115°)
2 tablespoons brown sugar
1½ cups unbleached white flour

1½ cups whole wheat flour
 (preferably stone ground)
2 tablespoons shortening
1 teaspoon salt

Dissolve yeast in warm water with brown sugar. Combine flours in a mixing bowl. Put 2 cups flour mixture, shortening, and salt in the food processor with the steel blade and process with quick on/off motions until mixture resembles cornmeal. Add ½ cup yeast mixture and process with 4 quick on/off motions. Add remaining yeast mixture and process with 4 quick on/off motions. Add remaining flour mixture, process with 4 quick on/off motions. Let machine run for about 15 seconds or until ball of dough forms. If dough seems sticky (it depends on weather and flour), add 1 to 2 tablespoons unbleached flour. Do not process more than 60 seconds. Place dough in a greased bowl. Grease surface of dough, cover and let rise in a warm place until dough doubles, about 45 to 60 minutes. Punch down and shape into a loaf. Preheat oven to 375 degrees F. Place in a buttered 8 × 4-inch loaf pan, cover, and let rise until dough has doubled, about 30 to 45 minutes. Bake for 45 minutes or until nicely browned. If bread browns too rapidly, cover loosely with foil for the last 20 minutes. Cool on wire rack.

Yield: 1 loaf

MOTHER'S SALLY LUNN BREAD

1 cup milk, scalded
½ cup sugar
½ cup melted butter or ¾ cup
  oil
2 teaspoons salt

1 package dry yeast
½ cup lukewarm water
3 eggs, beaten
5 cups flour, sifted

Combine milk, sugar, butter, and salt. Heat just a little but do not boil. Cool to lukewarm. Dissolve yeast in lukewarm water. Mix with milk mixture, add eggs, and blend well. Gradually add flour until smooth. Beat until all the air is out. Cover and let rise in a warm place until the dough has doubled in bulk. Stir down. Place on a floured board and shape into two loaves. Place in 2 greased 9 × 5-inch loaf pans and let rise again. Preheat oven to 350 degrees F. Bake for about 40 minutes or until golden brown. Old Southerners sometimes sprinkled loaf with sugar and ½ teaspoon nutmeg and served with 3 pints of sliced sweetened berries and fresh whipped cream for dessert.

Yield: 2 loaves

MUENSTER BREAD

The secret is the cheese, so please do not substitute any other cheese.

2 packages dry or compressed
  yeast
¼ cup warm water
1 cup warm milk

1½ tablespoons sugar
1½ teaspoons salt
½ cup butter, melted
3 to 4 cups flour

FILLING:
2 pounds Muenster cheese,
  grated

1 egg, beaten
3 tablespoons butter, melted

Dissolve yeast in warm water and set aside. Combine milk, sugar, salt, and butter in a large mixing bowl. Blend well and add yeast mixture. Beat in 2 cups flour until mixture is smooth. Add enough flour to make a soft, workable dough. Turn out on a lightly floured board and knead until smooth and satiny, about 8 minutes. Form into a ball and place in a warm, greased bowl, turning to grease the top. Allow to double in bulk, about 1 hour.

Punch down and let rise again, about 30 minutes. Meanwhile, combine filling ingredients and set aside. Brush a 9- or 10-inch cake pan with melted butter. Punch the dough down, place on a floured board, cover, and let rest for 10 to 15 minutes. Roll into a large circle 24 to 26 inches in diameter. If dough resists, cover and let rest again. Fold circle of dough in half and lay across half the prepared pan. Unfold the dough. Carefully lift and press dough to fit into the pan leaving a skirt of dough draped over the rim. Mound the cheese mixture on the dough, making it higher in the center. Pick up the skirt of the dough and begin to pleat in loose folds around the mounded cheese, lifting and rotating the pan as you progress. Gather the ends on top and twist into a knob. Encircle the bottom of the knob with both hands and give it a firm twist. If any dough is torn, pinch together firmly. Set aside for 15 minutes. Preheat oven to 375 degrees F. Give knob one more twist. Bake for 1 hour or until golden brown. Let bread cool on wire rack. Do not attempt to slice until cheese has congealed, about 40 minutes. Completely cooled bread can be reheated wrapped in foil for 20 minutes at 350 degrees F. Freezes well.

Serves 10 to 12

BACON AND CORN SPOONBREAD

¾ cup yellow cornmeal
1½ cups water
¼ cup butter
8 ounces Cheddar cheese, shredded
1½ cups cooked fresh corn (3 large ears) or 1 package (10 ounces) frozen corn, cooked

2 cloves garlic, minced
1 teaspoon salt
1 cup milk
4 eggs, separated
10 slices bacon, cooked and crumbled

Preheat oven to 325 degrees F. Combine cornmeal and water in a saucepan and cook over medium-high heat, stirring constantly until thick. Remove from heat and add butter and cheese. Stir until both are melted. Add corn, garlic, and salt. Stir in milk. Beat egg yolks until thick and lemon-colored; add bacon. Stir into cornmeal mixture. Beat egg whites until stiff but not dry and fold gently into cornmeal mixture. Pour into a lightly greased 2½-quart casserole or soufflé dish. Bake for 1 hour or more until knife inserted in center comes out clean. Serve with melted butter or syrup.

Serves 6

WHOLE WHEAT BREAD

1½ packages dry yeast
2½ cups lukewarm water
1 tablespoon sugar
1 egg, beaten
½ cup shortening, melted
2½ teaspoons salt

½ cup brown sugar, honey, or
  molasses
3 cups whole wheat flour
5 cups white or unbleached flour
¼ cup wheat germ

Dissolve yeast in ½ cup of the water. Add 1 tablespoon sugar and let stand for 45 minutes. Beat in egg, remaining water, shortening, salt, and brown sugar. Sift flours together and add wheat germ. Stir flour into mixture until a very thick batter is formed. Pour onto a floured board and knead in remaining flour, about 10 minutes. Place dough in a greased bowl and let rise until doubled in size. Punch down, turn over, and let rise again until doubled. Punch down and divide into 3 loaves. Place in 3 greased 9 × 5-inch loaf pans and let rise until doubled. Preheat oven to 400 degrees F. Bake for 15 minutes, reduce heat to 375 degrees F. and continue baking for 25 minutes. Bread is done when tapping it makes a hollow sound. This recipe can be doubled and extra loaves frozen.

Yield: 3 loaves

Variation: For Raisin Bread, add 3 cups plumped raisins to batter. For Cinnamon Bread, when dough has risen a second time, divide into 3 portions and roll out into rectangles. Brush with melted butter and sprinkle with cinnamon sugar. Roll up jelly-roll fashion and place in prepared pans for final rising. Bake as directed and ice with a thick glaze made from 1 cup powdered sugar, 2 tablespoons milk and ½ teaspoon vanilla.

CINNAMON BREAD STICKS

¼ cup butter, melted
1 package (3½ ounces) bread
  sticks (plain, long, thin)

½ cup sugar
1 teaspoon cinnamon

Preheat oven to 350 degrees F. Pour melted butter over bread sticks and roll to coat well. Roll buttered sticks in a mixture of the sugar and cinnamon. Place on shiny foil and bake for 10 minutes. Cool and wrap in foil or store in a plastic bag until ready to use. These may be frozen and heated briefly at 350 degrees F. before serving.

Yield: About 40

RIZ BISCUITS

5 cups flour
2 teaspoons salt
2 teaspoons baking powder
1 teaspoon baking soda
2 tablespoons sugar
1 cup shortening

1 package dry yeast
¼ cup lukewarm water
1¾ cups buttermilk, room
   temperature
Butter

Preheat oven to 450 degrees F. Sift together flour, salt, baking powder, baking soda, and sugar. Cut in shortening with a pastry blender or fork. Dissolve yeast in warm water. Add slightly cooled yeast to buttermilk and blend into dry ingredients. Form into a ball and place on a lightly floured board. Roll out the dough until thin and cut into small biscuits. Brush biscuits with melted butter and place on a cookie sheet in stacks of two. Let biscuits rise until doubled. Bake for 12 minutes. Serve warm.

Yield: 3 dozen

EASY TOMATO CHEESE BREAD

BREAD:
2 cups biscuit mix
⅔ cup milk

3 medium tomatoes, peeled and
   sliced ¼ inch thick

TOPPING:
1½ cups finely chopped yellow
   onion
2 tablespoons butter
¾ cup sour cream
⅓ cup mayonnaise
1 cup grated Cheddar cheese

1 teaspoon salt
¼ teaspoon pepper
¼ teaspoon leaf oregano
Pinch of sage
Paprika for garnish

BREAD: Preheat oven to 400 degrees F. Butter a 13 × 9 × 2-inch baking dish. Combine biscuit mix and milk. Knead lightly on a well-floured surface. Roll out dough until it is a little larger than the dish. Press into dish, pushing dough up on sides to form a ½-inch rim. Arrange tomato slices on top.
TOPPING: Sauté onion in butter until tender, add remaining ingredients, and spread over tomatoes. Sprinkle with paprika and bake for 25 minutes.

Serves 12

CORNBREAD DAVIS

This is a soft cornbread.

1 cup cornmeal
1 heaping teaspoon baking
  powder
1 teaspoon salt
½ teaspoon baking soda

1 cup sour cream
1 can (8½ ounces) cream-style
  corn
2 eggs, beaten

Preheat oven to 400 degrees F. Place a greased 8-inch iron skillet or muffin pan in hot oven while mixing batter. (Greasing pan with bacon drippings adds extra flavor.) Combine cornmeal, baking powder, salt, and baking soda. Add sour cream, corn, and eggs; mix thoroughly. Pour into hot pan and bake for 20 to 25 minutes or until golden brown.

Serves 6

Variation: For jalapeño cornbread add one can (4 ounces) chopped green chilies and chopped jalapeño pepper to taste.

SAVORY CHEESE LOAF

1 loaf (1 pound) day-old
  unsliced white bread
½ pound grated American
  processed cheese

½ cup butter, melted
1½ tablespoons grated onion
1 teaspoon Worcestershire sauce
½ teaspoon celery seed

Preheat oven to 350 degrees F. Trim crusts from top, sides and ends of bread. Slice vertically in thirds lengthwise; be careful not to cut through bottom crust! Slice vertically about 1½ inches apart crosswise. The loaf will have a checkerboard appearance from the top. Combine cheese, ¼ cup of the butter, onion, Worcestershire sauce, and celery seed. Spread between all the slices. Brush top and sides of loaf with melted butter and secure bread with toothpicks. Place loaf on a cookie sheet and bake for 20 to 25 minutes until cheese mixture is melted and light golden brown. Serve warm. To freeze, wrap unbaked bread in heavy-duty foil. When ready to serve, thaw and brush generously with melted butter. Bake as directed.

Yield: 1 loaf

SOFT PRETZELS

Children love to make these. Don't be limited to pretzel shapes—be creative!

1 package dry yeast	2 teaspoons sugar
1½ cups lukewarm water (105 to 110 degrees F.)	4 cups flour
	1 egg, beaten
1 teaspoon salt	Coarse kosher salt

Preheat oven to 400 degrees F. Dissolve yeast in warm water in a large bowl. Add salt, sugar, and flour. Stir until mixture is smooth and does not stick to the sides of the bowl. Place the dough on a floured board and knead to make a soft, smooth dough, about 10 minutes. Extra flour will be needed. Do not let the dough rise. Cut immediately into small pieces and roll into pencil-thin ropes. Shape into pretzel or other shapes. To shape like a pretzel: roll dough about 14 inches long; bend into a "U" shape; cross one end of the rope over the other about 3 inches from the ends; twist crossed ends a full turn; fold back toward middle of "U" and open slightly. Press ends into dough firmly. Place on a cookie sheet covered with foil and lightly floured. Brush with egg and sprinkle with salt. Bake for 15 minutes or until golden brown.

Yield: Approximately 3 dozen pretzels

CHAPTER V

FISH

*Galveston
and Galveston Bay*

Fifty-five miles southeast of Downtown Houston, on a narrow semitropical barrier island shaped and reshaped by the waves and hurricanes of the Gulf of Mexico, is Galveston, once the most prosperous and important commercial city in the Southwest. Despite the devastating 1900 storm, which killed more than six thousand people and ranks as the nation's worst natural disaster, many of the island's stone and carpenter-gothic buildings still stand, dating back as far as the late 1830s. At the wharves, which bustle with the export of sugar and the import of tea, the 160-foot 1877 square-rigger *Elissa* towers over weekending Houstonians. The embossed iron-front shops and restaurants along The Strand reflect the era when that thoroughfare was known as "The Wall Street of the Southwest."

Galveston's nineteenth-century charm exerts an almost irresistible appeal. This is where Cabeza de Vaca, the first European to set foot on Texas soil, landed in 1528, and where pirate chieftain Jean Laffite held sway. Many of the immigrants who settled the rest of Texas and the Southwest entered through this port. And even though upstart Houston eventually outstripped the Gilded Isle in population and prominence, Galveston maintains its grace and traditions.

Many of these customs center around the fishing and seafood industry. The marshes and inlets of Galveston Bay and other coastal waterways are prime breeding grounds for shrimp and oysters. Tasty blue crabs comb the bottom of the bay, there for anyone with a string and a chicken neck. Redfish, pompano, snapper, speckled trout, and other species churn the waters of the Gulf.

On the weekend after Easter, Galveston turns the annual Blessing of the Shrimp Fleet into a giant seafood festival. Boiled, fried, baked, and stuffed shrimp, iced shrimp to cart home by the coolerful, shrimp gumbo, and shrimp *en brochette*—they're all there to be sampled on the wharves and on the streets. But it doesn't take a special event to bring out the great seafood in Galveston and the smaller towns around the bay. At restaurants, waiters in immaculate uniforms serve elegant seafood. In little backroad cafes, patrons in T-shirts and cutoffs eat sweet boiled blue crabs over sheets of newspaper. Cracking and cleaning these delicacies is messy work but well worth it.

Italian, Greek, Mexican, and Cajun restaurants all have their own special hand with local seafood.

At the sides of the highway leading to and from Galveston and along the roads winding around the bay, vendors sell raw shrimp and oysters from refrigerated trucks. Houstonians often buy them to take back to the city or to their beach cottages and bayhouses, where the purchase supplements a feast of fresh-caught crabs and scale fish. Recipes like those in this chapter —Crab Quiche, Oyster Curry, Mother's Bayhouse Crab Salad, Different Shrimp Creole, Fish Fillets with Basil Sauce, and the like—demonstrate the varied ways to savor this briny bounty, whether you snag it in the Gulf or in the supermarket.

AUNT SARA'S BASS STEAKS

Bass steaks
Salt and pepper
Lemon juice

Mayonnaise
Parmesan cheese

Season bass steaks with salt and pepper. Sprinkle a teaspoon of lemon juice over each steak and let stand at room temperature for about 15 minutes. Prepare enough mayonnaise mixed together with a large quantity of Parmesan cheese to cover steaks. Coat steaks and broil until they flake, about 5 to 7 minutes. Cover with mayonnaise mixture again and return to broiler until bubbly and slightly browned, about 2 to 3 minutes. Take care not to overcook.

WHITE CLAM SPAGHETTI

4 cans minced white clams with
    juice
1 cup butter
5 cloves garlic, mashed
1 tablespoon fresh lemon juice
1 tablespoon grated onion
1 tablespoon chopped fresh
    parsley

Chopped chives to taste
Seasoned salt to taste
Ground white pepper to taste
1 cup heavy cream
3 tablespoons cornstarch or
    arrowroot
16 ounces spaghetti

Heat clams, juice, and butter in a saucepan. Add all remaining ingredients except cream, cornstarch, and spaghetti, and simmer for 15 minutes. Adjust seasoning. Mix a small amount of cream with cornstarch. Then combine with remaining cream. Add cream a little at a time to clam sauce until it reaches the right consistency to coat spaghetti not too thickly. Cook spaghetti according to package directions. Drain well and serve sauce on top.

Serves 5 to 6

CALIFORNIA CRAB SANDWICHES

1 cup grated Monterey Jack or
   Colby cheese
½ pound fresh or frozen crab
   meat
½ cup sour cream
¼ cup chopped water chestnuts
2 tablespoons finely chopped
   green onion

1 tablespoon lemon juice
1 teaspoon soy sauce
1 teaspoon seasoned salt
¼ teaspoon Tabasco
Pimiento slivers for garnish
3 English muffins, split, buttered,
   and toasted

Combine ½ cup of the cheese with all but pimiento and spread on muffins. Top with remaining cheese and broil until bubbly. Garnish with pimiento. This is also tasty served cold as a salad without the cheese topping.

Serves 6

CHESAPEAKE BAY CRAB CAKES

2 tablespoons minced onion
2 tablespoons butter or other fat
1 pound crab meat, cleaned
1 egg, beaten
½ teaspoon dry mustard

½ teaspoon salt
Dash of pepper
Dash of cayenne pepper
½ cup dry bread crumbs

Cook onion in 2 tablespoons butter until tender. Combine all remaining ingredients except crumbs. Shape into six cakes and roll in crumbs. Place cakes in a heavy frying pan which contains about ⅛ inch fat, hot but not smoking. Fry at moderate heat. When cakes are brown on one side, turn carefully and brown the other side. Cooking time will be approximately 5 to 8 minutes. Drain on absorbent paper.

Serves 6

Variation: Add 1 teaspoon Worcestershire sauce, 1 teaspoon lemon juice, ¼ teaspoon Old Bay Seasoning and 1 tablespoon minced parsley to above ingredients and cook in the same manner. Cakes may be fried in 2 tablespoons hot oil and drained on paper towels.

MARYLAND DEVILED IMPERIAL CRAB

½ to 1 green bell pepper, finely
   chopped
1 small onion, minced
4 tablespoons butter
1 tablespoon prepared mustard
1 tablespoon dry mustard
½ teaspoon salt

2 tablespoons brandy
½ cup Cream Sauce (below)
2 tablespoons fine dry bread
   crumbs
1 pound fresh lump crab meat,
   picked

Preheat oven to 400 degrees F. Sauté green pepper and onion in 2 tablespoons of the butter over low heat for 10 minutes. Stir in mustards, salt, brandy, Cream Sauce, and 1 tablespoon bread crumbs. Add crab meat, and heat for several minutes. Spoon into a baking dish or individual shells or ramekins. Sprinkle with remaining crumbs and dot with remaining butter. Bake 10 minutes for shells or 25 minutes for dish. Broil to brown tops.

Serves 4

CREAM SAUCE

1 cup milk
1 thin slice of onion
1 sprig parsley
2 tablespoons butter
2 tablespoons flour

Salt to taste
White pepper to taste
Dash of nutmeg
2 tablespoons heavy cream

Combine milk with onion and parsley and bring to a boil in a small saucepan. In an enameled or stainless steel saucepan, melt butter and mix with flour into a smooth paste. Strain the milk mixture and whip into flour mixture until it is thick and smooth. Simmer gently for 5 minutes, stirring occasionally. Add seasonings and cream.

Yield: 1¼ cups

CRAB QUICHE

1 cup mayonnaise
2 tablespoons flour
2 eggs, beaten
½ cup milk
1 package (6 ounces) frozen
　king crab, drained and picked
½ pound Swiss cheese, cut into
　¼-inch cubes

⅓ cup chopped green onions
Parsley
Mushrooms (optional)
9-inch pastry shell, baked and
　cooled

Preheat oven to 350 degrees F. Mix all filling ingredients thoroughly and spoon into pie shell. Bake for 30 to 40 minutes or until firm in center.

Serves 6

CRAB MEAT MORNAY

This can also be served in a chafing dish as an appetizer.

1 small bunch green onions,
　finely chopped
½ cup chopped fresh parsley
½ cup butter
2 tablespoons flour
1 pint half-and-half

½ pound sharp cheese, grated
Salt and pepper to taste
1 tablespoon sherry (optional)
1 pound white lump crab meat,
　drained, and picked

Sauté onions and parsley in butter. Stir in flour, cream, and cheese until melted. Add remaining ingredients, gently folding in crab meat last. Serve in chafing dish or patty shells.

Serves 4 to 6

CRAB MEAT SUPREME

½ cup butter
2 tablespoons flour
1½ cups light cream
2 egg yolks, beaten
1 teaspoon Worcestershire sauce

Dash of paprika
¼ cup sherry or to taste
1 pound fresh lump crab meat,
 picked

Preheat oven to 350 degrees F. Melt butter. Add and blend in flour over low heat. Stir in cream slowly and blend well. Add egg yolks, then seasonings. Gently stir in crab meat. Bake in a buttered casserole for 30 minutes.

Serves 4 to 6

MABEL'S CRAB DISH

2 tablespoons butter
1 pound lump crab meat, picked
Salt and pepper to taste
½ cup sweet cream

2 egg yolks, slightly beaten
Grated cheese
Additional butter

Preheat oven to 350 degrees F. Heat butter, crab meat, and seasonings in a saucepan for 5 minutes. Add cream and egg yolks and stir until heated through. Spoon into a buttered baking dish and sprinkle with grated cheese. Dot with bits of butter and bake until golden brown.

Serves 4

MOTHER'S BAYHOUSE CRAB SALAD
(RED BLUFF)

Boiled cold crab meat from 1 dozen large crabs or 1 to 2 pounds fresh lump crab meat.

1 cup (or more) mayonnaise
1 tablespoon capers
1 teaspoon lemon juice
1 cup coarsely chopped celery
4 water chestnuts, coarsely
 chopped

1 small onion, grated or finely
 chopped
Salt and pepper to taste

Mix all ingredients lightly and serve on lettuce cups. This is beautiful surrounded by hard-cooked-egg slices, tomato slices, green-pepper slices, pickles, and olives!

Serves 6

PEGGY'S DEVILED CRAB

½ cup minced onion
¼ cup minced celery
¼ cup minced green bell pepper
1 clove garlic, minced
1 tablespoon chopped parsley
¾ cup butter
2 cups soft bread crumbs
½ cup heavy cream
1 hard-cooked egg, chopped
1 tablespoon white wine vinegar

1 teaspoon Worcestershire sauce
¼ heaping teaspoon dried
 thyme, crumbled
1 teaspoon salt
Cayenne pepper or Tabasco to
 taste
2 eggs, beaten
1 pound fresh lump crab meat,
 washed and picked
Lemon wedges

Preheat oven to 450 degrees F. Sauté vegetables in ¼ cup of the butter for 10 minutes or until tender. Add 1 cup of the bread crumbs, cream, hard-cooked egg, and seasonings. Mix well. Add beaten eggs and crab meat. Melt remaining ½ cup butter and add remaining bread crumbs. Toss and reserve for topping. Pour crab mixture into 12 buttered ramekins or deep shells. Top with buttered crumbs. Bake ramekins in ¼-inch-deep hot-water bath for 10 minutes or until crumbs are golden. Serve with tiny lemon wedges. This may also be cooked in a shallow buttered 2-quart casserole in a ¼-inch water bath for 30 minutes or until crumbs are golden.

Serves 12

BAKED FISH

½ cup liquid margarine
Juice of 2 limes
Salt and pepper to taste
Pressed garlic to taste

3 pounds skinned fish fillets
½ cup Parmesan cheese
2 cans (3 ounces each) fried
 onions, crushed

Preheat oven to 400 degrees F. Beat margarine, lime juice, salt, pepper, and garlic until smooth. Spread liberally on both sides of fillets and marinate for 1 hour in a Pyrex baking dish. Sprinkle with Parmesan cheese and crushed onions. Bake for 15 minutes or until just done, depending on thickness of fish.

Serves 6 to 8

FISH FILLETS WITH BASIL SAUCE

2 tablespoons butter
2 tablespoons flour
½ cup sherry, sauterne, or
    chablis
½ cup chicken broth
2 teaspoons fresh basil or ½
    teaspoon dried basil

½ teaspoon thyme
2 tablespoons chives
Salt and pepper
2 pounds fish fillets
3 tomatoes, peeled and sliced

Preheat oven to 300 degrees F. Melt butter and stir in flour. Gradually add wine and broth, then the herbs and cook until thickened. Salt and pepper fillets and lay them in a greased casserole. Place the tomato slices on top. Pour sauce over all. Bake for 30 minutes or until done.

Serves 2 to 4

WHOLE GRILLED FISH

10 sprigs parsley
1 shallot, minced
½ cup butter, diced
6 to 8 pounds whole fish
    (salmon, seabass, bluefish)

½ teaspoon salt
¼ teaspoon pepper
2 cups dry white wine
Beurre Blanc Sauce (below)

Place parsley, shallot, and half the butter inside fish. Season inside and out with salt and pepper. Dot with remaining butter and place on heavy-duty aluminum foil. Shape foil to hold wine. Pour wine over fish and seal foil *tightly*. Place 4 to 5 inches from medium-hot coals. Cook 5-pound salmon for 1 hour (2-pound bass 45 to 60 minutes) until fish flakes easily. Remove parsley and bones. Serve with Beurre Blanc Sauce.

Serves 8

BEURRE BLANC SAUCE

12 ounces butter, chilled
¼ cup white wine vinegar
¼ cup dry white wine or lemon
 juice
1 tablespoon finely minced
 shallots or green onions

¼ teaspoon salt
⅛ teaspoon white pepper
Salt and pepper, to taste
Lemon juice, to taste

Cut butter into 24 pieces and chill. In a 6-cup medium-weight enamel saucepan, boil vinegar, wine, shallots, salt, and white pepper until reduced to about 1½ tablespoons. Remove pan from heat and beat in 2 pieces of butter. As butter melts, beat in another piece. Over very low heat, and beating constantly, continue adding butter piece by piece. The sauce will have the consistency of a light hollandaise. Remove from heat as soon as all the butter has been added. Beat in salt and pepper and lemon juice to taste.

Yield: 1½ cups

MAUDIE WESTON'S FRIED FISH FILLETS

5 medium to large fish fillets
1 cup buttermilk
1 stack Ritz crackers, rolled into
 crumbs

2 tablespoons dried parsley
1 teaspoon sweet basil
½ teaspoon oregano (optional)
Crisco oil

Soak fish in buttermilk for 1 hour to overnight. Drain slightly and coat with cracker crumbs to which other ingredients have been added. Set aside on wax paper for 45 minutes to 1 hour to dry. Fry in ¼-inch hot cooking oil for about 3 minutes on each side or until golden.

Serves 5

FROG LEGS

24 pairs frog legs, medium size	1 tablespoon minced garlic
Buttermilk to cover	2 tablespoons chopped shallots
Flour to coat	2 tablespoons minced parsley
¾ cup butter	2 tablespoons chopped chives
Salt and pepper	Juice of 1 large lemon

Wash and dry frog legs and cover with buttermilk for 30 minutes. Shake off excess buttermilk and dip frog legs in flour. Sauté in 6 tablespoons of the butter until golden brown and cooked through, about 10 minutes. Season with salt and pepper and place on a warm platter. Discard pan butter. Sauté garlic, shallots, parsley, and chives in remaining butter. Stir a few minutes over the heat and pour over frog legs. Pour lemon juice over all.

Serves 6

OYSTER CURRY

3 quarts oysters	2 tablespoons curry powder
1 cup butter	3 tablespoons chopped fresh
1 cup chopped celery	parsley
3 tablespoons minced green	1 teaspoon celery salt
onion	Salt and pepper to taste
1 cup flour	1 cup half-and-half
1 cup warmed oyster liquor	

The day before serving, drain oysters, reserving liquor. Run warm/hot water over oysters and drain again. Do this several times, refrigerating in between. It will prevent oysters from bleeding and making the sauce too thin.

Melt butter and sauté celery and green onion until softened. Add flour to make a paste. Slowly add warmed oyster liquor, blending until smooth. Add curry, parsley, celery salt, salt, pepper, and oysters. Mix well, stirring until sauce is thickened. Add half-and-half. Serve over toast, patty shells, or rice. This may be reheated in a double boiler or oven. This recipe can be divided easily.

Serves 16

EVA'S OYSTERS

2 quarts oysters
¾ cup butter
½ cup flour
3 cups oyster liquor
2 onions, diced
5 cloves garlic, crushed

1 large green bell pepper, diced
2 beef bouillon cubes
2 tablespoons A.1. sauce
Dash white pepper
1 cup cream
Sherry to taste

Boil oysters 5 minutes until they curl and drain, reserving liquid. Melt ½ cup of the butter, and add flour to make a paste. Stir in oyster liquor to make a thick sauce. Sauté onion, garlic, and green pepper in remaining ¼ cup of butter until soft. Add to cream sauce. Dissolve bouillon cubes in 1 cup water and add to cream sauce. Add A.1. sauce, pepper, and cream to sauce. Add oysters and sherry. Serve over toast or in a chafing dish.

Serves 8 to 10

SALMON-CUCUMBER MOUSSE

1 can (16 ounces) red salmon
2 envelopes unflavored gelatin
1 cup sour cream
3 to 4 tablespoons fresh lemon juice
1 cup mayonnaise
1 tablespoon grated onion, pulp and juice
1½ teaspoons prepared horseradish

½ teaspoon salt
¾ cup peeled, seeded, grated cucumber (about 1½ medium cucumbers)
Paprika, sliced stuffed olives, parsley, sliced unpeeled cucumbers for garnish

Drain salmon, reserving liquid. Pour hot water over salmon to remove grease. Remove skin and large bones; flake. Add enough water to salmon liquid to make ½ cup. Bring to a boil and pour over gelatin to dissolve. Cool. In a large bowl, beat sour cream, add lemon juice, mayonnaise, onion, and seasonings, mixing well. Fold in cucumber and salmon. Oil custard cups, individual molds or fish mold with mayonnaise and fill with mixture. Chill to set. Garnish with paprika, sliced stuffed olives or parsley and unpeeled cucumber slices. Flavor improves if this is made the day before.

Serves 6 to 8

HOT SEAFOOD SALAD

1 pound lump crab meat, picked
1 pound cooked shrimp
1 medium onion, chopped
1 large green bell pepper,
  chopped
1 cup chopped celery
1 can (4 ounces) chopped
  mushrooms
2 cans (8 ounces each) water
  chestnuts

4 hard-cooked eggs, chopped
1 small package (5 ounces)
  slivered almonds
1 pint mayonnaise
1 teaspoon salt
2 teaspoons Worcestershire sauce
Bread crumbs
Paprika

Preheat oven to 350 degrees F. Mix together all ingredients except bread crumbs and paprika. Place in a shallow 3-quart casserole. Sprinkle crumbs and paprika on top. Bake for 30 minutes. This is good as a cold salad either before or after cooking.

Serves 8

SEAFOOD CHANTILLY

3 tablespoons butter
3 tablespoons flour
1½ cups milk
1½ pounds fresh lump crab
  meat or 3 cans (7½ ounces,
  each) king crab, picked

5 egg whites
¾ cup mayonnaise
¼ cup grated Parmesan cheese

Preheat oven to 350 degrees F. Melt butter, add flour, and cook until bubbly. Add milk, and cook until thick, stirring constantly. Gently add crab meat and stir carefully with a fork. Place in a buttered shallow 1½-quart casserole. Beat egg whites until stiff and fold into mayonnaise. Cover crab meat with this mixture. Sprinkle with cheese. Bake until hot and run under the broiler to brown. Any flaked white fish, lobster, scallops, or shrimp can be substituted.

Serves 6

RED SNAPPER ITALIENNE

Salt and pepper
Paprika
Italian seasoning
6 medium snapper fillets

2 to 3 large onions, thinly sliced
3 to 4 large, juicy lemons
½ cup butter

Preheat oven to 500 degrees F. Line 2 pans with foil. Liberally sprinkle salt, pepper, paprika, and Italian seasoning on both sides of fillets. Place fillets in pans on a bed of sliced onions, reserving some of the onions for the top. Thinly slice 1 lemon and arrange over fillets. Squeeze remaining lemons over fish. Cut butter into small pieces and divide equally on top of fillets. Bake for 20 minutes. Spoon juices on top of each serving.

Serves 6

BAKED SHRIMP

1 ½ cups butter or margarine
2 cloves garlic, chopped
1 onion, chopped
1 stalk celery, chopped
1 cup white wine
2 to 3 ½ ounces frozen lemon
  juice, or to taste
1 tablespoon Worcestershire
  sauce

Dash oregano
Salt to taste
Freshly ground black pepper to
  taste
Cayenne to taste
Parsley
Several drops Tabasco
  (optional)
6 pounds shrimp, including heads

Preheat oven to 350 degrees F. Combine all ingredients except shrimp, and sauté until tender. Pour over shrimp in an oblong baking dish. Marinate for 30 minutes to 1 hour, turning frequently. Bake 30 to 45 minutes, turning every 10 minutes, until done to taste.

Serves 12

SHRIMP À LA MAISON

12 to 16 jumbo shrimp, peeled
  and butterflied
8 large mushrooms, finely sliced
4 artichoke hearts, halved
1 cup cold butter, cut into
  chunks

½ ounce Marsala wine
Pinch of salt
1 ounce chablis
Pinch of marjoram

Combine shrimp, mushrooms, and artichoke hearts in a large skillet with ½ of the cold butter, Marsala wine, and salt. Sauté slowly. Slowly add the chablis, and continue cooking until shrimp are firm and pink, about 3 to 4 minutes. Add marjoram and the remaining butter chunks. Serve when the butter is just melted.

Serves 2 but easily doubled

DIFFERENT SHRIMP CREOLE

4 onions, finely chopped
4 tablespoons butter plus 1 cup
  butter *or* ½ pound diced
  bacon
5 pounds raw shrimp, shelled and
  deveined
½ pound mushrooms, sliced
½ cup Madeira wine or good
  dry sherry
3 green bell peppers, thinly
  sliced

2 cloves garlic, minced
4 cups celery, chopped
½ cup minced parsley
3 cans (16 ounces each)
  tomatoes
½ teaspoon black pepper
1 teaspoon salt
1 teaspoon thyme
1 teaspoon curry powder
½ teaspoon cayenne
1 bay leaf

Sauté ¼ cup of the onions in 4 tablespoons of the butter until soft. Add shrimp and toss in butter until pink. Add mushrooms and Madeira. Set aside. In a large, deep, heavy pot, fry bacon or melt remaining cup of butter. Add remaining onions, peppers, garlic, celery, and parsley, and sauté until soft. Add tomatoes and spices. When heated through and beginning to boil, reduce heat and simmer for 45 minutes. Fifteen minutes before serving, remove bay leaf and add shrimp mixture. Cook for 15 minutes more. Serve immediately over steamed rice.

Serves 10 to 12

FRIED SHRIMP

2 large eggs, beaten
½ teaspoon salt
¼ teaspoon cayenne
1 tablespoon cornstarch

2 pounds fresh shrimp, shelled
and deveined
Cracker crumbs
Flour

Combine eggs, salt, cayenne, and cornstarch, and mix well. Fold in shrimp and let stand for 1 hour or more. Roll shrimp individually in mixture of equal parts cracker crumbs and flour. Fry in deep fat until golden brown. Eat immediately.

Serves 6

SALLY'S SHRIMP

½ pound fresh mushrooms,
thinly sliced
1 pound jumbo fresh raw
shrimp, peeled and butterflied

Lemon pepper
Paprika
½ cup butter, melted
½ cup fresh lemon juice

Preheat oven to 350 degrees F. Place mushrooms in a buttered Pyrex casserole. Place shrimp, cut side down, on top. Season with lemon pepper and paprika. Pour melted butter over shrimp and bake for 8 minutes. Pour lemon juice over shrimp and broil for 5 minutes or until shrimp are pink. Serve with wild rice.

Serves 2 to 3

BARBECUED SHRIMP

2 pounds shrimp, unpeeled
½ cup margarine, melted
1 cup olive oil
¼ cup soy sauce

¼ cup lemon juice
4 cloves garlic, crushed
1 heaping tablespoon Italian
seasoning

Preheat oven to 350 degrees F. Arrange shrimp in a shallow casserole. Combine all remaining ingredients. Pour over shrimp. Bake for 30 minutes or until done. Serve in soup bowls. Dip toasted French bread in sauce.

Serves 4 to 6

SHRIMP STROGANOFF

¼ cup minced onion
5 tablespoons butter
1 ½ pounds raw shrimp, shelled
  and deveined
½ pound mushrooms, quartered

1 tablespoon flour
1 ½ cups sour cream, at room
  temperature
1 ¼ teaspoons salt
Pepper to taste

In a large skillet, sauté minced onion in 4 tablespoons of the butter until soft. Add shrimp, and sauté until pink and just cooked, about 3 to 5 minutes. Transfer to a heated dish and keep warm. Add mushrooms and remaining tablespoon of the butter to the skillet and sauté over moderately high heat until browned. Sprinkle with flour, and cook, stirring, for 2 minutes. Reduce heat to moderately low and stir in shrimp mixture, sour cream, salt, and pepper. Continue stirring for 2 to 3 minutes or until shrimp are heated through, but do not boil. Serve over saffron rice tossed with artichoke hearts.

Serves 4

SHRIMP BROCHETTES

1 ½ pounds medium shrimp,
  shelled and deveined
3 ½ tablespoons olive oil
3 ½ tablespoons corn oil
⅔ cup fine dry bread
  crumbs

1 large clove garlic, finely minced
1 ½ tablespoons chopped parsley
¾ teaspoon salt
3 to 4 twists of pepper mill
3 lemons, cut into wedges for
  garnish

Wash shrimp in cold water and pat dry immediately. In a large mixing bowl, toss shrimp with 2 tablespoons of the olive oil, 2 tablespoons of the corn oil and half the bread crumbs. Add equal parts of oil and bread crumbs until all the shrimp have a light, even coating. Add garlic, parsley, salt, and pepper, and toss gently. Marinate at room temperature for 30 minutes to 2 hours. Skewer the shrimp lengthwise on thin metal skewers with the tail curled inward so that skewer pierces shrimp at 2 points. Grill over very hot coals for 3 minutes. Turn and grill 2 to 3 minutes more. Shrimp are done when a crisp, golden crust forms. Be careful not to overcook. Serve immediately with lemon wedges.

Serves 4

SHRIMP MARINADE/SAUCE

¼ cup olive oil
1 tablespoon chopped parsley
¾ teaspoon basil
½ teaspoon oregano
¾ teaspoon garlic salt *or* 2 cloves garlic, minced
¾ teaspoon salt

2 teaspoons coarsely ground fresh pepper
2 tablespoons lemon juice
½ pound shrimp, medium or large, peeled except for tail section

Combine first 8 ingredients and pour over shrimp. Refrigerate for 1 hour or more. Cook over hot coals or under broiler for 3 minutes on each side.

Serves 2

SCAMPI ALLA GUIGLIO

28 raw jumbo shrimp, about 1½ pounds, peeled except for tail section
1 cup butter, melted
½ cup olive oil
1 tablespoon lemon juice
¼ cup chopped shallots or green onions

3 to 4 cloves garlic, minced
Chopped parsley
Salt and pepper
Lemon slices
Crusty bread

Preheat broiler. Rinse and dry shrimp. In a 13 × 9-inch Pyrex dish, combine butter, olive oil, lemon juice, shallots, and garlic. Dip shrimp in this sauce and then lay them in the dish. Broil for 5 minutes. Turn and broil for 5 minutes more, or until done. Sprinkle with parsley, and serve with salt and pepper, lemon slices, and lots of crusty bread to soak up the sauce.

Serves 4

PAELLA

An adaptation from the Ritz Hotel in Madrid.

3 chorizo sausages, peeled and crumbled
¾ cup chopped onion
2 links Polish Kielbasa sausage, peeled and sliced
2 cloves garlic, chopped
12 pieces of chicken, 1 or more per person
1½ cups long-grain rice (not instant)
3 tablespoons olive oil
4 cups chicken stock
1 teaspoon saffron or 1 teaspoon turmeric

2 tablespoons salt
½ teaspoon pepper
1 or 2 fresh fish, skinned, boned, and cut into large pieces
24 to 36 raw shrimp, peeled
1 can mussels or 1 dozen fresh
8 artichoke hearts, frozen or canned
1 package (10 ounces) frozen green peas
1 jar (4 ounces) sliced pimientos

Preheat oven to 375 degrees F. Sauté chorizo sausage and onion in a very large skillet. Add Polish sausage, then garlic. Brown chicken pieces. Blot out any excess grease with paper towels. Add rice, olive oil, stock, saffron or turmeric, salt, and pepper. Cover, and cook until liquid is absorbed and rice cooked. Press fish pieces into rice. Decoratively arrange shrimp, mussels, and artichoke hearts on top. Sprinkle with peas and garnish with pimientos. Add additional chicken stock if needed to moisten. Bake, uncovered, for 25 minutes or until shrimp turns pink and mussels open.

Serves 12

SHRIMP TETRAZZINI

½ cup butter or margarine
1 bunch green onions, sliced
1 cup cold water
5 tablespoons flour
2½ cups chicken broth
½ cup clam juice
½ cup dry white wine
½ cup dry sherry
½ cup heavy cream
½ teaspoon oregano

1 cup shredded Parmesan cheese
2 tablespoons vegetable oil
1 pound fresh mushrooms, sliced
Dash of garlic salt
8 ounces thin spaghetti
2 pounds cooked medium shrimp
Salt and pepper to taste
Additional Parmesan cheese for
    topping

Preheat oven to 375 degrees F. Melt half the butter. Add green onions and cold water and bring to a boil. Reduce heat and simmer until water has boiled away; only the butter remains and the onions are soft. Stir in flour until smooth, and cook for about 3 minutes. Do not brown. Add broth, clam juice, wine, sherry, cream, and oregano. Cook, stirring constantly with a whisk, until sauce begins to boil. Stir in Parmesan cheese and set aside. Melt remaining butter with oil over high heat. In it sauté mushrooms with garlic salt until brown, about 4 to 5 minutes. Cook spaghetti according to package directions and drain well. Mix everything together with shrimp and season with salt and pepper. Pour into a 3-quart oblong Pyrex baking dish and sprinkle with additional Parmesan cheese. Bake uncovered for 15 to 20 minutes or until sauce is bubbly and top is brown.

Serves 10 to 12

SHRIMP BOAT

2 cups cooked shrimp
1 cup sliced ripe olives
1 cup thinly sliced fresh
    mushrooms
⅓ cup thinly sliced celery

2 tablespoons finely chopped
    green onion
1 tablespoon fresh lemon juice
2 large avocados, halved
Lettuce

DRESSING:

½ cup mayonnaise
2 tablespoons tarragon vinegar
1 tablespoon finely chopped
    parsley

¼ teaspoon dillweed
¼ teaspoon salt
¼ teaspoon onion powder
Dash of white pepper

Combine shrimp, olives, mushrooms, celery, and onion, and toss lightly with lemon juice. Cover and refrigerate. Mix dressing ingredients until smooth and creamy. Pour over salad and toss lightly. Cover and refrigerate until chilled, about 1 hour. To serve, mound salad mixture in avocado halves and place on a bed of fancy lettuce.

Serves 4

STEAMED SHRIMP

3 to 4 pounds raw shrimp, in
   shells, deheaded
2 stalks celery, cut in 3-inch
   pieces

2 onions, quartered
2 lemons, quartered
Salt
Red pepper

Wash shrimp in cold running water. Drain and place wet shrimp in large, heavy pan. Add celery, onions, and lemons. Season liberally with salt and pepper. Do not add water. Cover the pot and cook over medium heat. Stir frequently. When the shrimp are bright pink, about 10 to 12 minutes, test for tenderness. To serve hot, rinse immediately under running water and place on platter with celery and onions. To serve chilled, toss with ice cubes and refrigerate. To freeze, cool and pour, juices and all, into freezer bags.

Serves 6 as a main course

WILD RICE AND SHRIMP CASSEROLE

2 cups wild rice, uncooked
½ cup butter, melted
1½ pounds shrimp, cooked
Salt, pepper, Tabasco to taste
1 can (10½ ounces) cream of
   chicken soup

1 cup cream
1½ tablespoons onion powder
¾ teaspoon thyme
1½ tablespoons curry powder
   dissolved in ¼ cup hot water
Parsley for garnish

Preheat oven to 300 degrees F. Cook and drain 2 cups wild rice. Add melted butter and toss rice to mix thoroughly. Place half the rice in the bottom of a baking dish and add a layer of shrimp. Season with salt, pepper, and Tabasco. Top with remaining rice. Heat soup and cream. Season with onion powder, thyme, and curry. Pour over rice and bake for 45 minutes. Garnish with parsley.

Serves 10 to 12

SOLE STUFFED WITH SHRIMP AND GINGER

¼ pound fresh shrimp, shelled
and deveined
¼ cup finely chopped onion
2 tablespoons butter, melted
½ cup finely chopped celery
¾ cup finely chopped fresh
mushrooms
Salt and freshly ground pepper
to taste
1 tablespoon finely grated fresh
ginger

½ cup fine dry bread crumbs
1 tablespoon finely chopped
fresh coriander leaves
(cilantro)
8 small fillets of sole, skinned
¼ cup heavy cream
1 tablespoon soy sauce
½ cup chopped green onions

Preheat oven to 425 degrees F. Chop shrimp finely and set aside. Sauté onion in 1 tablespoon of the butter until wilted. Add celery and mushrooms and cook for 1 minute, stirring often. Season with salt and pepper. Stir in ginger and remove from heat. Scrape mixture into a mixing bowl. Add shrimp, bread crumbs, and coriander; blend well. Place 4 fillets, skinned side down, in a buttered shallow flameproof dish large enough to hold 4 fillets in a single layer. Season with salt and pepper and cover with filling. Arrange remaining 4 fillets, skinned side down, on top. Season with salt and pepper. Brush with remaining tablespoon butter. Combine cream, soy sauce, and green onions, and set aside. Put dish on stove and heat until butter starts to bubble. Transfer to oven and bake for 10 minutes. Spoon equal portions of cream mixture over fish and bake for 10 minutes more, basting occasionally. This may be prepared early in the day and refrigerated. Bring to room temperature before cooking.

Serves 4

GUMBO

¾ cup bacon fat
¾ cup flour
2 packages (10 ounces each)
    frozen chopped okra
1 green bell pepper, chopped
4 stalks celery, chopped
4 green onions, chopped
2 cloves garlic, mashed
8 cups stock (chicken or beef)

1 can (6 ounces) tomato paste
2 teaspoons pepper
1 teaspoon paprika
2 teaspoons salt
4 beef bouillon cubes
2 to 3 quarts cooked chicken or
    turkey, in chunks, and/or raw
    peeled shrimp
Tabasco to taste (optional)

Melt bacon fat. Add flour, and stir constantly over medium-heat until dark brown, taking care not to burn. This takes about 30 minutes. If mixture smells like burned bacon, throw away and begin again. Lower heat and add okra, green pepper, celery, onions, and garlic. Sauté until onions are soft. Add stock, tomato paste, seasonings, and bouillon cubes. Correct seasonings. Simmer for 2 hours. Add chicken, turkey, and/or shrimp 15 minutes before serving. Add Tabasco to taste. Freezes well.

Yield: 5 to 6 quarts

JAMBALAYA

1½ pounds smoked German
    sausage, cut in ¼-inch slices
1 to 2 pounds pork sausage or
    ground beef
3 tablespoons flour
2 onions, chopped
1 bunch green onions, chopped
1 green bell pepper, chopped
½ cup celery, diced
¼ teaspoon thyme

2 tablespoons fresh chopped
    parsley
4 cloves garlic, crushed
1 can (16 ounces) tomatoes
½ cup water
½ teaspoon salt
1 pinch cayenne or red pepper
1 cup raw rice
1 pound raw shrimp, peeled

Brown meat in a heavy iron skillet and remove. Pour off all but 3 tablespoons oil and add flour. Stirring constantly, brown flour to a dark roux over very low heat. This takes about 30 minutes. Add the next 7 ingredients and cook until soft. Add meat, tomatoes, and water. Season to taste with salt and cayenne pepper. This can be made a day or two in advance. To serve, bring jambalaya to a boil, add rice, cover, and lower heat to simmer. Cook for about 1 hour. When rice is done, add shrimp and toss until they turn pink.

Serves 8

JANIE LOWER'S POACHED TROUT IN WINE SAUCE

3½ cups fresh mushrooms, approximately ¾ pound	⅛ teaspoon salt
3½ tablespoons butter	Pinch of white pepper
2½ pounds fillet(s) of trout	¾ cup dry white wine (chablis)
2 tablespoons minced green onion	⅓ cup water

SAUCE:

2½ tablespoons flour	Lemon juice
4 tablespoons butter	Salt and pepper to taste
¾ to 1 cup heavy cream	⅓ cup grated Swiss cheese

Preheat oven to 350 degrees F. Toss mushrooms in 2 tablespoons of the butter over medium heat. Sauté 1 to 2 minutes and set aside. Arrange fillet(s) in a buttered baking dish. Sprinkle with onion, reserved mushrooms, and seasonings. Dot with remaining 1½ tablespoons butter. Add wine and enough water to just cover fish. Lay a piece of buttered brown paper over fish. Place in oven for 8 to 10 minutes until fish pierces easily.

SAUCE: Drain cooking liquid from fish into a stainless pan. Boil down to 1 cup. Remove from heat. Mix flour and 3 tablespoons of the butter and blend to a paste. Add this and ½ cup of cream to liquid, mixing well. Bring to a boil, and add more cream until sauce coats a spoon. Season with lemon juice, salt, and pepper. Spoon sauce over fish, sprinkle with Swiss cheese, and dot with remaining tablespoon butter. Place 6 inches from heat and broil for 2 to 3 minutes until sauce browns lightly.

Serves 6

FILLETS OF SOLE SAINT MORITZ

4 fillets of sole, skinned
Salt and white pepper
Fresh lemon juice
Worcestershire sauce
2 tablespoons finely chopped
   onion
2 tablespoons butter
2 tablespoons finely chopped
   shallots

2 cups dry white wine
2 ounces brandy
12 ounces small raw shrimp
16 oysters, shelled
2 cups heavy cream
BEURRE MANIÉ: 1 tablespoon
   butter blended to a paste with
   1 tablespoon flour
16 small mushroom caps, sautéed

Season fillets with salt, pepper, lemon juice, and Worcestershire sauce. Marinate for 15 minutes. Sauté onion in butter until transparent. Add shallots and sauté for ½ minute more. Do not brown. Pour in wine and brandy, and boil for 3 minutes. Remove from heat. Fold fillets in half and place on the onion mixture. Add shrimp and oysters, cover with aluminum foil, and cook for about 5 minutes or until done. Remove fillets, shrimp, and oysters from skillet and keep warm. Add cream to the skillet and boil for 3 minutes. Add the beurre manié paste little by little, until the sauce reaches the consistency of light cream. Add salt and pepper to taste. Arrange mushroom caps, shrimp, and oysters on top of the fillets, and pour the sauce over all.

Serves 4

CHAPTER VI

MEAT

Memorial Park and the Trail Rides

Admittedly, there are times when you have to look hard to find the Old West in Space Age Houston. Oilmen hang on to their good-old-boy drawls, lawyers and brain surgeons swear that they couldn't spend those hours on their feet without their handmade cowboy boots, and you can still buy a good saddle three blocks from the tallest building in town. But those touches tend to be obscured by the seas of men in three-piece suits and women in designer dresses. In Memorial Park, a verdant 1,503-acre expanse along Buffalo Bayou west of Downtown, joggers pace themselves with miniature tape players and headphones, just as they do in Golden Gate Park and Central Park.

But every year at the end of February, Houston digs up its Western roots for the Livestock Show and Rodeo. The most worldly sophisticates and staid bankers get duded up in chaps, Stetsons, prairie skirts, boots, and bandannas, heeding the citywide call to "Go Texan." During Rodeo Week, the only way to tell the urban cowboys from the gen-yew-ine rural variety is to scrutinize the labels on their jeans. Ranchers don't have signatures on their pockets.

The focus of much of the excitement, perhaps ironically, is Memorial Park, where twelve trail rides converge from all over South and East Texas, waiting to join the parade to the Astrodome that opens the Rodeo. One, Los Vaqueros Rio Grande Trail Ride, starts at the Mexican border and treks across 386 miles of semi-desert. Another, the Old Spanish Trail Ride, originates in Louisiana. The oldest of these parties, the Salt Grass Trail Ride, begins at Cat Springs, one of the first pioneer settlements in Texas.

The six thousand people who take part in these rides annually include doctors, lawyers, and businesspeople, as well as ranchers, who live in the surrounding communities. Giving up the comforts of central heat and innerspring mattresses, they spend from three days to three weeks on horseback, camping out in what often winds up being the coldest, wettest weather of the year. And yet the enthusiasm for this congenial hardship grows, perhaps because it provides a link with the state's heroic frontier past and a reminder that adversity shared can be better than comfort enjoyed alone.

One sacrifice the riders don't make is good food. Each of the trail rides has its own chuckwagons, and the range cooks are as carefully and critically chosen as the trail bosses. Barbecue, chili, cornbread, biscuits, ribs, and other cowboy fare tastes better as the miles wear on. True to their ranching heritage, Texas cooks have a way with beef, pork, and lamb; and that skill lives on in Houston's restaurants and backyards long after Rodeo season is over.

To bring a taste of Texas to your kitchen, round up some of the recipes that follow—Ranch Weekend Beef and Broth, Barbecue Beef Ribs, Texas Sirloin and One-Shot Steak Sauce, Black Jack Barbecue Sauce, or Mop Sauce. For a break from beef, try New Year's Ham, Veal Vermouth, Barbecued Butterfly Lamb, or any of the others included in this chapter. They're as delicious by candlelight as they are around a campfire.

BEEF BURGUNDY

5 medium onions, thinly sliced
2 tablespoons bacon drippings or Crisco
2 pounds boneless beef chuck, trimmed and cut into 1½-inch cubes
2 tablespoons flour
Salt and pepper to taste

Thyme to taste
Marjoram to taste
½ cup beef bouillon
1 cup dry red wine
½ pound fresh mushrooms, sliced
4 cups hot cooked rice

In a heavy skillet, cook onions in bacon drippings until brown. Remove onions from pan and set aside. Add beef and more bacon grease if necessary. Brown beef cubes well on all sides. Sprinkle beef with flour and seasonings. Stir in bouillon and wine. Simmer, covered, for 2½ to 3 hours or until meat is tender. If necesssary, add more bouillon and wine (1 part bouillon to 2 parts wine) to keep meat barely covered. Return onions to pan and add mushrooms. Cook 30 minutes longer, adding liquid if necessary. Adjust seasonings and serve over hot rice.

Serves 6

BEEF STROGANOFF AND WILD RICE

2 pounds fillet of beef, cut in
   1 × 2½-inch strips
6 plus tablespoons butter
1 cup chopped onion
1 clove garlic, minced
½ pound fresh mushrooms,
   sliced
3 tablespoons flour
2 tablespoons ketchup or tomato
   paste

½ teaspoon salt
½ teaspoon pepper
1 cup bouillon
½ to 1 cup dry white wine
1 tablespoon fresh dill or ½
   teaspoon dried
1½ cups sour cream

RICE:

2 packages (6 ounces each)
   Uncle Ben's Long Grain and
   Wild Rice
2 tablespoons butter

1 can (10½ ounces) beef
   bouillon
1 to 1¼ cans water

In a large, heavy skillet, sear meat in butter. Remove meat from skillet and drain on paper towels. In the same skillet, sauté onion and garlic until tender. Add sliced mushrooms and sauté until mushrooms begin to absorb liquid. Remove from heat and add flour, ketchup, salt, and pepper. Stir and cook over medium heat until smooth. Gradually add bouillon, and bring to a boil. Stir, reduce heat, and simmer until thickened. Over low heat, add wine and dill, and cook alcohol away. Taste; sauce should be very rich and rather strong and thick. Just before serving, add warm sour cream. When thoroughly combined, add meat, and heat over low heat until meat is warmed through. Watch carefully; do not boil.

RICE: Brown rice with butter in a large heavy saucepan or skillet, stirring constantly. When rice starts "popping," add one can beef bouillon and one can water. Stir well to be sure rice does not stick. Add seasoning packets, and cook, covered, until water is absorbed. Test a kernel or two. If still hard, add ¼ cup more water and cook until absorbed. Test again. *Do not stir rice until ready to serve.*

Serves 6 to 8

BARBECUE BEEF RIBS

5 pounds beef short ribs
3 cups Black Jack Barbecue
  Sauce (below)

Place ribs in a flat pan. Pour sauce over ribs, turning to coat. Pierce meat with a large fork. Marinate for 8 hours, turning once. Remove ribs from marinade and brush off excess. Broil or cook over coals for 10 minutes. Brush with marinade and cook for 4 to 5 minutes more. Heat remaining sauce and serve on the side. You can cook ribs in a 350 degree F. oven for 1½ hours.

Serves 4 to 6

RANCH WEEKEND BEEF AND BROTH

1 rump or well-trimmed chuck roast, 6 to 7 pounds, or 2 roasts, 3 pounds each	1 tablespoon rosemary
	1 tablespoon summer savory
	1 tablespoon oregano
3 quarts water	1 bay leaf
½ to 1 tablespoon cracked pepper	1 beef bouillon cube
1 tablespoon salt	4 small garlic cloves

Place roast in a large cooker and add water to just cover meat. Add remaining ingredients. Cover and cook on top of the stove over high heat until water begins to boil. Reduce heat and simmer for 8 to 10 hours. Do not add more water unless necessary. Before serving, remove roast from pan and shred meat with 2 forks. Strain broth. You now have a marvelous broth and lots of sandwich meat. One cup meat equals two sandwiches.

Serving Suggestions
  French Dip: Use buttered toasted French bread for sandwiches. Moisten 1 cup meat with a little broth. Spread bread with Dijon mustard, pile on meat, and serve each sandwich with a bowl of the broth to sip and/or use for a dip.
  Meat-Cheese Melt: Sauté ½ cup meat in 1 tablespoon butter. Pile the meat on a slice of toasted French bread. Top with slice of cheese and place under broiler until cheese bubbles.

Barbecue Beef: Heat ¼ cup of your favorite barbecue sauce plus 2 tablespoons water and 1 cup meat in a pan. Serve on buns.

Meat Salad Sandwich: Add ¼ cup mayonnaise, 1 tablespoon minced onion, and 1 tablespoon chopped celery to 1 cup meat. Salt and pepper to taste. Serve on rye bread.

Soft Meat Taco: Sauté 1 cup meat in 1 tablespoon butter, add 1 egg, stir, and cook until firm. Add ¼ cup Monterey Jack cheese and 1 teaspoon green taco sauce or canned green chilies.

Use your imagination! The broth makes an excellent base for many soups.

Serves: A *crowd!*

BLACK JACK BARBECUE SAUCE

1 cup strong black coffee
1 cup Worcestershire sauce
1 cup ketchup
½ cup cider vinegar
½ cup brown sugar

3 tablespoons chili powder
2 teaspoons salt
2 cups chopped onion
6 cloves garlic, minced

Combine all ingredients in a saucepan and simmer for 25 minutes over campfire or on the stove. Strain or purée in a blender or processor. Refrigerate between uses.

Yield: 5 cups

BURGUNDY BRISKET

7 pound lean brisket (do not
    trim fat)
1 large roasting bag

3 tablespoons seasoned salt
½ tablespoon pepper
2 cups red burgundy wine

Seal meat in bag with seasoned salt, pepper, and wine and marinate for 24 hours. Preheat oven to 325 degrees F. Put bag and meat in a large roasting pan that is at least 2 inches deep. Place in the oven with room for the bag to expand, and roast for 3 hours. Cool and refrigerate overnight. Preheat oven to 350 degrees F. Remove loose fat from brisket and reseal bag. Roast for 1 more hour.

Serves 8 to 10

MOP SAUCE

1 cup black coffee
½ cup ketchup
½ cup Worcestershire sauce
¼ cup butter
1 tablespoon ground pepper

1 tablespoon sugar
1 tablespoon salt
Dash hot sauce, to taste
   (optional)

Combine all ingredients in a saucepan. Heat until everything is well mixed. Use as a marinade for brisket or flank steak cooked over coals. Great for chicken, too!

Yield: 2½ cups

FILLETS OF BEEF WITH WALNUTS
AND MADEIRA SAUCE

½ pound mushrooms, finely
   chopped
3 shallots, finely chopped
4 tablespoons butter
6 beef fillets 1½ inches thick

½ cup walnuts, medium ground
½ cup soft bread crumbs
2 eggs, lightly beaten
3 tablespoons extra virgin olive
   oil

MADEIRA SAUCE:
1½ cups Quick Brown Sauce
   (below)

⅓ cup Madeira

Sauté mushrooms and shallots in 1 tablespoon of the butter until tender. Remove from skillet. Butterfly meat by cutting each fillet almost in half horizontally. Spread mushroom and shallot mixture inside and press together. Any remaining mixture may be used to stuff whole mushrooms. Mix ground nuts and bread crumbs. Dip each fillet in the lightly beaten eggs and roll in nut and crumb mixture. Refrigerate on an open rack for 3 to 5 hours. (This is important. If meat is closed in a wrapper, it will bleed. It needs to breathe.) When ready to serve, brown fillets in a mixture of 3 tablespoons butter and olive oil. Cook over high heat 3 to 5 minutes per side for a rare steak. Be careful not to burn. Cook the Quick Brown Sauce down to one cup. Add Madeira, and cook about 3 minutes. Serve sauce separately.

Serves 6

QUICK BROWN SAUCE

3 shallots or green onions, finely chopped
5 tablespoons butter
1 cup red wine
1 can (10½ ounces) beef bouillon
1 teaspoon tarragon
Pinch of thyme
3 tablespoons flour
Salt and pepper to taste

In a 4-cup saucepan, sauté the shallots or green onions in 3 tablespoons of the butter. Gradually add wine and bouillon and bring to a boil. Add tarragon and thyme and cook down for a few minutes. In a small saucepan, melt the remaining 2 tablespoons butter and mix with flour into a smooth paste. Gradually add enough flour paste to thicken the sauce. Simmer 5 minutes more and strain. Add salt and pepper to taste.

Yield: 1½ cups

DELICIOUS FLANK STEAK

2 pounds flank steak
3 tablespoons butter
2 tablespoons Dijon mustard
2 cloves garlic, chopped
1 teaspoon Worcestershire sauce
½ teaspoon salt
½ teaspoon pepper
½ cup dry sherry
1 cup sour cream
2 to 3 tablespoons brandy
¾ pound fresh mushrooms, sliced
Dash of sherry
2 tablespoons chopped fresh parsley

Place flank steak in a flat 13 × 9-inch Pyrex dish. Mix 1 tablespoon softened butter, mustard, garlic, Worcestershire, salt, and pepper together to form a paste. Spread the mixture on top of steak. Pour sherry over all and marinate in refrigerator for at least 6 hours. Remove the steak from the refrigerator to let it reach room temperature before broiling, about 3 hours. Place the meat in a preheated broiler pan, and quickly broil each side, about 5 minutes per side. Cut the steak into thin diagonal slices and set aside. Blend sour cream and brandy into the broiler pan juices. Sauté mushrooms in remaining butter over moderate heat for 5 minutes. Add sherry and pour over the steak slices. Place platter under the broiler for 1 minute longer. Garnish with parsley.

Serves 4

COMPANY FLANK STEAK

1½ to 2 pounds flank steak	Parsley
1 garlic clove, split in half	Tarragon Hollandaise Sauce
8 to 10 strips bacon	(below)

Butterfly or pound flank steak until ½ inch thick. Score meat diagonally with a knife and rub the split clove of garlic over both sides of the steak. Cook bacon until it starts to get crisp. Cover steak with bacon and sprinkle with chopped parsley. Roll into a long tight cylinder and secure with wooden skewers or toothpicks every 1½ to 2 inches. Cut meat between skewers to form pinwheels. Grill to desired doneness. Serve with Tarragon Hollandaise Sauce.

Serves 4

TARRAGON HOLLANDAISE SAUCE

4 egg yolks	2 teaspoons tarragon
2 tablespoons lemon juice	½ cup unsalted butter
½ teaspoon salt	

In a food processor, mix egg yolks, lemon juice, salt, and tarragon. Heat butter until bubbly. Turn on processor, then slowly add hot butter in a stream. Allow to cool.

Yield: ¾ to 1 cup

FLANK STEAK FLORENTINE WITH WILD RICE

3 or 4 flank steaks, 1½ pounds
    each
1 clove garlic
1½ teaspoons salt
1 package (10 ounces) frozen
    chopped spinach, thawed
1 package (8 ounces) cream
    cheese, softened

1 can (10½ ounces) condensed
    beef broth
¼ cup dry red wine
1 tablespoon flour
2 tablespoons cold water
1 package (6 ounces) long-grain
    and wild rice
1 jar (2 ounces) pimientos

Preheat oven to 350 degrees F. Pound steaks thin enough to roll easily. Mash garlic and salt. Rub evenly over meat. Cook spinach, drain, and add soft cream cheese; mix well. Spread mixture over steak surfaces. Roll steaks and tie securely with string. Place in a casserole large enough to hold all the steaks. Combine broth and wine and pour over meat. Bake, uncovered, for 1 hour, basting occasionally. Remove meat to a platter and keep warm. Drain excess fat from pan. Combine flour and water and stir into pan drippings. Cook over moderate heat until thickened. Prepare rice according to directions. Stir in pimientos. Serve with the gravy.

Serves 8

STEAK FLAMBÉ À LA HOTEL AVIZ

4 to 6 fillets of beef
1 to 2 bay leaves
3 to 4 tablespoons oil
2 tablespoons prepared mustard

½ cup Madeira
2 dashes cayenne red pepper
1 cup or less sour cream

Sauté fillets and bay leaves in oil for 3 to 4 minutes per side. Drain off excess oil if necessary. Make a sauce with the mustard, ¼ cup of the Madeira, and cayenne. Blend well and spoon over meat. Heat for about 20 seconds. Add remaining Madeira. Light with a match. After flame goes out, reduce sauce slightly. Add sour cream; stir into sauce well. Serve immediately. Meat should be medium rare.

Serves 4 to 6

HELMS MARINADE

¼ cup soy sauce
3 tablespoons honey
2 tablespoons red wine vinegar

¾ cup salad oil
1 ½ teaspoons garlic salt
1 ½ teaspoons powdered ginger

Combine ingredients to make marinade. Marinate flank steak or beef kabobs for 24 hours. Cook on grill over coals. This marinade also makes excellent fajitas by using skirt steak and slicing the meat in thin strips across the grain. Serve with warm flour tortillas.

Yield: 1 ¼ cups

MCVEA'S OVEN-ROASTING METHOD FOR BEEF

Roast
Salt

Pepper
Oil

Preheat oven to 500 degrees F. Set roast out for 3 hours or more to reach room temperature. Rub roast with salt, pepper, and oil. Place roast on a rack in an open pan or Dutch oven. Place pan in the center of the oven. *Warning:* Be sure roast is at least 8 inches from element. Close door. *Do not peek!!!* Cook as follows for rare roast and a rare treat:

Standing Rib	7 minutes per pound (bone in)
Standing Rib	5 minutes per pound (bone out)
Rib Eye	4 minutes per pound
Beef tenderloin, trimmed	3 minutes per pound

Turn off oven after the designated cooking time. Let stand in oven for 1 hour 45 minutes. The tenderloin will range from rare at thick end to medium well done at the tip. A sesame oil adds a savory nutty taste. This recipe also may be adapted to other meats, such as leg of lamb.

TEXAS SIRLOIN AND ONE-SHOT STEAK SAUCE

2 cups butter
½ cup finely chopped onion
2 cloves garlic, minced
½ cup bourbon whiskey
¼ cup Worcestershire sauce
1 tablespoon pepper

1 ½ teaspoons dry mustard
1 teaspoon salt
¼ teaspoon Tabasco
1 ½- to 2-inch-thick full sirloin
  steak

Melt butter in a saucepan; add onion and garlic. Cook slowly until onion is soft. Add remaining sauce ingredients and beat to mix. Brush sauce on both sides of steak and allow to sit for one hour. Grill over hot coals until done to desired degree. Serve steak in thin strips and pass sauce separately. Allow ⅓ to ½ pound of meat per person.

Yield: 3 cups sauce

CLIFT HOTEL CORNED BEEF HASH

¼ cup butter
1 onion, finely chopped
2 cups potatoes, finely diced
3 cups cooked lean corned beef,
  chopped fine

1 cup chicken broth
3 tablespoons A.1. sauce
1 small bay leaf
Salt to taste
Pepper to taste

Preheat oven to 350 degrees F. Melt butter in a large, ovenproof skillet or Dutch oven. Add chopped onion and sauté for 5 minutes. Add potatoes, and cook for 5 minutes more. Add corned beef, chicken broth, A.1. sauce, bay leaf, salt, and pepper. Bake uncovered for 45 minutes or until all the broth has evaporated. Cool and refrigerate overnight. Press into a large nonstick skillet and fry over medium heat until bottom is crisp. Turn over and fry on other side until crisp.

Serves 3 to 4

COUNTRY GROUND BEEF AND VEGETABLE STEW

Super on cold days with jalapeño cornbread!

1 ½ to 2 pounds ground chuck
1 cup coarsely chopped onion
1 large clove garlic, crushed
1 can (16 ounces) stewed
    tomatoes
1 can (8 ounces) tomato sauce
2 ¼ cups tomato juice
2 beef bouillon cubes
1 chicken bouillon cube
1 ½ cups boiling water
⅛ teaspoon ginger
¼ teaspoon dry mustard
¾ teaspoon oregano
1 teaspoon marjoram, crushed
1 teaspoon sweet basil, crushed
4 teaspoons dried parsley or ¼
    cup fresh minced parsley
½ teaspoon cumin powder
1 teaspoon salt

1 teaspoon seasoned salt
1 teaspoon freshly ground
    pepper
1 bay leaf
1 ½ tablespoons brown sugar
2 to 3 medium potatoes, peeled
    and chopped
3 to 4 medium zucchini or
    yellow squash, sliced in
    ½-inch rounds
1 green bell pepper, chopped
1 package (10 ounces) frozen
    corn
2 to 3 medium carrots, washed
    and sliced
1 to 2 tomatoes, chopped
    (optional)
A few stalks celery with leaves,
    chopped

In a large, heavy Dutch oven, sauté beef quickly until it loses its color. Pour off all but 2 tablespoons of grease. Add onion and garlic; sauté for 5 to 10 minutes. Add stewed tomatoes, tomato sauce, tomato juice, and bouillon cubes dissolved in 1 ½ cups boiling water. Add seasonings and brown sugar gradually, to taste. Start with these amounts; you may end up using at least twice as much, depending on your taste! While the mixture is slowly simmering, add vegetables in the order given. Use whatever vegetables you like; be creative! Simmer for 45 minutes until vegetables are tender. If you plan to freeze this, omit potatoes and add preboiled ones when ready to serve.

Yield: 3 quarts

GREEN PEPPER STEAK

2 pounds round steak, cut in
  ½-inch strips
1 clove garlic, minced
2 tablespoons olive oil
2 large green peppers, cut in thin
  strips
2 large onions, coarsely chopped
½ pound mushrooms, halved

2 teaspoons salt
½ teaspoon pepper
¾ cup burgundy wine
5 to 6 pinches curry powder, or
  more
Chicken or beef bouillon, if
  necessary

In a heavy skillet, brown meat and garlic in 1 tablespoon olive oil. In another skillet, sauté peppers and onions in remaining oil. When tender, add mushrooms, salt, and pepper. Mix with beef and add burgundy wine. Cook slowly, uncovered, for 30 minutes. Add curry powder and simmer for 1 hour. If sauce is too thick, add chicken or beef bouillon. This can be made the day before.

Serves 4

SAUSAGE STUFFED ACORN SQUASH

3 acorn squash
Butter, melted
Salt and pepper to taste
¾ pound ground beef
¼ pound sausage

½ cup chopped celery
⅓ cup chopped onion
1 can cream of mushroom soup
Bread crumbs, buttered
½ teaspoon sugar

Preheat oven to 400 degrees F. Cut squash in half lengthwise and remove seeds. Brush edges and insides with butter and season with salt and pepper. Bake, cut side down, for 45 minutes. Meanwhile, brown beef, sausage, celery, and onion in skillet. Add soup, and cook, stirring constantly, until heated through. Fill squash with meat mixture, cover with buttered bread crumbs, and sprinkle with ½ teaspoon sugar. Return to oven and bake for 20 minutes.

Serves 6

WILD RICE AND SAUSAGE DRESSING

This is a meal in itself when served with a green salad.

2 tablespoons butter
1 medium onion, chopped
1 can (4 ounces) mushrooms, drained
1 pound mild smoked link sausage, sliced thin

Sage to taste
1 box (6 ounces) Uncle Ben's Long Grain and Wild Rice

Melt butter in a large skillet. Add onions, and brown until clear. Add mushrooms, and sauté. Add sausage, and cook for 10 to 15 minutes. Add sage. This may be done earlier in the day and set aside to let season. Cook wild rice according to package directions. When done, add the sausage mixture. Toss and serve.

Serves 10 as a side dish or
6 as an entree

SMOTHERED LIVER, BACON, AND ONIONS

3 medium white onions, sliced
2 cans (10½ ounces each) beef broth
12 slices bacon

1½ to 2 pounds calf's liver
Flour
Salt
Pepper

Preheat oven to 350 degrees F. Place sliced onions in a 2-quart casserole, add 1 can broth, and bake, covered, for 1 hour and 30 minutes. Meanwhile, fry bacon until crisp. Drain and set aside. Reserve drippings. Cut liver into strips and dredge in flour. In a large, heavy skillet, brown each slice quickly in reserved bacon drippings. Remove liver and set aside. Reduce heat; add cooked onions and their broth. Simmer slowly, about 10 minutes, stirring and scraping the bottom to blend in all the drippings. Stir 1 tablespoon flour into ½ can of broth and add to the skillet to thicken gravy. Add liver and heat thoroughly. Pour liver and gravy onto a platter and top each slice with 2 pieces of bacon.

Serves 6

GUERRIERO SPAGHETTI

SAUCE:

¾ cup chopped onion
1 clove garlic, chopped
3 tablespoons fat or bacon
   drippings
2 pounds canned Italian tomatoes
2 cans (6 ounces each) tomato
   paste

1 cup water
1 tablespoon sugar
1½ teaspoons salt
½ teaspoon pepper
1 bay leaf
1½ teaspoons oregano

MEATBALLS:

¼ cup bread crumbs
½ cup milk
2 eggs, beaten
1 pound ground beef
¼ pound ground pork
½ cup Parmesan cheese

½ cup chopped onion
1 clove garlic, minced
½ teaspoon salt
Pepper to taste
1 tablespoon Italian seasoning
3 tablespoons olive oil

SAUCE: Sauté onions and garlic in fat. Add remaining ingredients, and cook, covered, for 1 hour.

MEATBALLS: Soak bread crumbs in mixture of milk and egg. Add all the remaining ingredients except oil. Form into balls and sauté in oil until brown. Drain on paper towels and add to sauce. Cook meatballs in the sauce, covered, for 1 hour. Serve over spaghetti.

Serves 6 to 8

SPAGHETTI CASSEROLE

Easy crowd pleaser with a different twist.

2 tablespoons butter
1 clove garlic
1 teaspoon sugar
1 teaspoon salt
Pepper to taste
1½ pounds lean ground beef
2 cans (8 ounces each) tomato
   sauce

1 package (8 ounces) spaghetti
1 package (3 ounces) cream
   cheese, softened
1½ cups sour cream
6 green onions, chopped
½ pound Cheddar cheese, grated

Preheat oven to 350 degrees F. Put the butter in a cold skillet. Add garlic, and mash with sugar, salt, and pepper. Cook until butter is melted, then add meat and brown. Add tomato sauce, and simmer, uncovered, for 20 minutes. Cook spaghetti according to package directions. Combine cream cheese, sour cream, and green onions. Place spaghetti in a greased 13 × 9-inch casserole. Top with cream-cheese mixture and then meat mixture. Sprinkle Cheddar cheese on top. Bake, uncovered, until hot and bubbly, about 30 minutes.

Serves 6 to 8

SWEET AND SOUR MEAT LOAF

SAUCE:

1 can (16 ounces) stewed tomatoes
½ cup brown sugar

¼ cup vinegar
1 teaspoon prepared mustard
⅓ cup chopped green pepper

MEAT:

2 pounds ground meat
2 eggs, slightly beaten
½ medium onion, minced
½ cup Pepperidge Farm cornbread dressing

2 tablespoons prepared sauce (above)
1 teaspoon salt
½ teaspoon garlic salt
½ teaspoon black pepper

Preheat oven to 350 degrees F. Mix together sauce ingredients. Simmer until sugar dissolves. Combine meat ingredients and shape into a loaf. Place loaf in a shallow pan. Pour ¼ cup sauce over top of meat loaf. Cook, uncovered, for 1 hour. Heat remaining sauce and serve with meat.

Serves 6

LAMB SHANKS

1 tablespoon olive oil
4 lamb shanks
½ teaspoon salt
Freshly ground pepper

4 thin slices lemon
1 clove garlic, minced
1 bay leaf
½ cup (or more) strong coffee

Heat oil over moderately high heat in Dutch oven or heavy pot with a tight lid. Sprinkle shanks with salt and pepper and lightly brown in oil. Add lemon, garlic, bay leaf, and coffee. Heat until liquid boils. Cover pot tightly, reduce heat, and simmer shanks slowly for 1 hour. Check seasonings and add more coffee if desired. Cook another ½ hour until meat is very tender. Remove meat to hot platter and keep warm. Reduce liquid to gravy consistency by boiling rapidly.

Serves 4

BARBECUE BUTTERFLY LAMB

1 bottle good red wine
2 packages Good Seasons Garlic
    salad dressing mix
    (powdered)
½ jar Spice Islands rosemary
½ jar Spice Islands thyme

½ jar Spice Islands fines herbes
½ cup red wine vinegar
1 cup olive oil (less if lamb is
    fatty)
1 leg of lamb (8 pounds), boned,
    butterflied, glands removed

Mix first 7 ingredients together. Marinate the leg of lamb in this mixture for 24 to 48 hours. Barbecue on open fire, 4 inches from heat, 10 minutes on each side, or until crusty on outside and pink on inside.

Serves 8 to 10

BUTTERFLY LEG OF LAMB

1 cup dry red wine
1 cup beef stock
2 tablespoons orange marmalade
2 tablespoons wine vinegar
1 tablespoon minced onion
1 tablespoon rosemary
1 tablespoon marjoram

1 large bay leaf, crumbled
1 teaspoon salt
½ teaspoon minced fresh ginger
    or ¼ teaspoon powdered
    ginger
1 leg of lamb, boned and
    butterflied by butcher

Combine all ingredients except leg of lamb in a saucepan and simmer for 20 minutes, stirring occasionally. At least 2 hours, but not more than 24 hours, before cooking, pour marinade over lamb. Turn frequently. Cook meat over charcoal fire for between 20 to 40 minutes, basting with marinade and turning often.

Serves 8 to 12

KANSAS CITY ROAST RACK OF LAMB

2 racks of lamb, 9 ribs each,
  shinbone removed and bones
  trimmed
2 cloves garlic, crushed
1 tablespoon Worcestershire
  sauce

1 teaspoon rosemary
3 tablespoons butter, softened
Freshly ground pepper

SAUCE:
6 ounces chili sauce
10 ounces currant jelly
¼ cup butter

2 tablespoons mint sauce or mint
  jelly

Preheat oven to 400 degrees F. Score fat side of the racks. Mix garlic, Worcestershire sauce, rosemary, and butter, and spread over scoring. Grind pepper over top. May be prepared a day ahead to this point. Bring lamb to room temperature before baking. Place in an open pan and bake for 20 to 25 minutes. Meanwhile, mix chili sauce, currant jelly, butter, and mint jelly over medium heat until heated through. Carve 2 ribs together. Serve with sauce.

Serves 6 to 8

ROAST RACK OF LAMB
WITH HERBAL MUSTARD COATING

½ cup Dijon mustard
2 tablespoons soy sauce
1 clove garlic, crushed
1 tablespoon rosemary

¼ teaspoon ginger
2 tablespoons olive oil
1 rack of lamb, 8 to 10 ribs

Preheat oven to 400 degrees F. Mix mustard, soy sauce, garlic, rosemary, ginger, and olive oil to make a paste. Trim fat from lamb and discard it. Coat lamb with paste. Do this several hours ahead of time if possible. Roast in a shallow roasting pan till meat thermometer reads 170 to 180 degrees F., depending on desired doneness. This coating may also be used on a leg of lamb in a 325 degree F. oven, cooking till meat thermometer reads 170 to 180 degrees F., depending on desired doneness.

Serves 4 to 5

AMY'S INDONESIAN SATÉ

½ pound pork loin
½ teaspoon salt
Freshly ground pepper
2 teaspoons cumin seeds
⅓ cup salad oil
⅜ cup onion slices

2 teaspoons brown sugar
2 tablespoons soy sauce
Generous dash of ginger
2 limes
½ cup cooked rice

Cut pork loin into 1½-inch cubes. Marinate in salt, pepper, cumin seeds, and salad oil for 20 minutes. Add onion slices, brown sugar, soy sauce, and ginger, and marinate for 24 to 48 hours. Thread pork on skewers, packing tightly. Reserve ½ cup marinade; pour remaining marinade over pork. Broil 4 inches below flame, turning and basting for 15 minutes. Sprinkle juice of 2 limes over pork just before serving. Degrease reserved marinade, stir into cooked rice, and serve with pork.

Yield: 1 serving. Multiply for any number!

SISTER'S BAKED HAM

½ cured ham, preferably the
    butt end
Ground cinnamon
Ground cloves

Yellow mustard
Whole cloves (optional)
Sugar

Preheat oven to 250 degrees F. Cut away all the skin from the ham but leave the fat. Rub ham with ground cinnamon and ground cloves so that it is completely covered. Wrap airtight in heavy foil and bake for 3 hours. Cool, and scrape cinnamon and cloves off and throw away. Coat ham with mustard. If desired, score fat in diamond pattern and put a whole clove in each diamond. This is not necessary for flavor. Sprinkle liberally with sugar. Brown in 350 degree F. oven for about 30 minutes. Watch carefully so sugar does not burn. Allow to cool before carving. This ham is always moist.

VICKSBURG STUFFED HAM

Medium-size ham	2 tablespoons brown sugar
1 tablespoon vinegar	Steaming water

DRESSING:

1 cup ham fat, chopped fine	1 tablespoon mustard seed
3 cups bread crumbs	½ teaspoon black pepper
1 cup chopped parsley	2 tablespoons brown sugar
1 cup chopped celery	2 tablespoons vinegar
¾ cup chopped onion	1 egg
1 tablespoon dry mustard	Dash thyme
1 tablespoon celery seed	

Preheat oven to 300 degrees F. Cut off ham hock. Add vinegar and brown sugar to water, and steam ham until meat is tender enough to feel loose at the bone. Remove bone and all fat. Bone should twist out easily. Reserve a cup of the fat and meat trimmings. Combine dressing ingredients. Fill bone cavity with dressing. Depending on size of ham, dressing amount may need to be doubled. Cover outside of ham about 2½ inches thick with remaining dressing. Wrap securely in cheesecloth and tie tightly with cord. Bake for 30 minutes to 1 hour until crust forms nicely. Chill for 24 hours and slice very thin.

Serves: An army!

NEW YEAR'S HAM

1 boneless cooked ham (Hormel Cure 81)	2 cups pineapple juice
Cloves, whole	1½ cups brown sugar
2 cups crushed pineapple	2 tablespoons Dijon mustard
	Ginger ale

Preheat oven to 350 degrees F. Stud ham with lots of cloves. Combine pine-apple, pineapple juice, sugar, and mustard in blender, and blend well. Pour over ham. Bake 1 hour. Reduce oven temperature to 300 degrees F. and cook 2 more hours. Baste with ginger ale. The more often it is basted, the better ham will be. (Hams which have been "cooked in water" do not ab-sorb the juices as well.) For a real treat, have your butcher slice the ham and tie it back together before cooking.

STUFFED PORK ROAST

3- to 4-pound center-cut pork
   loin roast
1 medium onion, chopped
3 tablespoons olive oil
½ pound ground veal or lean
   pork
1 bunch fresh spinach, cooked,
   drained, and chopped
¼ cup fresh bread crumbs

½ cup freshly grated Parmesan
   cheese
1 teaspoon rosemary
½ cup shelled pistachio nuts
1 clove garlic
1 teaspoon salt
½ teaspoon freshly grated
   pepper
1 egg, slightly beaten

Preheat oven to 350 degrees F. Trim away fat covering pork loin. Remove bones by cutting down along ribs. Reserve to use as a roasting rack. Cut along backbone to remove meat. (If the tenderloin is on the opposite side of ribs, remove it, halve it lengthwise, and place it in center of roast before rolling and tying it.) Cut meat lengthwise. Cut to, but not through, the op-posite side of roast, and lay meat open. Sauté onion in olive oil over medium heat for 3 to 4 minutes or until translucent. Crumble ground meat into pan and continue cooking until it loses its pinkness. As meat cooks, break it up with a spatula. Remove pan from heat and stir in chopped spinach, bread crumbs, Parmesan cheese, rosemary, pistachios, and garlic that has been crushed in a mortar with pestle. Add salt and pepper. Stir in beaten egg. Taste and adjust seasoning so it is exaggerated somewhat. Place stuffing down the center seam of roast. Compress stuffing into a firmly packed mound. The roast must be rolled so that it will be sliced across the grain. Wrap meat around stuffing. Turn roast seam down and wrap cotton twine around it at 1-inch intervals. Tie securely. Place roast on bones in shallow roasting pan and cook for 25 minutes per pound. When roast is done, remove to a platter and serve with a sauce made from the pan drippings. Place pan over high heat and add 2 cups water. Boil while scraping crust on pan bottom. When reduced to half the original volume, season and strain into a sauce dish.

Serves 6 to 8

AUSTRIAN PORK CHOPS

2 tablespoons Hungarian paprika	1 large white onion
½ cup plus 1 tablespoon flour	1 can (16 ounces) sauerkraut,
Salt and pepper	drained
6 very large pork chops or 8	2 tablespoons butter
medium ones	1 cup beef bouillon
Bacon drippings or butter	1 cup sour cream

Preheat oven to 350 degrees F. Mix 1 tablespoon of the paprika, ½ cup flour, salt, and pepper. Dredge pork chops and brown in bacon drippings or butter using enough to prevent sticking. Cut onion into rings and add when turning the chops. When the chops are brown and onions are still crunchy, transfer chops to a baking dish and top each with a mound of sauerkraut, then onion rings. Set aside. Melt butter. Dissolve remaining tablespoon of the paprika in butter. Add remaining tablespoon of the flour, salt and pepper, and stir until smooth. Remove from heat, add bouillon, and bring to a boil. Remove from heat, stir in sour cream, and heat gently until sauce is smooth. Pour over pork chops. Bake for 40 minutes or until done.

Serves 6

PORK TENDERS PAPRIKA

1 tenderloin of pork, sliced ½	1 tablespoon Hungarian paprika
inch thick	¼ cup white vermouth
2 tablespoons oil	¼ cup chicken broth
1 small onion, chopped	1 cup sour cream or yogurt
2 cloves garlic, pressed or	Salt to taste
chopped	

Sauté pork in oil until juices run clear when sliced. Remove from skillet. Sauté onion, garlic, and paprika slowly in oil. Add vermouth and broth and cook down. Add pork slices and sour cream or yogurt. Heat through but do not boil. Serve over noodles.

Serves 6

MARIPOSA PORK

Salt and pepper to taste
8 butterfly pork chops
Vegetable oil
3 tablespoons Dijon mustard
½ cup red wine
1½ cups beef stock or Bovril
1 tablespoon soy sauce
½ cup orange juice
1 can (8 ounces) mandarin
  oranges

1 can (8 ounces) pineapple
  chunks
2 tablespoons cornstarch,
  dissolved in 2 tablespoons
  water
Salt to taste
¼ teaspoon black pepper

Salt and pepper pork chops. In a small amount of oil in a hot skillet, sear chops on one side for 4 minutes. Turn and cook for another 4 minutes. Combine mustard, wine, stock, and soy sauce, and add to chops. Cover, and reduce heat to simmer for 20 minutes. Turn chops and add orange juice and canned fruits with juices if desired. Simmer gently for another 15 minutes. Remove chops and fruit to a warm platter with fruit on top of chops. Thicken the sauce with cornstarch, season with salt and pepper, and serve on the side.

Serves 8

VEAL VERMOUTH

1½ pounds thin veal steak
2 tablespoons flour
¼ cup butter
1 clove garlic, minced
½ pound mushrooms, sliced

½ teaspoon salt
Dash of pepper
1 tablespoon lemon juice
⅓ cup dry vermouth
2 tablespoons snipped parsley

Flatten veal with mallet until ¼ inch thick. Cut into 2-inch squares and flour each piece. Melt butter in skillet, and sauté veal, a few pieces at a time, until golden brown on both sides. Return all meat and garlic to skillet. Heap mushrooms on top. Sprinkle with salt, pepper, and lemon juice. Add vermouth, cover, and cook over low heat for 20 minutes until veal is fork-tender. A little more vermouth may be added if needed. Sprinkle with parsley just before serving. Can be prepared ahead and reheated in oven.

Serves 4

CÔTES DE VEAU NORMANDE

4 veal chops or scallops
Salt and pepper
¼ cup butter
1 cup sliced mushrooms
4 tablespoons Calvados
    (applejack brandy), warmed

1 cup cream
2 tart apples, peeled and
    quartered
Butter

Season veal with salt and pepper, and sauté in butter until golden on both sides. Add sliced mushrooms, and simmer gently for 10 minutes. Pour Calvados into skillet, light it, and when flame dies out, stir in cream. Remove chops and set aside. Reduce sauce, stirring constantly until smooth and thick. Sauté apples in butter. Arrange chops and apples on dish and cover with sauce.

Serves 4

VEAL CASSEROLE

2½ pounds veal
½ cup flour
2 teaspoons paprika
2 teaspoons salt
1 teaspoon pepper
½ cup butter
2 cloves garlic
1 to 1½ cups water

1 beef bouillon cube
2 cups sour cream
2 cups sliced water chestnuts
1 teaspoon basil
⅛ teaspoon rosemary
1 teaspoon lemon juice
¼ cup dry sherry

Preheat oven to 350 degrees F. Pound veal and cut into strips 1 inch by 2 inches. Dip veal in a mixture of the flour, paprika, salt, and pepper. Heat butter and garlic to sizzling. Brown veal, adding more butter if necessary. Remove veal and garlic from pan and discard garlic. Add water and bouillon cube and stir till dissolved. Add sour cream, lower heat and mix thoroughly. Add veal, water chestnuts, and remaining ingredients, and stir. Pour into a deep casserole and bake, covered, about 1 hour. Serve with wild rice. This can be made 1 day ahead.

Serves 6 to 8

CHAPTER VII

MEXICAN

The Near North Side

Just off Houston Avenue, not far from Downtown, are places that could almost be in northern Mexico—all-night restaurants where *mariachis* entertain patrons as they eat *cabrito* and *enchiladas verdes*, a park where a statue of a *vaquero* on a plunging bronco captures the attention of brown-eyed children playing soccer, shops selling scented candles and *piñatas*.

Texas shared a common history with Mexico from the Spanish Conquest in the 1500s until Texas independence in 1836, first as a Spanish colony and then as a Mexican territory. As residents of the Department of Brazos, settlers near what was to become Houston sent representatives to the state government at Saltillo, but the federal authorities in Mexico City still considered Texas a remote northern frontier. Disgruntled at this treatment, many of the Mexican farmers and craftsmen in the area sided with the American and German Texans in the War of Independence. A third of the men who fought with Sam Houston against Santa Anna had Spanish surnames.

Characterized by their melodic language and by a strong family system and religious traditions, Houston's Mexican community has maintained a more separate identity than most of the city's other ethnic groups. Although there has always been intermarriage, especially with Irish, Italian, and other predominantly Catholic nationalities, those outsiders have often been absorbed into the warm and expansive Mexican-American community, rather than anglicizing their spouses.

Today, about 15 percent of Houston's population is Mexican-American. Some are descendants of the original colonists from the days of the Spanish Empire; others are recent immigrants. Although virtually every neighborhood in town has its share of the Spanish-surnamed residents, the North Side is the section with the most distinctly Latin flavor, the section with the *curanderos* (herbal healers) and the fiestas.

Mexican music and Mexican food quickly became part of the common Texas culture. Cowboys learned to play the guitar and compose ballads in English that mimicked the sentiments of Spanish love songs. Mexican dance tunes and European polkas merged into rollicking *conjunto*. Latin rhythms and American jazz evolved into *salsa*.

With the possible exception of chicken-fried steak and cream gravy, there's almost no distinctively Texan dish that doesn't take at least some of its flavor from the rich heritage of Mexican *cocina*. Mexican cooking is more American Indian than it is Spanish. It was developed by people working with primitive kitchens and limited ingredients. It owes its appeal to the inventiveness of its creators, who were able to make an otherwise monotonous diet interesting by combining the same things in different ways.

Mexican cuisine is not a single, unwavering style. The food prepared in Veracruz isn't the same as the dishes served in Mexico City; the *burritos* in Sonora don't taste like those in Houston. The Republic of Mexico, of which Texas was a part, covered a vast area, and there were regional differences.

Still, certain ingredients are common to most Mexican cooking: peppers, onions, garlic, cheese, beans, tomatoes, chocolate, cornmeal (*masa*), cumin (*comino*), and cilantro. The recipes that follow bring these elements together in interesting ways, some traditional, others "authentic" departures. Treat yourself and your guests to Guacamole, Arlene's Green Turkey Burritos, Lolita's Fajitas, Salsa Pico de Gallo, or Red Snapper Veracruz. Most of these dishes are easy, economical, and *muy sabroso*.

GUACAMOLE

An old favorite with a different twist!

3 to 4 ripe avocados, mashed
Juice of 3 small lemons
½ cup mayonnaise
1 tablespoon vegetable oil
2 cloves garlic
¼ cup Danish blue cheese (optional)
2 tablespoons grated onion
¼ teaspoon Lawry's Seasoned Salt

⅛ teaspoon freshly ground pepper
⅛ teaspoon salt
1/16 teaspoon cayenne
¼ to ½ teaspoon Tabasco
1/16 teaspoon garlic salt
Dash of sugar
½ teaspoon chili powder
1 teaspoon bacon pieces or Bacon Bits

Blend all ingredients except 2 tablespoons of the lemon juice and bacon pieces. Put in glass or ceramic container. Level, and cover with 2 tablespoons lemon juice. When ready to serve, stir in lemon juice and top with bacon.

Serves 4 to 6

ARLENE'S GREEN TURKEY BURRITOS

1 large onion, chopped
2 cloves garlic, minced
2 tablespoons butter
4 cups cooked chopped turkey
  (½ frozen breast)
½ cup green taco sauce
1 or 2 chopped avocados
1 teaspoon cumin
4 tomatoes, chopped

1 can (4 ounces) green chilies,
  chopped
2 bunches green onions, chopped
½ teaspoon coriander
1 can (15 ounces) refried beans
12 large flour tortillas
⅔ cup shredded Cheddar cheese
1 pint sour cream

Sauté onion and garlic in butter until soft. Add turkey, taco sauce, avocado, and cumin. In separate bowl, combine tomatoes, chilies, half of green onions, and coriander. Heat refried beans.

Assembly: Heat tortillas and spread each one with hot beans. Cover with turkey mixture, add a layer of tomato mixture, and sprinkle with cheese. Roll up and dress with sour cream and more chopped onion.

Serves 12

SANTA ROSA PIE

1 can (16 ounces) refried beans
1 can (6 ounces) avocado dip
1 can (4½ ounces) chopped
  black olives, drained
3 medium green onions, chopped
1 can (4 ounces) chopped green
  chilies, drained

1 medium tomato, diced
1 cup shredded Cheddar cheese
1 cup sour cream
4 tablespoons Jalapeño Sauce *or*
  Picante Sauce (see Index)

On serving plate, spread beans into pie shape 8 to 9 inches in diameter. Cover with avocado dip. Combine olives and green onions. Spread over pie. Mix chilies and tomato. Spread on top. Cover with cheese, frost with sour cream, and spread jalapeño sauce over top. Serve with home-fried flour or corn tortilla chips.

Serves about 20

Variations: 1. Add layer of taco-seasoned hamburger meat. 2. Use Monterey Jack instead of Cheddar cheese. 3. Preheat oven to 350 degrees F. Layer beans, olives, onions, chilies, tomatoes, and cheese into Pyrex dish. Bake for 30 minutes. Frost with avocado, sour cream, and jalapeño sauce.

FRITOLE

This is a common breakfast dish in Mexico. It also would make a quick and easy lunch or hors d'oeuvre.

Day-old rolls or French bread
Refried beans (homemade if
    possible)

Monterey Jack cheese or Queso
    Blanco
Sliced pickled jalapeño peppers

Slice French bread or rolls in half. Cover liberally with refried beans. Cover beans with thin slices of cheese and dot with several jalapeño rings. Place under broiler until cheese melts.

CHALUPAS

6 corn tortillas
1 cup cooking oil
½ pound ground beef
1 tablespoon bacon drippings
½ teaspoon cumin
¼ teaspoon chili powder
1 teaspoon salt
1½ cups bean dip
2 cups grated cheese—Monterey
    Jack or Cheddar

Pepper to taste
6 teaspoons finely chopped
    onions
¾ cup chopped fresh tomatoes
3 cups finely chopped iceberg
    lettuce
¾ cup guacamole
6 tablespoons sour cream

Preheat oven to 350 degrees F. Fry each tortilla in hot oil until crisp. Drain on paper towels and set aside. Sauté meat in bacon drippings. Add cumin, chili powder, and salt. Remove from heat. Spread each tortilla with ¼ cup bean dip. Layer about 2 tablespoons meat mixture on top. Sprinkle ⅓ cup of the grated cheese over meat. Place on cookie sheet and bake until heated through, about 10 minutes. While piping hot, place on individual plates. Sprinkle each chalupa with pepper, 1 teaspoon onion, 2 tablespoons chopped tomatoes, ½ cup lettuce, 2 tablespoons guacamole, and 1 tablespoon sour cream. Serve immediately. If you are serving a crowd, put garnishes on table. Prepare each chalupa with bean dip, meat, and cheese. Then let guests build their own.

Serves 4 to 6

LOLITA'S FAJITAS

This is a great dish for a casual party. Put a variety of garnishes on the table and let guests build their own creations.

3 pounds fajita meat (beef skirt steak). If unavailable, use flank steak, but meat must be tenderized. Use ½ pound per person.

MARINADE:

½ cup butter, melted
Juice of 2 medium lemons

¼ cup Worcestershire sauce
¼ cup soy sauce

GARNISH:

Flour tortillas
Blender Picante Sauce (see Index) (or any brand)
Guacamole (see Index)

Salsa Pico de Gallo (see Index) (optional)
Sour cream (optional)

Marinate meat for 2 to 3 hours, turning once. Place meat on grill over hot coals and cook for 5 to 10 minutes on each side or until done. Slice cooked steak against the grain in narrow strips not more than ¼ inch thick. Place several strips of meat on hot flour tortilla. Add picante sauce, Guacamole, Salsa Pico de Gallo, or whatever sounds good. Roll up and enjoy!

Serves 6

MOTHER'S CHILI CON CARNE

This chili takes time to prepare but is well worth the effort. As with any well-seasoned recipe, it is always better the next day.

6 large dried chili pods
1 pound beef (preferably round steak)
1 pound pork
1 to 2 tablespoons bacon drippings

5 large cloves garlic, chopped
1 heaping tablespoon oregano
1 tablespoon cumin
1 tablespoon flour
1 tablespoon chili powder
Salt to taste

Prick chili pods several times with fork. Cover with water and bring to a boil. Boil slowly until pods are tender and pulp begins to leave skin. Rinse pods carefully under running water to loosen seeds, which have a bitter taste. Strain pulp and set aside, or mix in blender with a little water and set aside. Cube meat and fry in bacon drippings until almost brown. Add garlic and continue browning. Add oregano and cumin, then chili pod pulp, flour, and chili powder, mixing well after each addition. Cover with hot water and mix thoroughly. Add salt. Cook slowly until meat is tender. If necessary, add more hot water as chili cooks down.

Serves 4

PICADILLO

Do not be dismayed by the long list of ingredients. This is not difficult to make, and the result is well worth the effort.

2 pounds ground beef
1 cup chopped onion
2 teaspoons minced garlic
⅔ cup chopped green bell pepper
1 can (16 ounces) tomatoes, undrained and coarsely chopped
2 ¼ teaspoons salt
¼ teaspoon pepper
¼ teaspoon cayenne pepper
½ teaspoon cumin
½ teaspoon oregano
¼ cup Worcestershire sauce
2 cans beef broth

2 cans (6 ounces each) tomato paste
1 jar (4 ounces) chopped pimientos
1 can (6 ounces) chopped black olives
1 cup slivered almonds
1 can (4 ounces) chopped green chilies or 4 jalapeño peppers, seeded and chopped
1 cup dark raisins
8 cups peeled cubed potatoes (optional)
1 can (8 ounces) mushrooms (optional)

Brown beef. Skim off fat. Add onion, garlic, green pepper, tomatoes, salt, pepper, cayenne, cumin, oregano, and Worcestershire sauce. Cook over moderate heat until vegetables are soft. Add remaining ingredients, and simmer for 1 hour. Serve in chafing dish with tortilla chips or serve over Spanish Rice (see Index).

Serves 8 to 10 as an entree or
20 as an hors d'oeuvre

MEXICAN RED BEANS

This can accompany your Mexican dinner or may just be served over rice with salad and cornbread.

2 large onions, chopped
1 garlic clove, minced
¼ cup bacon drippings
1 whole ham hock
1 package (16 ounces) pink or
   red beans
1 cup cubed ham

1 can (16 ounces) tomatoes
2 tablespoons chili powder
1 bay leaf
1 teaspoon thyme
Pinch of sugar
Salt and pepper to taste

In a Dutch oven or heavy pot, sauté onions and garlic in bacon drippings. Add ham hock, beans, and enough water to cover. Add the remaining ingredients. Then add 2 cans of water. Cook, covered, for 6 to 8 hours. If you have soaked the beans overnight, cook for about 4 hours. Stir occasionally and add more water if needed. If thickening is needed, remove ½ cup of beans, mash thoroughly, and return to the pot. The results should be thick and meaty.

Serves 10

BARBECUED CABRITO

Young goat, cut into two hind quarters, two fore quarters and two slabs of ribs, or any portions.

Beer
Texas Barbecue Sauce (below)

Wash meat and arrange in large pan. Marinate for 24 hours in beer, turning often. Brown meat over coals, basting often with Texas Barbecue Sauce. After browning meat, continue cooking over indirect heat at about 350 degrees F. until tender to taste. Baste often to keep meat moist. After 1 hour or so over low coals, meat may be brought in and placed in oven. Cover with foil when it is brown enough. Total cooking time is about 3½ hours. Carve and serve extra Barbecue Sauce over meat.

Serves: A crowd
One hind quarter feeds about 8
to 10 people

TEXAS BARBECUE SAUCE

1 tablespoon salt
1 teaspoon barbecue seasoning
  mix
½ teaspoon pepper
3 tablespoons brown sugar
¼ cup ketchup

¼ cup Worcestershire sauce
3 tablespoons Dijon mustard
1 teaspoon liquid smoke
1 cup strong coffee
½ cup vinegar
1 cup Wesson oil

Mix ingredients in order given, using rotary beater when adding oil. Simmer slowly until thickened. Keep hot. This makes enough for about 6 pounds of meat.

Yield: 3 cups

BAY CITY JALAPEÑO PIE

1 can (7 ounces) pickled
  jalapeño peppers, cut in circles
  or strips

1 pound sharp Cheddar cheese,
  grated
6 eggs, beaten

Preheat oven to 350 degrees F. Line greased 8 × 8-inch pan with jalapeños. Sprinkle cheese over peppers. Pour eggs over cheese, and bake for 30 minutes. Cut into small bite-size squares for appetizers or large squares for main course.

Yield: 12 large squares or
36 small ones

CHILI CON QUESO

4 cloves garlic, minced
1½ cups chopped onion
1 cup chopped chili poblano
  peppers
1 cup chopped red or green bell
  peppers
½ cup corn oil

1½ teaspoons cumin
1 teaspoon chili powder
2 pounds processed American
  cheese, cubed
2 cups sour cream
Tabasco or jalapeño juice to
  taste (optional)

Sauté garlic, onion, and peppers in the corn oil until they begin to get tender. Add cumin and chili powder, and cook about 3 minutes longer. Do *not* brown vegetables. Reduce heat and add cheese; cook slowly, stirring, until cheese melts. Just before serving, stir in sour cream. Taste and add Tabasco or jalapeño juice if necessary. Serve in chafing dish with tortilla chips.

Yield: 1½ quarts

DIVINE CHILI RELLENO CASSEROLE

1 cup half-and-half
2 eggs
⅓ cup flour
3 cans (4 ounces each) whole green chilies *or* 1 can (3 ounces) pickled jalapeño peppers

½ pound Monterey Jack cheese, grated
½ pound sharp Cheddar cheese, grated
1 can (8 ounces) tomato sauce

Preheat oven to 350 degrees F. Beat half-and-half with eggs and flour until smooth. Split chilies or peppers open, rinse out seeds, and drain chilies on paper towels. Mix cheeses and set aside ½ cup for topping. In deep 1½-quart casserole, make alternate layers of remaining cheese, chilies, and egg mixture. Pour tomato sauce over top and sprinkle with reserved cheese. Bake for 1¼ hours or until cooked in center.

Serves 4

BLENDER PICANTE SAUCE

This picante sauce will keep forever in the refrigerator.

1 can (12 ounces) mild pickled jalapeño peppers, drained
1 can (4 ounces) green chilies
1 large green bell pepper
2 medium onions
2 cans (18¾ ounces each) tomatoes, undrained

¾ cup vinegar
1 garlic clove
1 teaspoon oregano
1 teaspoon cumin
2 teaspoons salt

Blend ingredients in blender on high speed for several minutes. Refrigerate until ready to use. If you prefer a milder sauce, add more tomatoes. If you can't find mild jalapeños, remove seeds from regular jalapeños to get a milder flavor. To make sauce very hot and spicy, add fresh hot peppers.

Yield: Approximately 6 cups

SALSA PICO DE GALLO

This makes a tasty dip or a delicious garnish for fajitas, burritos, or enchiladas. It keeps for days in the refrigerator or can be frozen in plastic containers.

2 pounds tomatoes
2 small onions
6 fresh jalapeño peppers, seeded

10 pieces fresh cilantro
Salt to taste
Juice of 1 lemon

Chop tomatoes, onions, jalapeños, and cilantro in small pieces. Do not use blender or processor. Mix together. Add salt and lemon juice. Mix well.

CHEESE ENCHILADAS

These enchiladas can be assembled ahead of time without the sauce and refrigerated. When ready to serve, cover with sauce, cook, and serve immediately.

2 tablespoons chili powder
2 onions
2 teaspoons plus 1 cup oil
1 can (15 ounces) tomato sauce
2 cups water
¼ teaspoon cumin

Salt to taste
1 pound Monterey Jack cheese
12 corn tortillas
½ pound Cheddar cheese, grated
1 cup sour cream

Preheat oven to 375 degrees F.

SAUCE: Sauté chili powder and ⅓ cup chopped onion in 2 teaspoons of the oil for about 5 minutes. Add tomato sauce, water, cumin, and salt. Simmer about 1 hour or until slightly thickened.

ASSEMBLY: Cut Monterey Jack cheese into 12 sticks about the diameter of a tortilla and thickness of a finger. Pass each tortilla through heated oil and then quickly through enchilada sauce until just softened. Roll 1 stick Monterey Jack and 1 tablespoon minced onion in each tortilla. Place seam side down in casserole. Top with enough enchilada sauce to just cover. Bake immediately until bubbly, about 25 to 30 minutes. Sprinkle Cheddar cheese evenly over top and return to oven until cheese melts. Serve immediately with a dollop of sour cream on each.

Serves 6

Variation: Substitute chicken filling for cheese.

2 whole chicken breasts, halved
1 package (12 ounces) cream cheese
2 jalapeño peppers, minced

1 onion, finely minced
6 ounces Monterey Jack cheese, grated

Cook chicken, remove from bones and cut into ½-inch pieces. Mix chicken, softened cream cheese, jalapeños, onion, and Monterey Jack.

CHICKEN BREASTS WITH CHILIES

6 whole chicken breasts, halved
Salt and pepper to taste
¼ cup butter
¼ cup cooking oil
1 large onion, thinly sliced
2¼ pounds chili poblano peppers, or 20 to 22 canned green chilies

1 cup milk
½ teaspoon salt
2 cups sour cream
¼ pound Cheddar cheese, grated

Preheat oven to 350 degrees F. Remove bones and skin from chicken breasts and cut each into 3 fillets. Season with salt and pepper. In heavy skillet, sauté chicken in butter and oil until light brown on both sides. Remove from pan. Sauté onion in same pan until soft but not brown. Set aside 3 chili poblano peppers. Cut remaining peppers into strips and remove seeds. Add pepper strips to onions, cover, and cook 8 minutes, or less if using chilies. Remove seeds from remaining peppers. Combine peppers, milk, and salt in food processor or blender. Mix until smooth. Add sour cream, and blend a few seconds more. Arrange half the chicken in 9 × 11-inch ovenproof dish. Cover with half the pepper strips and onions, then half the sauce. Repeat layers. Sprinkle with cheese, and bake for 30 minutes.

Serves 8 to 10

CHICKEN PORTUGUESE

This is a great dish to serve a crowd.

2 whole chicken breasts, halved
2 onions
¾ teaspoon cumin
2 cloves garlic
1 tablespoon butter
1 green bell pepper, chopped
1 chili poblano pepper, chopped
   (if unavailable, increase
   amount of green chilies)
Fresh or canned jalapeño peppers
   to taste

1 can (15 ounces) tomatoes,
   drained
1 teaspoon chili powder
½ can (4 ounces) green chilies
¼ cup chicken stock, reserved
¾ pound Velveeta cheese, cubed
½ cup sour cream
Fried tortilla strips or chips

Cover chicken with water. Add 1 quartered onion, ½ teaspoon of the cumin, and 1 of the garlic cloves. Simmer until tender. Cool in stock; reserve ¼ cup stock. Remove bones from chicken and tear into large bite-size pieces. Set aside. In butter, sauté 1 chopped onion, 1 chopped garlic clove, green pepper, poblano pepper, and jalapeño. Add tomatoes, chili powder, remaining ¼ teaspoon cumin, green chilies, stock, Velveeta cheese, and chicken. Simmer, stirring constantly. When heated through, turn off heat and stir in sour cream. Serve over tortilla strips or tortilla chips. This also is good over Spanish Rice (see Index). May be doubled or tripled.

Serves 4

CHICKEN SOPA

4 whole chicken breasts
1 onion, finely chopped
2 cans (4 ounces each) chopped
    green chilies, drained
Oil or bacon drippings
2 cans (10¾ ounces each)
    cream of chicken soup

2 cans (5⅓ ounces each)
    evaporated milk
10 to 12 corn tortillas
8 ounces Swiss cheese, grated

Preheat oven to 325 degrees F. Cook chicken, cut into bite-size pieces, and set aside. Cook onion and chilies in bacon drippings or oil until tender. Drain. Combine soup and milk and heat through. Add onion and chilies. Cut tortillas into strips. Place strips in 3-quart casserole, layer chicken over tortillas, and cover with soup mixture. Top with cheese and bake for 45 minutes. (Note: Be sure soup mixture soaks down to bottom layers!)

Serves 6 to 8

ENCILATRADA

This is hot!

3 to 4 pounds chicken, cut up
2 pounds boneless pork
1 large onion, coarsely chopped
3 cloves garlic, minced
3 cans (7 ounces each) Herdez
    Mexican green hot sauce
1 can (6 ounces) pickled
    jalapeño peppers, finely
    chopped

1 whole bunch fresh cilantro
    (coriander), minced
1 teaspoon cumin
1 teaspoon garlic salt
Salt and pepper to taste

Place chicken, pork, onion, and garlic in enough salted water to cover, and cook until meat is tender. Bone and skin chicken. Shred or dice chicken and pork. Put meat in 3-quart saucepan. Add hot sauce, jalapeños, cilantro, and spices. Add salt and pepper. Simmer for 10 to 15 minutes. Serve hot as a dip with tortilla chips. Freezes well.

Yield: 1½ to 2 quarts
Variations: 1. Use as filling for enchiladas. 2. Roll in large flour tortilla to

make a burrito. 3. Make flautas by rolling a heaping tablespoon of mixture in corn tortilla. Deep-fry in corn oil until crisp. Serve with Guacamole (see Index) and sour cream.

ENCHILADAS VERDES

1 cup cooked shredded chicken
2 cups grated Monterey Jack
  cheese
1 pint sour cream
1 onion, chopped
3 jalapeño peppers, seeded and
  chopped

12 corn tortillas
Oil
1 cup heavy cream
1 cup Salsa de Tomatilla
  (below)

Preheat oven to 350 degrees F. Mix chicken, 1 cup of the cheese, sour cream, onion, and jalapeños. Soften tortillas by dipping in hot oil. Fill with above mixture, roll up, and place in ovenproof dish. Combine cream and Salsa. Pour over enchiladas, and top with remaining cheese. Bake for 45 minutes or until bubbly.

Serves 4

SALSA DE TOMATILLA

25 to 35 fresh tomatillas,
  (canned ones may be
  substituted)
½ yellow onion, coarsely
  chopped

10 jalapeño peppers, seeded
1 to 10 cloves garlic
2 to 3 cups fresh cilantro with
  stems removed

Remove husks from tomatillas and cut in quarters. Sauté tomatillas and onion over medium heat for 20 minutes or until soft. Stir frequently. Add jalapeños and garlic, and sauté for 5 minutes more. Remove from heat and let cool. Add cilantro and mix in blender until smooth. Chill. Serve with chips or meat or use for Enchiladas Verdes (above).

Yield: 2 cups

RED SNAPPER VERACRUZ

2 limes
1 ¾ to 2 pounds red snapper
  fillets
Salt

5 tablespoons olive oil
Fresh cilantro (coriander) for
  garnish

SAUCE VERACRUZ:

½ cup chopped onion
3 cloves garlic, crushed
4 tablespoons olive oil
3 large tomatoes, peeled, seeded,
  and chopped
1 large bay leaf
½ teaspoon oregano
12 green olives, cut in half
2 tablespoons capers

2 jalapeño peppers, seeded and
  cut in strips (fresh, if
  possible)
½ teaspoon salt
¼ teaspoon pepper
1 tablespoon fresh chopped
  cilantro (or ½ teaspoon
  dried)
1 tablespoon lime juice

Preheat oven to 325 degrees F. Squeeze lime juice over fish and set aside until ready to cook. To make the sauce, sauté onion and garlic in oil until soft. Stir in remaining ingredients. Season to taste. Cook over medium heat for 10 minutes or until some of the liquid has evaporated. Salt fillets and sauté in oil on both sides. Drain and remove to ovenproof casserole or platter. Cover with sauce and bake for 10 to 15 minutes. Garnish with fresh cilantro and serve.

Serves 6

SPANISH RICE

1 cup uncooked rice
3 tablespoons bacon drippings
1 medium onion, finely chopped
1 clove garlic, minced
1 ½ cups canned tomatoes
1 tablespoon minced green bell
  pepper

1 teaspoon cumin
1 can chicken broth
Salt and pepper to taste
1 cup cooked green peas
  (optional)

Brown rice in bacon drippings. Add remaining ingredients. Cover and cook slowly until all liquid is absorbed, about 25 minutes.

Serves 6

SHRIMP AND SCALLOP CEVICHE

2 pounds shrimp, cooked, peeled, and cut in thirds
1 pound raw scallops, thinly sliced
1 cup fresh lime juice (about 6 limes)
6 tablespoons finely chopped red onion
4 tablespoons chopped fresh parsley

2 tablespoons finely chopped green bell pepper
½ cup olive oil
½ teaspoon oregano
Dash of Tabasco
1 teaspoon salt
Freshly ground pepper to taste
2 avocados

Combine shrimp and raw scallops in large bowl. Add lime juice, cover, and let stand at room temperature for several hours. Drain and discard juice. Add all remaining ingredients except avocados. Toss lightly and chill for 1 hour. Serve with avocado slices.

Serves 6

JACKIE'S TORTILLA SOUP

A meal in itself.

1 onion, chopped
1 jalapeño pepper, chopped
2 cloves garlic, minced
1 can (14½ ounces) stewed tomatoes
4 cups stock (chicken or beef)
1 can tomato soup
1 teaspoon cumin
1 teaspoon chili powder (or less, to taste)

Salt and pepper to taste
½ teaspoon lemon pepper
2 teaspoons Worcestershire sauce
4 corn tortillas, sautéed lightly
Avocado
Cheddar or Monterey Jack cheese, grated
Sour cream (optional)

Sauté onion, jalapeño pepper, garlic, and tomatoes in large kettle for several minutes. Add remaining ingredients except tortillas, avocado, cheese, and sour cream. Simmer for 1 hour. About 10 to 20 minutes before serving, tear tortillas into bite-size pieces and add to soup. Place cubed avocado and grated cheese in individual bowls and ladle hot soup on top. Top with spoonful of sour cream.

Serves 4 to 6

BEST EVER PRALINES

1 cup whipping cream, unwhipped
1 box (1 pound) light brown
   sugar

1 generous tablespoon vanilla
   (preferably Mexican)
1 cup pecans

Combine cream and brown sugar. Cook to 242 degrees F. on a candy thermometer. Remove from heat. Add vanilla and beat until creamy. Add pecans and drop by spoonfuls onto wax paper. Cool.

Yield: 12 to 18

BOO'S PUERTO RICAN FLAN

This is especially pretty when made in a heavy bundt pan. After unmolding, fill the center with strawberries.

15 heaping tablespoons sugar
8 eggs
Dash of salt
1 can (14 ounces) sweetened
   condensed milk
1¾ cups milk

1 can (8½ ounces) cream of
   coconut
1 teaspoon vanilla
1 can (18 ounces) coco rallado
   (grated coconut in heavy
   syrup)

Preheat oven to 350 degrees F. Caramelize sugar. Pour into flan mold and, using oven mitts, gently swirl caramel around edges of pan until pan is coated 2 inches up sides. Cool. (It will make cracking noises.) In blender or food processor, combine all remaining ingredients except coco rallado. Blend well and pour into prepared mold. Drain coco rallado and drop in small chunks evenly into custard. Place mold in hot water bath and bake for 1 hour and 15 minutes or until done. (Flan is done when it is firm and not too shaky.) Cool for 25 minutes on wire rack. Run knife around edge to loosen from pan. Be sure it is completely loose. Place serving tray with raised edge on top of mold and invert quickly. Scrape out as much syrup as possible and serve at room temperature. This is best made and served on the same day. (For easy cleanup of pans, fill with water and heat until caramel dissolves.)

Serves 12

FLAN

2 cups sugar
12 egg yolks
Pinch of salt
1 can (5⅓ ounces) evaporated
  milk

1 quart milk
1 teaspoon vanilla

Preheat oven to 350 degrees F. Caramelize 1 cup sugar. Divide into 10 to 12 individual custard cups or baking dishes. Beat egg yolks with remaining sugar and salt. Combine milks, and scald. Beat in egg mixture. Add vanilla. Place custard cups in large pan of water. Divide flan evenly into cups and bake for 40 to 60 minutes or until firm. When cool, refrigerate until ready to serve. Run a knife around edge and invert onto serving dish. Flan will stay fresh for 3 to 4 days in refrigerator.

Serves 10 to 12

CHAPTER VIII

GAME
The Coastal Marshes

Not long ago, in geological terms, the coastal marshes southeast and south-west of Houston were the bottom of the Gulf of Mexico. Nowadays, they provide a congenial habitat for ducks, geese, and other waterfowl, while the drier meadows support deer, dove, pheasant, and quail. In some places, the rich alluvial soil is twenty to thirty feet deep. The climate is ideal for rice and sugar cane and for the tall wild grasses that have grown there since the land rose up from the sea. With unabashed enthusiasm, turn-of-the-century land promoters and railroad companies touted the area as the land where anything grows.

Each fall, Houstonians oil their rifles and shotguns, break out their waders and camouflage shirts, and head for these coastal fields and marshes to hunt game. Ranchers and farmers lease their land for this seasonal purpose, and local guides contribute their cunning, spreading squares of white cloth on the rice fields to fool the geese into thinking others of their species are feeding peacefully.

Houstonians with ranches host hunting parties on holidays and week-ends, but Houston hunting parties aren't like those in the Southeast. They're occasions for old clothes and hip flasks, for tall drinks and even taller tales. Since frontier times, women have hunted along with men, especially on dove shoots; but a weekend deer hunt is still considered a valid excuse for an all-male retreat. Often on these occasions, there's more action around the poker table than there is in the woods.

A good hunt will produce a volume of meat or birds that would strain the capacity of the largest refrigerator-freezer, so many families with hunters have separate freezers in their garages. The white-paper and plastic-wrapped birds, roasts, and fillets generally last well past the New Year. Since they also make popular house gifts, nonhunters with hunting friends often find themselves collecting favorite game recipes. Most concoctions that win prizes at Texas chili cookoffs have some sort of game in them—venison, squirrel, or one of the less conventional species, like opossum or armadillo.

The early Czech, Silesian, and German settlers earned a reputation for equal skill with a rifle and a cookpot. Their recipes merged with those from

Mexico, Cajun southern Louisiana, Appalachia, and the refined Southeast to make Texas game cookery what it is today. Doves Chasseur, Mexican Mallards, Pheasant à la Crème, Quail in Orange Sauce, Antichukas, Venison Chili con Queso, Wild Game Gumbo, and the other recipes in this section reflect this mingling and provide delicious alternatives for what to do with what the modern Jim Bowie or Daniel Boone brings home from the hunt.

CHARCOAL DOVE

12 doves (mourning or
  white-winged)
8 ounces Italian salad dressing
1 teaspoon Worcestershire sauce
  or to taste

Seasoned salt
Lemon pepper seasoning
Jalapeño peppers
12 strips bacon

Fillet doves from breastbone and marinate in salad dressing and Worcestershire sauce for 30 minutes to an hour. Sprinkle with seasoned salt and lemon pepper. Wrap a whole breast (two fillets) around a thin strip of jalapeño, then wrap a slice of bacon around the dove. Place on a skewer and cook over open coals for 15 minutes or until bacon is cooked.

Serves 4 to 6

DOVES CHASSEUR

16 doves or 8 teal
Salt and pepper
Flour
8 slices bacon
⅛ teaspoon Tabasco
4 tablespoons Worcestershire
  sauce

⅔ cup water, consommé, or red
  wine
12 ounces mushrooms, drained
2 tablespoons butter
1 teaspoon lemon juice
Chopped parsley for garnish

Dry doves and season with salt and pepper inside and out. Dust lightly with flour. In a Dutch oven large enough for single layer of birds, cook bacon until crisp. Remove, drain, and set aside. Brown birds on all sides in hot bacon drippings. With breasts down over low heat, add Tabasco, Worcestershire, and ⅔ cup liquid. Cover and cook for 20 minutes. Stir, turn birds breast up, and continue cooking, covered, for 20 minutes. Add more liquid if necessary. While birds are cooking, sauté mushrooms lightly in butter and lemon juice. Add mushrooms to doves for final 15 minutes of cooking. Before serving, crumble bacon over doves. Garnish with parsley and serve with rice. If doves are breasted, cut sauce in half.

Serves 8

GRILLED DUCK BREASTS

4 unskinned duck breasts	1½ teaspoons salt
1 clove garlic, split	¼ teaspoon freshly ground
2 tablespoons oil	black pepper

Rub both sides of duck breasts with cut side of garlic and a little oil. Season with salt and pepper. Place duck, skin side up, on a very hot grill and cook for 2 minutes. Turn pieces, skin side down, and cook for 6 minutes more for rare or 8 minutes more for medium rare. *Do not overcook.* Adjust the height of the grill so skin becomes crisp and dark brown but does not burn. Slice on the bias and arrange on plates.

Note: To broil instead of grill, place duck on a rack over a broiling pan and place 1½ to 2 inches below broiling unit. Broil for 2 minutes, skin side down, then 6 to 8 minutes, skin side up.

Serves 4

JANET'S DUCK

1 cup white wine	Honey
4 tablespoons salt	2 teaspoons curry powder
¼ cup vinegar	2 teaspoons black pepper
4 small cloves garlic, pressed	4 tablespoons butter, melted
4 ducks	½ cup frozen orange juice,
Water	undiluted
4 apples, quartered	¼ cup brandy

Combine wine, salt, vinegar, and garlic cloves. Pierce underside of ducks with ice pick. Place ducks in a Dutch oven, pour wine mixture over ducks and add enough water to cover. Soak in refrigerator overnight.

Preheat oven to 250 degrees F. Pat ducks dry with paper towels. Place apple quarters in each cavity, spread honey inside and out, and sprinkle each duck with ½ teaspoon curry powder and ½ teaspoon pepper. Bake, uncovered, for about 4 hours. Mix melted butter with orange juice and baste often. Pour warm brandy over duck and flame. Degrease pan drippings for sauce.

Serves 6 to 8

DUCK STEW

STEP 1:

4 to 5 cups cubed duck breast
   meat (10 to 12 ducks)
Salt and pepper
Garlic salt

Cinnamon
Allspice
Flour to dust
½ cup olive oil, more if needed

STEP 2:

3 onions, chopped
3 ribs celery, chopped
Garlic clove, crushed

¼ cup seedless raisins
2 tablespoons flour
4 cups hot water

STEP 3:

Dash of Tabasco
Sprinkle of allspice
Sprinkle of cinnamon
Sprinkle of powdered cloves
1 bay leaf
1 teaspoon Worcestershire sauce
½ tablespoon salt
½ tablespoon pepper
½ tablespoon sage
½ tablespoon marjoram
½ tablespoon rosemary
½ tablespoon thyme
1 tablespoon sugar
1 tablespoon butter
1 tablespoon Parmesan cheese

¼ green bell pepper, cut in
   squares
Rind of one large orange, cut in
   squares
¼ cup shredded coconut
¼ cup Madeira wine
1 can (2 ounces) mushrooms,
   drained
½ cup orange juice
½ cup sliced ripe olives
   (optional)
1 cup applesauce
1 cup pecan halves
1 pound smoked sausage, sliced
Fresh parsley, chopped

STEP 1: Season duck meat with the spices and flour well. Heat olive oil in enameled Dutch oven and brown duck well. Remove duck, reserving oil, and set aside.

STEP 2: In same oil, sauté onions, celery, garlic, and raisins until wilted. Remove sautéed ingredients, reserving oil, and set aside. Make a roux in oil by adding flour, and brown, taking care not to burn. Add sautéed ingredients to roux. Stirring well, add hot water.

STEP 3: Add remaining ingredients except parsley. Add duck, and simmer over low heat, covered, for 1½ hours. Watch carefully and stir occasionally. Add parsley and serve over rice. Can be made a day ahead and refrigerated in the same pot. Reheat slowly, stirring often.

Serves 12 to 16

MEXICAN MALLARDS

2 cups mild pickled jalapeño
  juice
2 lemons
1 bottle white wine (chablis)
2 teaspoons celery salt
2 teaspoons freshly ground
  pepper

8 mallard duck breasts
½ cup butter
1 teaspoon Creole mustard
½ pound bacon slices

In a large pan, combine 1 cup of the jalapeño juice with juice and rind of 1 of the lemons, wine, 1 teaspoon of the celery salt, and 1 teaspoon of the pepper. Add duck breasts and marinate in refrigerator for 24 hours. Remove from marinade. Melt butter in a small pan and add remaining jalapeño juice, lemon juice, mustard, and remaining celery salt and pepper. Baste breasts, wrap in bacon, and cook over charcoal fire for about 10 to 15 minutes on each side. Baste continually. Cook until medium rare. *Do not overcook.*

Serves 6 to 8

NEVER-FAIL WILD DUCK

1 large duck or 2 small ones
Salt and pepper to taste
2 tablespoons thyme

4 oranges
6 bacon strips
2 cups red wine

Preheat oven to 300 degrees F. Rub inside and outside of duck with salt, pepper, and thyme. Cut 2 of the oranges into quarters and stuff into cavity. Place duck, breast down, in deep pan or casserole. Cover with strips of bacon. Pour wine over duck and bake for 1 hour, basting frequently. If desired, squeeze the juice of 1 or 2 of the remaining oranges into wine. Cook down pan juices for sauce.

Serves 2 to 3

WILD DUCK BREASTS
WITH GREEN PEPPERCORN SAUCE

4 whole wild duck breasts
1½ teaspoons salt
½ teaspoon white pepper
2 tablespoons flour
3 tablespoons butter
6 shallots, chopped
2 to 3 tablespoons green
   peppercorns, canned in water,
   drained and mashed

2 tablespoons cognac
½ cup brown gravy or chicken
   stock
1½ cups heavy cream
1 tablespoon arrowroot
   (optional)
2 tablespoons chopped parsley

Preheat oven to 180 degrees F. Bone and skin duck breasts. Remove tendon and pound breasts thin. Season with ½ teaspoon of the salt and the pepper. Dredge with flour and shake off excess. Melt butter in large skillet, and sauté meat over medium heat for about 3 minutes on each side. The meat should be slightly pink inside. Drain, and keep warm in oven. Sauté shallots in pan drippings for 30 seconds. Add peppercorns, cognac, gravy or stock, and remaining salt, and bring to a boil. Add cream and bring to a second boil. Thicken with arrowroot if desired. Add parsley. Slice meat diagonally and cover with sauce.

Serves 4 to 6

Variation: This sauce is also good with steak fillets.

ROAST GOOSE WITH CUMBERLAND SAUCE

8 cups fresh bread cubes
½ cup chopped onion
½ cup chopped celery
2 tablespoons butter
1 cup fresh orange juice
2 tablespoons coarsely shredded
   orange rind
1 cup chopped fresh parsley
½ teaspoon thyme leaves
½ teaspoon ground sage
2 teaspoons salt
Freshly ground pepper
1 goose, 4½ to 5 pounds
Cumberland Sauce (below)

Preheat oven to 400 degrees F. Spread bread cubes out for an hour before making stuffing. Sauté the onion and celery in butter until soft. Mix with bread cubes in a large bowl. Add orange juice, orange rind, and seasonings. Toss lightly but thoroughly. Rinse the goose inside and out with cold water and dry thoroughly. Remove any stray pinfeathers. Fasten neck skin to back with skewer. Spoon stuffing into cavity, packing lightly. Roast for 15 minutes, remove from oven and lower temperature to 325 degrees F. Remove grease from pan and return goose to oven for about 1 hour and 15 minutes or 15 minutes per pound. Serve with Cumberland Sauce.

Serves 6

CUMBERLAND SAUCE

½ cup port wine
1 cup fresh orange juice
1 tablespoon lemon juice
1 cup red currant jelly
½ cup chopped onion
1 teaspoon dry mustard
¼ teaspoon ground ginger
Several drops of Tabasco
1½ tablespoons arrowroot or
   cornstarch
1 tablespoon coarsely shredded
   orange rind
1 tablespoon coarsely shredded
   lemon rind

Combine port, orange and lemon juices, jelly, onion, mustard, ginger, and Tabasco in a large saucepan. Bring to a boil, stirring occasionally. Be careful, as this sauce may foam up and over the sides of the pan. Strain the sauce. Combine arrowroot with a little of the hot sauce and mix well. Stir this into remaining sauce and cook over low heat, stirring constantly, until slightly thickened. Do not boil. Add orange and lemon rind.

Yield: 3 cups

PHEASANT À LA CRÈME

1 pheasant
1 chicken or pheasant liver
5 tablespoons butter plus extra
3 tablespoons oil
3 tablespoons minced onion
3 tablespoons finely chopped
   carrot
¼ teaspoon thyme

1 bay leaf, crushed
Salt and freshly ground pepper
   to taste
4 tablespoons brandy plus extra,
   warmed
1¼ cups whipping cream
1 slice white bread, decrusted
   and toasted

Truss the pheasant. In a large heavy pan, brown the bird and the chicken liver in 5 tablespoons of the butter and oil. Set liver aside. Add onion, carrot, thyme, bay leaf, salt, and pepper. Cover, and simmer for 20 minutes. Pour off excess fat, and flame with brandy. Add cream, and simmer until pheasant is tender, approximately 1½ to 2 hours. Mash the liver with a little butter and brandy and spread on toast. Place the bird on this. Strain the sauce, correct seasoning, and pour over the pheasant.

Serves 2 to 3

PHEASANT IN RED WINE

10½ tablespoons butter
12 small button mushrooms, caps
   and stems separated
12 small white onions
1 to 2 tablespoons sugar
2 pheasants with livers (chicken
   livers may be substituted)

4 shallots, finely chopped
2 tablespoons olive oil
2½ cups red burgundy wine
2 tablespoons flour
Salt and freshly ground pepper
   to taste

Preheat oven to 350 degrees F. Melt 2 tablespoons of the butter in sauté pan and lightly sauté mushroom caps. Season with salt and pepper and set aside. Cook onions in gently boiling salted water until tender. Drain. Melt 2 tablespoons of the butter in the pan. Add sugar, and stir until well blended. Add onions and cook slowly until glazed. Keep warm. Chop liver finely and sauté in ½ tablespoon of the butter. Mix with shallots and place in cavities of cleaned birds. Sauté the pheasants in oil and 4 tablespoons of the butter until golden on all sides and almost tender. Transfer to large covered casserole and keep warm. Pour wine into same pan, and cook over high heat. Add mushroom stems and continue to cook until liquid is reduced by half. Thicken with last 2 tablespoons of the butter and flour worked together, dropped by bits and stirred into sauce. Simmer for several minutes. Strain into a bowl, cool, and skim off grease. Pour over pheasant and adjust seasonings. Add onions and mushroom caps. Cover and bake in a moderate oven for 1½ to 2 hours until tender.

Serves 4 to 6

BAKED QUAIL OR DOVE

12 quail or doves
½ cup butter
½ cup green onions, finely chopped
½ cup celery, finely chopped
2 cups chicken broth

1 pound fresh mushrooms, sliced
½ cup white wine
2 cans (10¾ ounces each) golden mushroom soup
1 cup water
Salt and pepper to taste

Preheat oven to 325 degrees F. Sauté birds in butter and transfer to covered baking dish. Sauté onions and celery and transfer with pan drippings to a large bowl. Add broth, mushrooms, wine, soup, and water. Season with salt and pepper. Pour over birds, cover, and bake for three hours. If using breasted birds, make half the amount of sauce.

Serves 4 to 6

GRILLED QUAIL

2 cups wine vinegar or herb vinegar
1 cup vegetable oil
4 tablespoons lemon juice
4 whole lemon rinds
3 cloves garlic, crushed

2 bay leaves
1 tablespoon soy sauce
1 tablespoon A.1. sauce
1 tablespoon vermouth
Freshly ground pepper to taste
10 to 12 quail

Combine all ingredients and marinate quail for at least 8 hours. Cook on grill over slow fire, basting often. Cooking time will depend on how hot your coals are. *Do not overcook.*

Serves 4 to 6

GRILLED QUAIL WITH TARRAGON

8 quail
Salt and freshly ground pepper
8 teaspoons butter

8 teaspoons crushed tarragon
16 strips bacon

Season quail with salt and pepper and place about 1 teaspoon butter in each cavity. Sprinkle generously inside and out with tarragon. Close each cavity by holding legs up close to breast and wrapping securely with two strips of bacon. Secure with toothpicks or small skewers. Grill over charcoal or broil in oven, turning until bacon is very crisp.

Serves 4

QUAIL IN ORANGE SAUCE

1 teaspoon seasoned salt
½ cup flour
¼ teaspoon pepper
8 quail
½ cup oil
½ onion, chopped
½ green bell pepper, chopped

1 clove garlic, minced
1 carrot, sliced
1 cup chicken broth
1 cup dry white wine
1 tablespoon grated orange rind
1 teaspoon Worcestershire sauce
Sour cream at room temperature

Preheat oven to 350 degrees F. Combine salt, flour, and pepper in a paper bag. Shake quail individually in bag until lightly coated with seasoned flour. Heat oil in skillet and quickly brown birds over medium-high heat. Remove to ovenproof casserole. Sauté onion, green bell pepper, and garlic in remaining oil. Add carrot, broth, and wine. Cover and simmer for 15 minutes. Strain sauce over birds and sprinkle with orange rind and Worcestershire sauce. Cover and bake for 45 minutes. Turn off heat and leave in oven for an additional 30 minutes. Serve with a dollop of sour cream.

Serves 4

STUFFED QUAIL

12 quail	Salt and pepper
1 pound pork sausage	¼ cup butter
12 strips bacon	2 cups red wine
1 cup flour	Water

Preheat oven to 325 degrees F. Stuff quail with sausage. Secure a strip of bacon around each breast and roll in flour seasoned with salt and pepper. Melt butter in a large skillet and cook quail, breast down, until brown. Place in baking dish or pan. Add enough seasoned flour to the drippings to thicken. Stir in wine and enough water to yield a thin gravy. Pour over quail, cover, and cook for about 1 hour and 15 minutes. If gravy loses its wine flavor, add 1 cup wine 15 minutes before serving.

Serves 4 to 6

ANTICHUKAS

4 pounds venison backstrap	¼ teaspoon oregano
½ cup red wine vinegar	¼ teaspoon cumin
1½ tablespoons salt	¼ teaspoon paprika
1 tablespoon peppercorns	¼ cup olive oil
3 to 4 jalapeño peppers,	½ teaspoon crushed red pepper
stemmed, seeded, and chopped	flakes, or to taste
½ clove garlic, peeled and	
mashed	

Cut backstrap into 1- to 1½-inch cubes. Place in a large, deep bowl. Combine remaining ingredients except olive oil and red pepper. Pour over backstrap and marinate overnight. Preheat broiler. String meat on green cane skewers. Add olive oil and red pepper to marinade and baste as it cooks. Broil and serve en brochette. This is also good with beef tenderloin.

Serves 8 to 10

VENISON MEATBALLS

MEATBALLS:

1 pound lean trimmed venison, ground

½ pound venison pan sausage or any hot sausage

4 slices stale bread made into crumbs

½ medium onion, grated

1 teaspoon salt

½ teaspoon nutmeg

½ teaspoon garlic salt

1 egg

SAUCE:

1 cup chili sauce

½ cup grape jelly

1 teaspoon Colman's dry mustard

MEATBALLS: Preheat oven to 375 degrees F. Combine all ingredients and roll into small meatballs. Place on cookie sheet and bake for 30 minutes. Serve in chafing dish covered with sauce. Or freeze raw meatballs on cookie sheet and put into plastic bags when frozen. Defrost and bake as above.

SAUCE: Combine all ingredients and heat until well blended.

Yield: 4 dozen

Variation: Meatballs are also good in spaghetti sauce.

VENISON CHILI CON QUESO

1 pound finely ground venison

1 tablespoon oil

1 onion, chopped

3 or more jalapeño peppers, seeded and chopped

1 pound American cheese, grated

1 can (8 ounces) tomato sauce

Brown meat in 1 tablespoon oil or in a nonstick pan. Add onion, and sauté until tender. Add remaining ingredients, and cook until cheese is melted. Serve in chafing dish with tortilla chips. Freezes well and doubles well.

Serves 10

VENISON ROAST

Venison roast (4 pounds)
Marinade for Venison Roast
   (below)
8 strips bacon
2 onions
4 stalks celery
Bunch of fresh herbs or bouquet
   garni

Salt and pepper to taste
2 carrots
Juice and rind of 1 lemon or
   orange
½ cup Madeira (optional)

Marinate roast for 2 to 3 days. Preheat oven to 500 degrees F. Place venison and Marinade for Venison Roast in roasting pan. Arrange strips of bacon on venison and cook for 20 minutes. Reduce oven temperature to 350 degrees F. Add remaining ingredients and continue cooking for 30 minutes for each pound. Baste occasionally.

Serves 6

MARINADE FOR VENISON ROAST

1¼ cups oil
2½ cups Madeira
2 ribs celery
1 bouquet garni
1 clove garlic
6 sprigs parsley

1¼ cups red wine vinegar
1 onion, sliced
6 crushed juniper berries
   (optional)
Pinch of rosemary
Twist of orange rind

Put all ingredients in a large pan, bring to a boil, and simmer for 10 minutes. Let cool and pour over roast. Meat may be marinated for 2 to 3 days. Turn the meat occasionally. This should be done in a glass or china dish, not an enamel or metal one.

Yield: Approximately 6 cups

MIGHTY HUNTER VENISON STROGANOFF

½ venison backstrap, cut in thin
   strips or cubed, *or* 3 pounds
   lean venison stew meat
Salt and pepper
Flour
Chopped garlic to taste
3 medium onions, sliced

¼ cup butter or more
8 ounces mushrooms, fresh, or
   canned and drained
¼ teaspoon marjoram
½ teaspoon oregano
½ cup burgundy wine
1 cup sour cream

Season meat with salt and pepper and dredge with flour. In Dutch oven or heavy skillet, sauté garlic and onions in butter until soft and browned. Remove and set aside. Add more butter if necessary, and brown venison. Return garlic and onions to pan. Add flour and water, if gravy needs thickening, and adjust seasonings. Cover and simmer for 1½ hours. Add mushrooms, herbs, and wine, and simmer for 15 minutes more. Just before serving, add sour cream. Serve over white or wild rice or egg noodles.

Serves 6 to 8

VENISON SAUTÉ WITH SAUCE QUEST

3 tablespoons butter
1 small clove garlic, crushed
Six ¾-inch slices venison
   backstrap
Salt and pepper
¾ teaspoon minced onion

¼ cup brandy, warmed
1½ heaping tablespoons Grey
   Poupon mustard
2 heaping tablespoons sour cream
Parsley for garnish

Melt half the butter with garlic in a sauté pan over medium heat. When butter has melted, discard garlic. Place backstrap in pan and sprinkle with salt, pepper, and onion. Brown lightly, turn, and add remainder of butter. Cook to medium rare. *Do not overcook.* Pour in brandy and light. As flames die, quickly add mustard and blend around meat. Remove meat to plates or serving platter. Remove pan from heat and blend in sour cream. Pour over meat and garnish with parsley.

Serves 2 to 3

VENISON MINCEMEAT

2 pounds cooked venison,
  chopped or coarsely ground
4 pounds apples, unpeeled and
  chopped (about 8 pippin)
2 pounds raisins
4 cups brown sugar
¾ pound suet, chopped, or 1 ½
  cups butter

8 ounces currants
½ teaspoon ground cloves
1 teaspoon mace
½ teaspoon nutmeg
2 teaspoons salt
1 ½ teaspoons cinnamon
1 lemon, seeded and ground
5 cups cider, more or less

Mix first 12 ingredients in a large pot. Cover with cider, being careful not to add too much, as sugar dissolves quickly. Cook very slowly for about 1 hour until fruits are tender. It will be soupy at this point, but consistency will change as it cools. Refrigerate or store in sterile fruit jars. Keeps indefinitely if sealed in sterile fruit jars. Use as a relish or pie filling.

Yield: 6 cups

WILD GAME GUMBO

2 geese *or* 4 ducks *or* 12 to 16
  doves
3 quarts chicken stock
1 bay leaf
4 yellow onions
6 stalks celery
1 cup flour
½ cup bacon drippings
2 green bell peppers, chopped
¼ cup chopped parsley

4 cloves garlic, crushed
1 can (8 ounces) tomato sauce
3 cups fresh sliced okra or 2
  packages (10 ounces each)
  frozen okra
2 tablespoons Worcestershire
  sauce
½ teaspoon Tabasco
1 tablespoon salt
1 tablespoon pepper

Boil game in chicken stock with bay leaf, 1 coarsely chopped onion, and 2 coarsely chopped stalks of celery until tender. Remove meat from bones, cut into small pieces, strain stock and discard vegetables. Return meat to stock to keep moist. In a heavy pan or iron skillet, cook flour in bacon drippings until glossy and chocolate-colored, stirring often. This takes about 30 to 45 minutes. Put this roux in a soup pot. Chop remaining onions and celery. Add to the roux along with peppers, parsley, and garlic. Cook for 10 minutes. Stir stock into roux by pints. Add remaining ingredients, including meat. Simmer for 1 hour. This freezes well.

Yield: 4 to 5 quarts

WILD GAME PÂTÉ

Meat from 4 to 6 ducks *or* 3 to 4
  geese *or* 12 to 14 doves
3 tablespoons cognac
Salt and pepper
1 can (1 ounce) truffles
  (optional)
8 ounces lean raw pork
8 ounces raw pork fat
½ cup onion, minced
2 tablespoons butter
1 tablespoon salt

½ teaspoon freshly ground
  pepper
½ teaspoon thyme
⅛ teaspoon allspice
1 clove garlic, mashed
2 large eggs
Sheets of fresh pork fat ⅛ inch
  thick (fatback) *or* blanched
  salt pork *or* bacon
Bay leaves

Preheat oven to 350 degrees F. Slice ⅓ of the meat (breast) into thin 1-inch strips. Place strips in bowl with cognac and sprinkling of salt and pepper. Marinate for at least 30 minutes. Add truffles with juice. Grind remaining game with pork and pork fat. Sauté onion in butter until soft and combine with ground meat. Beat in salt, pepper, thyme, allspice, garlic, and eggs. Add liquid from marinade. Blend well. Line loaf pan(s) with sheets of pork or bacon. Put in half the ground meat mixture. Layer marinated breast slices evenly on top. Cover with rest of meat mixture. Top with bay leaves and cover with blanched salt pork or bacon to seal. Cover top with foil. This can be frozen or refrigerated for two days before cooking. Bake in water bath for 1½ to 2 hours. Pâté is done when it shrinks from sides and fat is clear yellow (170 to 175 degrees F. on meat thermometer). Remove terrine from pan(s) and weight down with cans or a brick. When cool, refrigerate with weights. Unmold, and scrape off excess fat. Decorate with aspic and green onions or tomatoes. This will keep 7 to 10 days.

Yield: 7 to 8 cups

CHAPTER IX

PICKLES AND RELISHES

Rosenberg

The Brazos River bottomlands southwest of Houston were the site of one of the oldest Anglo-American settlements in Texas. In 1821, William W. Little, Joseph Polley, and other members of the original Stephen F. Austin colony built a pioneer blockhouse at a bend in the river and then began planting their crops. The rich black soil was ideal for cotton, sugar, vegetables, and pecans. The region came to be known as Fort Bend County. Livestock thrived, and the Karankawa Indians who inhabited the areas were friendly, although rumors that they practiced cannibalism alarmed some of the squeamish.

In the decades between the Texas War of Independence and the War Between the States, European immigrants flocked to the area, bringing their crafts and their costumes, their dances and their savory food. The community of Rosenberg, now just beyond the reach of Houston's farthest suburbs, was popular with Czechs, who were called Bohemians by their neighbors. Any task that could be done as a group usually was. The work went quicker, and there was a built-in excuse for celebration when it was done. Songfests, dances, picnics, and church socials were all enthusiastically carried out.

Rosenberg weddings were elaborate affairs, with mountains of food. Preparations for the feast began days in advance. Tables groaned under the weight of soups, pork roasts, sausages, pecan pies and *kolaches*—square pastries filled with poppy-seed paste or fruit preserves. A polka band kept up a brisk pace for hours, so that guests could work off some of the meal and then return to the table for more.

As Houston encroaches from the northeast, this area keeps its hard-working, fun-loving pioneer past alive with barbecues and lavish wedding receptions and especially with the annual Czech Festival in the fall, preserving its heritage in much the same way a good cook preserves snap beans or okra—with just the right amount of pepper and spice.

The recipes that follow have that same lasting spark. Cranberry Conserve, No-Cook Pickles, Apple and Pear Chutney—they all contribute that touch of zest that keeps food—and life itself—interesting.

APPLE AND PEAR CHUTNEY

1 pound tart apples, peeled and
    chopped
6 firm pears, peeled and sliced
2 large cantaloupes, peeled and
    sliced
2 mangoes, peeled and sliced
1 can crushed pineapple or 1
    fresh pineapple, peeled and
    chopped
12 tomatoes, peeled and chopped
5 large onions, peeled and
    chopped
3 cloves garlic

6 hot red peppers, chopped
2 green bell peppers, chopped
6 cups brown sugar
1 quart cider vinegar
1 cup raisins
½ cup currants
1 cup chopped walnuts
1 tablespoon mustard seed
Juice of 2 limes
½ teaspoon powdered ginger
½ teaspoon powdered cloves
3 jars candied ginger, chopped

Mix chopped fruit, tomatoes, onions, garlic, red and green peppers, sugar, and vinegar in a large pot. Cook until mixture is thick and smooth, stirring frequently. This may take several hours. Add the remaining ingredients, and cook for about 45 minutes. Remove from heat and let stand until cool. Chill overnight. Bring to a boil and pack in hot sterilized jars immediately.

Yield: 18 pints

CRANBERRY CONSERVE

1 large orange
4 cups fresh cranberries,
    approximately 1 pound
1 cup golden raisins

½ cup chopped walnuts
¼ cup honey
¾ cup sugar
1½ teaspoons ginger

Quarter orange and remove seeds. Put orange and cranberries through a food chopper or processor. In a large bowl, stir the mixture with the raisins, nuts, honey, sugar, and ginger. So that flavors may blend, chill in refrigerator for several hours. Store in glass jars in refrigerator. Conserve will keep at least a month.

Yield: 4 cups

FRESH MINT JELLY

2 cups fresh mint, leaves and
    stems, washed and packed
    firmly
2¼ cups unsweetened apple juice

Juice of 1 lemon
3 cups sugar
1 package (3 ounces) Certo
3 drops green food coloring

Put mint leaves and stems in a large pan and crush to release the mint flavor. Add the juice and bring to a boil. Cover, remove from heat, and let stand for 10 minutes. Strain and measure the infusion. There should be 1¾ cups. Pour infusion into another large pot. Add lemon juice and sugar and bring to a boil over high heat, stirring constantly. As soon as it boils, add Certo and food coloring. Boil hard for 1 minute. Remove from heat. Skim and pour into sterilized jelly jars. Seal with paraffin.

Yield: 4 to 5 8-ounce jars of jelly

SPICED ORANGE JELLY

2 tablespoons fresh grated orange
    peel
1 teaspoon whole allspice
½ teaspoon whole cloves
2 cups freshly squeezed orange
    juice
⅔ cup water

⅓ cup freshly squeezed lemon
    juice
1 package (1¾ ounces)
    powdered pectin
5 sticks cinnamon
3½ cups sugar

Tie orange peel, allspice, and cloves in a cheesecloth bag. In a 4-quart saucepan, combine orange juice, water, and lemon juice; stir in pectin. Add spice bag and cinnamon sticks. Bring to a full rolling boil and boil 1 minute, stirring constantly. Add sugar; stir well. Bring back to a full rolling boil. Boil 1 minute, stirring constantly. Remove from heat and discard spice bag. Skim off foam. Pour jelly mixture into hot sterilized jars, filling to within ½ inch of the top. Place a cinnamon stick in each jar. Wipe top of jars clean. Seal with melted paraffin or process in boiling water bath for 5 minutes.

Yield: About 5 cups

NO-COOK PICKLES

7 cucumbers, thinly sliced
2 cups sugar
1 cup onions, thinly sliced

1 teaspoon celery seed
1 cup white vinegar
1 tablespoon coarse or kosher salt

Mix together all ingredients. Let stand for 1 to 2 hours. Put in jars and seal. These are good to use the next day and will keep in the refrigerator for months.

Yield: 3 pints

MICROWAVE STRAWBERRY JAM

4½ cups crushed strawberries
1 box (1¾ ounces) powdered
    fruit pectin

7 cups sugar
¼ to ⅓ cup lemon juice

Place crushed fruit and pectin in 3-quart casserole. Stir well and microwave on high, for 8 to 10 minutes, until mixture reaches a full rolling boil. Add sugar and lemon juice and stir well. Microwave on high uncovered, for 8 to 10 minutes more, until mixture reaches a full rolling boil, then boil for one minute. Skim off foam with a metal spoon and stir for about 5 minutes before spooning into sterilized jars. Seal with ⅛ inch hot paraffin or store in refrigerator or freezer.

Yield: 8 cups

CHAPTER X

POULTRY

Humble

Less than an hour north of Houston, the coastal plains end and the Great Southern Forest begins. Deep into this country is the Big Thicket, where wild orchids, azaleas, and dogwoods brighten the green-dappled wilderness of towering yellow pines and magnolias stretching up over one hundred feet.

The forest extends into the northern suburbs of Houston. In fact, Houston Intercontinental Airport is surrounded by a sea of woodsy green spreading north and east to the horizon. Until recently, this was country, the western extreme of the Deep South. In 1826, Joseph Dunman, a Tennessee farmer, settled in the area and established an outpost called Hunters' Paradise, because of its abundant game. Just before the Civil War, an enterprising man named Pleasant Smith Humble arrived in the fledgling community. A self-educated attorney and businessman, he operated a ferry across the San Jacinto River, ran a commissary, and appointed himself justice of the peace. He also set up a post office. Envelopes addressed to local farmers and ranchers would say "Deliver to Humble." Gradually, Humble became the name of the town.

Throughout the nineteenth century, ranching and logging were the mainstays of Humble's economy. The Big Thicket Lumber Mill was the primary employer in the area. Then, in 1904, a wildcat driller named C. E. Barrett struck oil just outside town. Apparently, the unassuming village of Humble was situated right on top of a salt dome—an underground geological "bubble," in this case filled with petroleum. The community boomed. The population, which was 75 in 1895, swelled to 25,000 by 1910.

Barrett's discovery brought with it the usual mixture of prosperity and confusion. Barrooms and boardinghouses sprang up like mushrooms in an East Texas cow pasture after a good spring rain. In 1912, the Humble Oil Company, which later became Exxon, moved its headquarters to Houston, but the Humble field kept on producing. Two decades later, in the midst of the Depression, another oil strike came in near the neighboring lumber town of Conroe, creating more jobs and more work for the Texas Rangers and other lawmen brought in to quell the frequent fracases among the roughnecks.

The cooks in the oilfield boardinghouses were experts at the hearty Southern fare that had sustained the ranchers and loggers in the Big Thicket from the days of the Spanish Empire. Turnip and mustard greens, black-eyed peas, stewed okra, cornbread, biscuits with cream gravy, and other rib-sticking specialties were devoured at every meal. But the real test of a good Southern cook was the chicken—chicken and dumplings, chicken stew, chicken and sausage gumbo, and, especially, fried chicken. Recipes for batter and seasonings were guarded like maps to buried treasure. The temperature of the oil had to be exactly right, the consistency of the batter just so, to make the crust crunchy, the meat soft and moist.

That pride in poultry preparation didn't confine itself to boardinghouse kitchens, of course. Cooks throughout the Houston area have winning ways with fowl. Some of the best are revealed on the pages that follow—Choleta's Zippy Fried Chicken, Cranberry-Glazed Chicken, Dijon Chicken, Honeyed Chicken, Jalapeño Fried Chicken, Stuffed Cornish Hens, and lots more. Approach them all with the two prime ingredients of good Southern cooking—a light hand and a good heart.

BAKED STUFFED CHICKEN

1 whole chicken
1 teaspoon dried mixed herbs
  (thyme, oregano, savory, etc.)
3 tablespoons olive oil
6 tablespoons butter
½ cup chopped onions
2 cups zucchini, cut in julienne
  strips
3 ounces ricotta or cream cheese

1 teaspoon chopped fresh
  marjoram (may substitute ¼
  teaspoon dried or other fresh
  herbs)
1 egg, beaten
¼ cup freshly grated Parmesan
  cheese
½ teaspoon salt
¼ teaspoon pepper

Preheat oven to 450 degrees F. At least 1½ hours before cooking, split chicken down entire length of back. Open out, breast side up, and flatten with firm whack, fracturing breast bone and rib cage. (Try not to tear skin.) Marinate for 1 hour in mixture of dried herbs and olive oil. Drain. Using 2 tablespoons of the butter, cook onions until clear. Salt zucchini and squeeze out excess juice. Sauté in remaining butter for several minutes. Cool. Combine onion, zucchini, ricotta cheese, marjoram, egg, Parmesan cheese, salt, and pepper. Taking one handful at a time, force stuffing between flesh and skin of chicken. Begin with drumsticks and thighs. When all stuffing is in place, fold neck skin flap over and tuck it underneath bird. Place chicken, breast side up, in a shallow roasting pan. Mold surface with your hands to force skin and stuffing into plump version of natural form. Bake, uncovered, for 10 minutes. Reduce oven temperature to 375 degrees F. Continue baking for 50 minutes more or until done.

Serves 4

BRAZILIAN CHICKEN

4 chicken breasts, halved,
   skinned and boned
1 can (14 ounces) hearts of palm

Melted butter
Salt and white pepper to taste
Parsley and paprika for garnish

SAUCE:
3 egg whites
1 tablespoon lemon juice
Salt and white pepper

1 cup butter, melted and
   bubbling hot

Preheat oven to 400 degrees F. Flatten chicken breasts slightly. Wrap each one around a stalk of heart of palm. Brush with melted butter and season with salt and pepper. Bake, uncovered, for 20 to 25 minutes, basting several times with drippings.

SAUCE: Place egg whites, lemon juice, salt, and pepper in a blender. With blender on medium speed, slowly drip hot melted butter into blender to make a good emulsion. Garnish chicken with parsley and paprika, serve with the sauce (Hollandaise may be substituted).

Serves 4
Sauce Yield: Approximately
1½ cups

BREAST OF CHICKEN BEAU MONDE

½ pound fresh mushrooms,
  sliced
4 tablespoons margarine
4 whole chicken breasts, halved
  and boned
2½ teaspoons Beau Monde
  seasoning

1 cup chopped green onions
½ cup dry white wine
1½ teaspoons tarragon
1 cup sour cream

Sauté mushrooms in 3 tablespoons of the margarine. Remove mushrooms and set aside. Add remaining margarine to skillet. Sauté chicken until brown. Sprinkle with Beau Monde while browning. Add green onions, wine, and tarragon. Simmer over low heat for 30 minutes or until tender. Remove chicken to serving platter. Stir sour cream and mushrooms into sauce. Pour over chicken and serve with rice or noodles.

Serves 4 to 6

CHICKEN ANDALUZA

2 large whole frying breasts
1¼ teaspoons salt
½ teaspoon freshly ground
  pepper
4 teaspoons cornstarch
4 teaspoons vegetable oil
1 egg white
1 cup dry sherry
⅓ cup dark raisins
½ cup sliced almonds, toasted in
  butter

7 tablespoons butter
6 tablespoons minced green
  onions
3 large cloves garlic, minced
1 cup coarsely chopped
  pimiento-stuffed olives
2 teaspoons brown sugar
3 tablespoons finely chopped
  fresh parsley
Fresh orange slices

Bone the breasts and cut into thin strips. Put on a glass plate and sprinkle with ¾ teaspoon of the salt and the fresh pepper. Let stand 20 minutes. Sprinkle with cornstarch and oil and gently turn to mix, letting stand another 20 minutes. Fold in the unbeaten egg white and let stand an additional 30 minutes. Heat the sherry and pour over the raisins and let soak for 1 hour. Toast the almonds in a little butter and set aside. Sauté the chicken in the butter for about 5 minutes until opaque. Remove and keep warm. Increase heat and add the onions and garlic; sauté briefly. Add the sherry, raisins, olives, brown sugar, remaining ½ teaspoon salt, and sauté a few minutes. Return chicken to skillet and add the parsley. Turn gently to mix. Sprinkle with almonds. Serve over rice. Serve orange slices on the side, to be squeezed over the chicken if desired.

Serves 4

CHICKEN AND WILD RICE

1 package (6 ounces) long-grain and wild rice
3 cups cooked diced chicken
1 cup mayonnaise
1 box (10 ounces) frozen French-cut green beans
1 can (10½ ounces) cream of celery soup
1 small onion, chopped
1 can (8 ounces) water chestnuts, sliced

Preheat oven to 350 degrees F. Cook rice according to package directions. Combine rice and remaining ingredients. Salt and pepper, if desired. Bake 45 minutes. Freezes well before baking.

Serves 8 to 10

KAREN'S CHICKEN SOUFFLÉ

9 slices white bread, cut in pieces
4 cups cooked, cubed chicken
1 can (8 ounces) sliced mushrooms, drained
¼ cup margarine, melted
1 can (8 ounces) sliced water chestnuts, drained
½ pound sharp Cheddar cheese, grated
½ cup mayonnaise
4 eggs, well beaten
2 cups milk
1 teaspoon salt
1 can (10½ ounces) cream of mushroom soup
1 can (10½ ounces) cream of celery soup
1 jar (2 ounces) pimientos, drained
2 cups bread crumbs

Line a buttered 9 × 13-inch casserole with bread. Cover with chicken. Sauté mushrooms in margarine and spoon over chicken. Add layers of water chestnuts and cheese. In a separate bowl, combine mayonnaise, eggs, milk, and salt. Beat well and pour over cheese. Combine soups and pimientos, and pour over casserole. Cover with aluminum foil and refrigerate for 8 hours or overnight. Preheat oven to 350 degrees F. Bake casserole, uncovered, for 30 minutes. Top with bread crumbs and bake for an additional 20 minutes.

Serves 8 to 10

CHICKEN CURRY

1 chicken	¼ teaspoon ground ginger
1 onion	¼ teaspoon ground cardamom
1 stalk celery	1 tablespoon turmeric
1 carrot	¼ teaspoon cayenne
1 chicken bouillon cube	½ teaspoon salt
½ pound fresh mushrooms	½ cup milk
3 tablespoons butter	½ cup unsweetened coconut
1 cup minced onion	1½ cups chopped celery
2 cloves garlic, minced	½ cup chopped green bell
1 green or tart apple, cut in small	pepper
pieces	2 teaspoons slivered lemon peel
4 tablespoons curry powder	½ cup dried currants
4 tablespoons cornstarch	¼ cup slivered candied ginger
½ cup heavy cream	

Cover chicken with water. Add onion, celery, carrot, bouillon cube, and seasonings of your choice. Simmer until tender. *Do not overcook.* Cool, bone, and cut chicken into bite-size pieces. Set aside. Cook stock until reduced to 2½ cups. Reserve. Sauté mushrooms in butter. Remove and set aside. Add onion and garlic; sauté until golden. Add apple and curry powder; stir until blended. Remove from heat. Combine cornstarch and cream. Add to curry mixture along with seasonings. Cook over low heat, stirring, until mixture becomes thick and creamy. Put milk and coconut in a blender. Blend for several minutes on high speed. Strain. Add this and 1 cup reserved stock to sauce. Bring to a boil, stirring constantly. Reduce heat and simmer, uncovered, for 15 to 20 minutes, stirring occasionally. Add chicken, celery, green pepper, lemon peel, and mushrooms. Cook for 10 minutes, adding remainder of broth as mixture thickens. Remove from heat, and gently stir in currants and ginger. Serve over rice with your favorite condiments. Try peanuts or cashews, sieved hard-cooked eggs, chutney, sliced bananas, raisins, chopped avocados, and shredded coconut. If you are not serving this immediately, pour it into a casserole. Reheat for 15 minutes at 300 degrees F. Freezes well.

Serves 10

CHICKEN AND SPINACH CASSEROLE

1 large stewing chicken (about 5 pounds) or 2 fryers
5 ounces fine egg noodles
¼ cup butter
¼ cup flour
1 cup milk
2 cups sour cream
⅓ cup lemon juice
2 teaspoons Lawry's Seasoned Salt
½ teaspoon cayenne
1 teaspoon paprika
1 teaspoon salt

2 teaspoons pepper
1 package frozen chopped spinach, cooked and drained
1 can (6 ounces) mushroom pieces and juice
1 can (8 ounces) sliced water chestnuts, drained
1 jar (4 ounces) chopped pimientos, drained
½ cup chopped onion
½ cup chopped celery
1½ cups grated Cheddar or Monterey Jack cheese

Cook chicken in seasoned water. Reserve stock. Debone and cut into bite-size pieces. Cook noodles according to package directions. Drain. Melt butter in a large saucepan. Stir in flour. Slowly add milk and 1 cup reserved stock. Cook over low heat, stirring constantly, until thickened. Add sour cream, lemon juice, and seasonings. Mix well. Add noodles, spinach, mushrooms, water chestnuts, pimientos, onion, and celery. Preheat oven to 300 degrees F. Spoon a layer of spinach mixture into a buttered 3-quart casserole. Add a layer of chicken. Repeat. Top with cheese. Bake, uncovered, for 25 to 30 minutes or until bubbly. *Do not freeze.*

Serves 10 to 12

CHICKEN CHINESE

4 whole chicken breasts, halved
½ cup butter or margarine,
    melted

½ cup soy sauce
4 tablespoons Worcestershire
    sauce

Preheat oven to 350 degrees F. Arrange chicken in ovenproof dish. Combine remaining ingredients. Baste chicken with sauce while baking for 45 minutes. This is also good barbecued.

Serves 4 to 8

Variation: Add 2 tablespoons orange juice and 1 teaspoon orange peel or 1 tablespoon honey to marinade.

CHICKEN DURKEE WITH RICE

CHICKEN:
Chicken breasts
Durkee Famous Sauce
Salt
Lemon pepper

Fines herbes
Marjoram or rosemary
Paprika

RICE:
1 cup rice
1 can (10½ ounces) chicken
    consommé

1⅛ cups water
1 tablespoon butter
1 teaspoon salt

Preheat oven to 350 degrees F.
CHICKEN: Wash and pat chicken breasts dry. Coat liberally with Durkee Sauce. Lay chicken, skin side up, in a shallow broiler pan. Sprinkle with salt, lemon pepper, fines herbes, marjoram or rosemary, and paprika. Bake on the middle oven rack for 1 hour or until golden brown. Stir drippings in bottom of pan and use for gravy.
RICE: Combine rice, consommé, water, butter, and salt in a container with a tight lid. Place on the bottom rack of the oven and bake with the chicken for 30 minutes to 1 hour. The leftover chicken makes a great salad.

Serve ½ to 1 chicken
breast per person

CHICKEN FLORENTINE

6 tablespoons clarified butter
1 egg
½ cup milk
2 large chicken breasts, halved,
    skinned and boned
½ cup flour
¾ cup butter

2 cups sliced fresh mushrooms
½ cup white wine
Salt to taste
Pepper to taste
1 bag (10 ounces) fresh spinach,
    cooked and drained
4 slices mozzarella cheese

Preheat broiler. In a heavy skillet, heat clarified butter until bubbling. Beat egg into milk. Pound chicken breasts to ¼ inch thick. Dip chicken in flour and then in egg mixture. Place chicken in the hot clarified butter. Do not disturb until edges are browned. Turn and brown edges on other side. This should take about 2 minutes. Remove chicken from skillet and set aside. Clean skillet. Melt ½ cup of the butter, return chicken to pan, and cook over medium heat for 2 minutes. Add mushrooms and wine. Cook for 5 minutes more. Season with salt and pepper. Place cooked spinach in a lightly buttered and salted ovenproof dish. Season with salt and pepper. Arrange chicken over spinach. Spoon half of the mushroom mixture on top. Add cheese and top with remaining mushroom mixture. Dot with remaining ¼ cup butter, cut in chunks. Place under broiler until cheese melts and casserole is slightly glazed.

Serves 4

CHOLETA'S ZIPPY FRIED CHICKEN

1 fryer, cut in pieces
Salt and pepper
Juice of 1 lemon
2 cups buttermilk

Vegetable oil
2 cups flour
Salt and pepper

Rinse chicken and pat dry. Season with salt and pepper. Place chicken in a pan and squeeze lemon juice over all the pieces. Pour buttermilk over chicken and marinate for several hours. Heat 1½ to 2 inches of oil in a heavy skillet. Roll chicken in flour seasoned with salt and pepper. Fry in hot oil about 10 minutes per side or until done.

Serves 4 to 6

CHICKEN IN CHUTNEY SAUCE

1 chicken, cut in pieces
Salt and pepper
4 tablespoons oil
1 tart apple, chopped
1 stalk celery, chopped
1 onion, chopped
1 carrot, chopped
2 tablespoons curry powder
2 tablespoons flour

½ cup orange juice
½ cup chicken broth
2 teaspoons grated orange rind
⅓ cup chopped chutney
1 bay leaf
Raisins, optional
2 oranges, peeled and sectioned,
   and fresh mint for garnish

Season chicken with salt and pepper. Brown in oil in a heavy skillet. Remove chicken and keep warm. Add apple, celery, onion, and carrot to skillet. Cook, stirring, for 4 minutes. Sprinkle with curry powder and flour. Cook and stir for another minute. Gradually add orange juice, broth, orange rind, chutney, bay leaf, and raisins, if desired. Bring to a boil and season with salt and pepper. Return chicken to skillet. Reduce heat and simmer, covered, for about 30 minutes or until tender. Garnish with orange sections and fresh mint.

Serves 4

CHICKEN IN A PACKET

1 cup raw rice for every 4
   packets of chicken
For each packet:
1 teaspoon margarine or butter
2 teaspoons dehydrated onion
   soup mix

¼ chicken *or* 1 chicken breast
Freshly ground pepper
2 teaspoons margarine or butter
2 teaspoons cream
Paprika

Preheat oven to 350 degrees F. Partially cook the rice by halving the amount of water normally used. On a sheet of heavy aluminum foil, layer the ingredients in the above order, beginning with the partially cooked rice. Wrap packet tightly and bake for 1 hour. You can make as many packets as you want at one time and freeze them before baking. Take them to a sick friend or a new mother or save them for a rainy day.

Each packet serves 1

CHICKEN PIZZA

2 whole fryer breasts
1 package (8) refrigerator
   crescent rolls or your favorite
   pizza dough
¼ cup cooking oil
1 large onion, sliced into thin
   rings
1 large green bell pepper, seeded
   and sliced into thin rings

½ pound fresh mushrooms,
   sliced
½ cup ripe olives, sliced
1 can (10½ ounces) pizza sauce
   with cheese
1 teaspoon garlic salt
1 teaspoon oregano
¼ cup Parmesan cheese
2 cups grated mozzarella cheese

Preheat oven to 425 degrees F. Skin and bone chicken; cut chicken into 1-inch pieces. Press dough triangles into a lightly oiled 12-inch pizza pan, sealing at perforated edges. Heat oil in a heavy skillet. Add chicken, onion, green pepper, mushrooms, and olives. Cook, stirring, for about 5 minutes. Spread pizza sauce over crust. Spoon chicken mixture evenly over sauce. Sprinkle with garlic salt, oregano, and Parmesan cheese. Top with mozzarella, and bake for approximately 20 minutes.

Makes 1 pizza

CHICKEN SCAMPI

1 fryer, cut in pieces and boned
1 tablespoon salt
½ teaspoon pepper
¼ cup margarine
3 small onions, chopped
1 clove garlic, minced

3 tablespoons chopped parsley
½ cup white wine
1 can (8 ounces) tomato sauce
1 teaspoon sweet basil
1 pound large shrimp, cleaned
Parsley for garnish

Rub chicken with salt and pepper. In heavy skillet, melt margarine and fry chicken until brown. Add all remaining ingredients except shrimp and parsley for garnish. Simmer for about 30 minutes. Increase heat until sauce boils. Add shrimp. Reduce heat, and cook, uncovered, for 3 to 4 minutes. Stir thoroughly. Garnish with parsley and serve with your favorite rice.

Serves 4 to 6

CHINESE CHICKEN

10 ounces chicken breasts,
  lightly cooked and cubed
3 tablespoons oil
1 heaping cup cashew nuts
6 green onions, sliced

1 bamboo shoot or 1 can (8
  ounces) water chestnuts,
  cubed
6 fresh mushrooms, sliced

SOUP MIXTURE:

2 chicken bouillon cubes
⅔ cup hot water
1½ tablespoons sake
½ teaspoon salt
2 teaspoons sugar
¼ teaspoon garlic powder

1½ tablespoons Kikkoman soy
  sauce
1 tablespoon cornstarch
1 tablespoon water
3 tablespoons frozen English
  peas, thawed

Sauté chicken quickly in hot oil. Add nuts, and sauté lightly. Add onions, bamboo shoot, and mushrooms. Dissolve bouillon cubes in hot water. Add sake, salt, sugar, garlic powder, and soy sauce. Pour over chicken. Sauté quickly for several minutes more. Combine cornstarch and water. Stir into chicken mixture. Add peas, and simmer until thickened. Serve with rice.

Serves 4

CRANBERRY-GLAZED CHICKEN

1 chicken (about 2½ to 3
  pounds), cut in pieces
Salt and pepper to taste
1 can (8 ounces) whole-berry
  cranberry sauce

¼ cup margarine
2 tablespoons soy sauce
1½ tablespoons lemon juice

Preheat oven to 400 degrees F. Season chicken with salt and pepper. Place, skin side down, in baking dish. In a saucepan, heat remaining ingredients until margarine and cranberry sauce are melted. Pour sauce over chicken. Bake, uncovered, for 30 minutes. Turn chicken and bake 20 to 30 minutes more. Serve with rice.

Serves 4

CHICKEN SUPERB

8 chicken breasts, halved
Vegetable oil spray
3 cans (8½ ounces each) artichoke hearts, drained
2 cans (8 ounces each) sliced mushrooms, drained, *or* 2 cups fresh mushrooms sautéed in 1 tablespoon butter, drained
1 cup butter
½ cup flour

3 cups milk
¼ pound sharp Cheddar cheese, grated
5 ounces Swiss cheese, grated
⅓ cup tomato sauce
½ teaspoon cayenne pepper
8 small garlic cloves, pressed
2 tablespoons salt
Pepper to taste

Boil chicken in water until tender and debone. Preheat oven to 350 degrees F. Coat a shallow 3-quart casserole dish with vegetable spray. Quarter artichoke hearts and layer in bottom of dish. Next layer chicken and then mushrooms. Melt butter over low heat. Add the flour, blending well. Gradually add the milk, and cook, stirring into a smooth cream sauce. Add remaining ingredients and blend until smooth. Pour cream sauce over the casserole and bake, uncovered, for 30 to 35 minutes or until bubbly. This can be made ahead and frozen.

Serves 16

GOLDEN CHICKEN

1 fryer, skinned and cut in pieces
¼ cup margarine
1 can (4 ounces) sliced mushrooms, drained
1 tablespoon flour

2 tablespoons Worcestershire sauce
1 bay leaf
Juice of ½ lemon
1 can beef broth

Preheat oven to 350 degrees F. Brown chicken in margarine. Remove to 9 × 13-inch ovenproof dish. Add remaining ingredients to pan and bring to a boil. Pour sauce over chicken, and bake, uncovered, for 1 hour. Serve with rice or potatoes.

Serves 3 to 4

DIJON CHICKEN

3 whole chicken breasts, halved
1 cup butter, melted
Salt and pepper to taste
1 jar (8 ounces) Dijon Poupon
　　mustard made with white wine

1 cup seasoned bread crumbs
　　(Italian)

Preheat oven to 325 degrees F. Smother chicken with butter, salt, and pepper, and bake, uncovered, for 1 hour.

Remove from oven. Pour off drippings and reserve. Cover chicken with mustard and sprinkle with bread crumbs. Drizzle reserved drippings over all. Increase oven temperature to 375 degrees F. Return chicken to oven and cook for 15 minutes more.

Serves 4 to 6

JOHN QUIN'S GARLIC CHICKEN

20 cloves garlic
1 hen or chicken (about 3 to 4
　　pounds)
1 teaspoon rosemary
Freshly ground pepper to taste
2 tablespoons olive oil
2 tablespoons butter
6 stalks celery, sliced ¼ inch
　　thick

2 onions, chopped
3 cooking apples, quartered
½ fresh pineapple, cubed
½ cup honey
3 teaspoons curry powder
½ cup white wine

Preheat oven to 350 degrees F. Pour boiling water over whole garlic cloves. Let stand several minutes. Drain and peel. Wash chicken and dry. Place garlic cloves, rosemary, and pepper in cavity. Tie legs together and wings to sides of chicken. Brush with olive oil and set aside. Melt butter and any remaining olive oil in large cast-iron or enamel casserole. Sauté celery and onions until limp. Place chicken in casserole and surround with apples, pineapple, celery, and onions. Pour honey over this, sprinkle with curry powder, and pour wine over all. Bake, covered, for about 2 hours for hen or 1 hour for chicken. Be sure to serve garlic cloves to spread on French bread.

Serves 4 to 6

GRACE'S LEMONY CHICKEN CUTLETS

3 whole chicken breasts, halved
    and boned
¼ cup flour
½ teaspoon salt
⅛ teaspoon pepper

3 to 6 tablespoons butter
1 cup water
1 chicken bouillon cube
Juice of ½ lemon
1½ lemons, thinly sliced

Pound chicken breasts to make cutlets. Dip chicken in flour seasoned with salt and pepper. Save excess flour. Melt butter in skillet. Cook chicken until lightly browned on both sides. Remove chicken and reduce heat. Combine water and remaining flour. Add with bouillon and lemon juice to skillet. Cook, stirring to loosen anything cooked onto bottom of skillet. Return chicken to the skillet. Arrange lemon slices on top of chicken. Cover, and simmer for 5 minutes or until chicken is tender.

Serves 4

CHICKEN-ARTICHOKE CASSEROLE

2 large whole chicken breasts,
    halved
1 bay leaf
1 cup sherry
Salt and seasoned pepper
½ pound fresh mushrooms,
    sliced
½ cup chopped green onions

2 tablespoons butter, melted
Garlic salt
2 cans (8½ ounces, each)
    artichoke hearts, drained and
    quartered
¾ cup mayonnaise
½ cup sour cream
1 cup grated Parmesan cheese

Preheat oven to 350 degrees F. Cook chicken until tender in water seasoned with bay leaf, ½ cup of the sherry, salt, and pepper. Remove meat from bones and cut in bite-size pieces. Sauté mushrooms and green onions in butter and garlic salt. Place chicken and artichoke hearts in a 2-quart casserole. Add mushrooms and onions. Fold in mayonnaise, sour cream, remaining sherry, and ½ cup of the Parmesan cheese. Mix well. Wipe sides of casserole clean and top with remaining cheese. Bake, uncovered, for 20 minutes or until cheese browns. Serve with rice or green noodles.

Serves 6

HONEYED CHICKEN

¼ cup butter or margarine
½ cup honey
¼ cup prepared mustard
1 teaspoon salt

1 teaspoon curry powder
1 chicken (about 3 pounds) cut
   in pieces or 6 to 8 pieces of
   chicken

Preheat oven to 375 degrees F. Melt butter or margarine in shallow 3-quart baking dish. Stir in honey, mustard, salt, and curry powder. Roll chicken pieces in mixture and arrange in a single layer in dish. Bake, uncovered, for 1 hour or until tender. Baste while baking. Serve with curried rice.

Serves 4

HOT CHICKEN SALAD

3 cups cooked bite-size chicken
1 can (10½ ounces) cream of
   mushroom soup
1 cup Hellmann's mayonnaise
2 tablespoons finely chopped
   onion
1½ cups sliced celery

1½ tablespoons lemon juice
⅛ teaspoon pepper
½ cup slivered almonds
2 cups crushed potato chips
1 cup grated sharp Cheddar
   cheese

Preheat oven to 375 degrees F. Combine all ingredients except potato chips and cheese. Place in 9 × 13-inch casserole. Top with potato chips and cheese. Bake, uncovered, for 25 minutes.

Serves 8

JALAPEÑO FRIED CHICKEN

1 can (12 ounces) pickled
   jalapeño peppers
2 cups milk
1 fryer, cut in pieces

Flour
Salt
Paprika

Drain the jalapeños, reserving the juice. Remove seeds from the peppers.

Grind the jalapeños along with some of the juice in a blender or food processor. Add to the milk and soak the chicken in the mixture for at least 4 hours. Drain. Dredge the chicken in flour seasoned with salt and paprika and fry as you would regular Southern fried chicken. For a party, you can use drumettes or chicken bits.

Serves 2 to 4

LEMON AND SOY CHICKEN

3 tablespoons shredded lemon
  rind
¾ cup lemon juice
¾ cup water
¾ cup corn oil
3 tablespoons soy sauce

3 cloves garlic, minced
3 teaspoons salt
3 teaspoons pepper
3 small chickens, cut in pieces
1½ cups flour
2 tablespoons paprika

Combine lemon rind, juice, water, oil, soy sauce, garlic, 1 teaspoon of the salt and 1 teaspoon of the pepper. Pour over chicken, cover, and refrigerate for at least 3 hours or overnight. Preheat oven to 400 degrees F. Remove chicken from marinade and drain on paper towels. Reserve marinade. Combine flour, paprika and remaining salt and pepper. Coat chicken with flour mixture. Shake off any excess flour and place chicken, skin side down, in two shallow pans. Bake, uncovered, for 30 minutes. Turn and pour marinade over chicken and continue baking 30 minutes or until tender. Baste occasionally.

Serves 12 to 14

POLYNESIAN CHICKEN

1 can pineapple slices and juice
½ cup soy sauce
½ cup sherry
¼ cup lemon juice
2 teaspoons dry mustard
1 tablespoon oil

Dash of Tabasco
2 broiling chickens, halved or
  quartered
1 tablespoon cornstarch
⅓ cup cold water
4 teaspoons brown sugar

Combine juice drained from pineapple with soy sauce, sherry, lemon juice, mustard, oil, and Tabasco. Pour over chicken and marinate for at least 3 to 4 hours. Drain chicken and reserve marinade. Preheat grill or broiler. Cook chicken slowly, turning frequently. Baste often with marinade. When chicken is almost done, combine cornstarch with water. Add brown sugar and remaining marinade. Cook over low heat, stirring constantly until thickened. Heat pineapple slices on grill or under broiler. Serve chicken with gravy and garnish with pineapple slices.

Serves 4 to 8

POULET AU VIN

4 whole chicken breasts, halved
Salt and pepper
Flour
½ cup butter
Oil
½ cup small julienne strips of ham
½ cup chopped green onions or shallots
½ cup finely chopped onion
2 cloves garlic, minced

½ to ¾ cup fresh sliced mushrooms
1 tablespoon margarine
2 tablespoons flour
Pepper to taste
Pinch of cayenne
¼ to ½ cup dry white wine or vermouth
1 cup chicken stock, warm
Water chestnuts, pine nuts, or almonds, toasted (optional)

Season chicken with salt and pepper, and dust with flour. Melt butter in skillet and add a little oil. Sauté chicken until golden. Remove to buttered ovenproof casserole. Preheat oven to 350 degrees F. Sauté ham, onions, and garlic in same skillet. Using another pan, briefly sauté mushrooms in margarine over high heat. Add to ham mixture along with flour, pepper, and cayenne. Brown mixture slightly while stirring. Blend in wine and warm stock. Simmer for 2 to 3 minutes. Pour over chicken and bake for 45 to 60 minutes. Serve over a mixture of white and wild rice which has been cooked in broth. Add water chestnuts, pine nuts, or almonds to rice if desired.

Serves 6

POPPY-SEED CHICKEN

2 to 3 whole chicken breasts
1 stalk celery, sliced
1 medium onion, quartered
Salt and pepper to taste
1 can (10½ ounces) cream of
  chicken soup
1 cup sour cream

¼ cup white wine or vermouth
1 can (4 ounces) mushrooms,
  drained
1 cup crushed Ritz crackers
4 tablespoons butter, melted
2 to 3 tablespoons poppy seeds

Cook chicken in water seasoned with celery, onion, salt and pepper until tender. Preheat oven to 350 degrees F. Cut chicken into large pieces and place in greased casserole. Combine soup, sour cream, wine, mushrooms, salt and pepper. Pour over chicken. Toast Ritz crackers in melted butter. Top casserole with crackers and sprinkle with poppy seeds. Bake 30 minutes, uncovered, until bubbly.

Serves 4 to 6

FOIES DE VOLAILLES AUX CHAMPIGNONS FRAIS

1 pound chicken livers
Flour
Salt and pepper
4 tablespoons butter
6 green onions, chopped
1 teaspoon tarragon

½ pound fresh mushrooms,
  thickly sliced
1 cup sour cream
4 slices whole wheat bread,
  toasted

Dredge chicken livers in flour seasoned with salt and pepper. Melt butter in heavy skillet and add livers. When livers start to brown, add onions. Continue cooking until onions start to turn golden brown. Add tarragon and mushrooms, stirring well to coat with butter. When mushrooms are tender, remove from heat and stir in sour cream. Serve on toast.

Serves 4

STIR-FRIED CHICKEN AND BROCCOLI

8 chicken thighs
¼ teaspoon ground ginger
¼ teaspoon pepper or to taste
3 tablespoons peanut oil
1 bunch fresh broccoli, thinly
    sliced
1 cup sliced green onions
1 cup sliced fresh mushrooms
1 can (8 ounces) sliced water
    chestnuts

¾ cup plus 2 tablespoons
    chicken broth
1 teaspoon salt
½ teaspoon sugar
1 tablespoon cornstarch
Grated Parmesan cheese
    (optional)

Skin, bone, and cut chicken into bite-size pieces. Season chicken with ginger and pepper. In a large frying pan or wok, heat oil to high temperature. Add chicken, and stir-fry until browned. Push chicken to one side and add vegetables. Stir-fry vegetables for 3 minutes. Combine ¾ cup of the broth, salt, and sugar. Add to chicken. Reduce heat to medium high, cover, and cook for 2 minutes. Stir remaining 2 tablespoons broth into cornstarch to make a smooth paste. Add to chicken, and cook for 1 minute. Remove from heat. Stir in Parmesan cheese. Serve immediately.

Serves 6

WORLD'S EASIEST CHICKEN

3 whole chicken breasts, halved
    or combination of breasts and
    thighs
1 can (10½ ounces) cream of
    mushroom soup
1 can (10½ ounces) cream of
    chicken soup

1 can (10½ ounces) cream of
    celery soup
½ cup dry vermouth
¼ cup grated Parmesan cheese
1 package slivered almonds
    (optional)

Preheat oven to 350 degrees F. Place chicken in a 9 × 13-inch casserole. Mix remaining ingredients and pour over chicken. Bake, uncovered, for about 1 hour and 15 minutes. Serve with rice.

Serves 4 to 6

SWEET AND SOUR CHICKEN

4 whole chicken breasts, halved
1 jar (10 ounces) apricot
   preserves
1 bottle (8 ounces) Russian
   dressing
1 envelope dry onion soup mix

Preheat oven to 350 degrees F. Place chicken in shallow baking dish. Mix remaining ingredients and pour over chicken. Bake, uncovered, for 45 minutes to 1 hour. Serve with rice.

Serves 6 to 8

CORNISH HENS WITH CRANBERRY SAUCE

2 Cornish hens, halved
   lengthwise
Salt and pepper
2 slices bacon, cut in half
1 tablespoon lemon juice
1 chicken bouillon cube
1 cup hot water
2 tablespoons flour
1 cup water
3 tablespoons whole-berry
   cranberry sauce
1 can (4 ounces) sliced
   mushrooms, drained or ½
   pound fresh mushrooms, sliced

Preheat oven to 375 degrees F. Season hens with salt and pepper. Place, cut side down, in large shallow roasting pan. Place ½ slice bacon on each half hen. Sprinkle with lemon juice. Dissolve bouillon cube in 1 cup hot water and add to pan. Bake for 1 hour and 15 minutes or until juice runs clear when thigh is pierced with fork. Baste often with pan drippings. Remove hens to serving platter. Pour pan drippings into medium saucepan. Blend flour into drippings. Cook over low heat, stirring constantly, until browned. Gradually add 1 cup water. Cook, stirring constantly, until smooth and thickened. Stir in cranberry sauce and mushrooms. Add salt and pepper to taste. Simmer 10 minutes. Serve with rice.

Serves 4

STUFFED CORNISH HENS

1 small box (6 ounces) wild and
   long-grain rice
¼ pound fresh mushrooms,
   sliced
4 green onions, chopped
1 teaspoon tarragon
1 tablespoon butter

½ orange, peeled, seeded, and
   cut in pieces
2 tablespoons chopped pecans
2 Cornish game hens, room
   temperature
Salt and pepper to taste
1 cup dry white wine

Prepare rice according to package directions. (Only half of the rice will be used.) Sauté mushrooms, onions, and tarragon in butter for several minutes. Add *half* the rice, orange pieces, and pecans, and mix well. Preheat oven to 400 degrees F. Stuff hens with rice mixture. Season outsides of hens with salt and pepper and place them in a baking dish. Pour wine over hens and place in oven. Immediately reduce oven temperature to 350 degrees F. Bake, uncovered, for 1 hour or until tender. Baste frequently.

Serves 2 to 4

CHAPTER XI

SALADS AND DRESSINGS

Buffalo Bayou

From the Turning Basin at the head of the Houston Ship Channel, where tankers and cargo ships loaded with oil or grain turn to head back out to the Gulf of Mexico, to the wooded parks and residential areas west of Downtown, to its start as a cluster of springs in the Central Texas ranch country, Buffalo Bayou snakes in and out of Houston, linking the manmade metropolis with the gentle wonders of nature.

The early settlers named the stream for its abundant buffalo fish—a large relative of the succulent Southern catfish. "Bayou" was a word the Louisiana French picked up from the Choctaw Indians, who applied it to medium-size meandering streams in marshy coastal areas.

Buffalo Bayou drove some pioneers to poetry and others to desperation. In his diary, a settler named Joseph Chambers Clopper described the stream as "crystal clear and teeming with fish. . . . Flowering shrubbery . . . overhang its grassy banks and dip and reflect their variegated hues in its unruffled waters." Others cursed the same waterway as a snag- and alligator-infested navigator's nightmare, riddled with jutting cypress knees and overhung with troublesome branches. In the early days of the republic, navigation along the bayou was so hazardous that one captain reported in his log, as if it were an accomplishment, that he had only lost the cook on a recent voyage to the Allen brothers' outpost.

That overgrown aquatic trail between Galveston Bay and Allen's Landing bore little resemblance to the dredged and widened Houston Ship Channel into which it has evolved. International vessels ply its waters; oil refineries, petrochemical plants, and sprawling tank farms—huge oil storage facilities—crowd its banks. At night the sky glitters with electric lights and gas flares.

West of Downtown, Buffalo Bayou reverts to type. Well within the city limits, it becomes a tunnel of ferns, wild dogwood, and cypress limbs draped with Spanish moss, mustang grape, and trumpet vine.

Nutria, raccoons, and even wild mink burrow along the banks. Much of the land along the bayou has been retained as public parks. Jogging and bike paths run close to the stream. The Houston Arboretum and Nature Center, a piece of densely forested bayou bottomland in Memorial Park, is preserved exactly as it was when the city was founded—except for its winding nature trails and a few identifying signs on vines and trees. Wildlife and conservation groups sometimes hold canoe trips up the bayou, and the huge lots that spread along its southern bank were chosen as the sites of some of the city's most beautiful homes. To some, the appeal of that verdant splendor so close to the city's Space Age spires is irresistible.

Buffalo Bayou adds an element of cool, refreshing greenery to Houston in much the way that a salad adds that flavor to a meal. Some salads are so complete you can make a warm-weather supper out of them; others are the perfect complement to more substantial courses. This chapter contains some of both, plus a broad selection of dressings and marinades. Cobb Salad, Paella Salad, Green Greek Salad, Molded Gazpacho—they all capture a taste of Nature at her best.

BEEF VINAIGRETTE

Fantastic for a picnic! This is a great way to use leftover roast beef.

2 cups julienne strips cold roast beef

1 cup raw onion rings
2 tablespoons capers

DRESSING:

½ cup, or less, olive oil
2 tablespoons tarragon vinegar
1 clove garlic, crushed
1 teaspoon salt

¼ teaspoon dry mustard
⅛ teaspoon pepper
2 tablespoons chopped parsley for garnish

Toss beef with onions and capers. Combine ingredients for dressing and toss with beef. Chill for at least 1 hour. Sprinkle with parsley and serve.

Serves 6

COBB SALAD

½ head iceberg lettuce, finely chopped

½ bunch watercress, finely chopped

1 small bunch chicory, finely chopped

3 tablespoons minced fresh chives

3 small tomatoes, peeled, seeded, and finely chopped

2½ cups cooked white chicken meat, finely chopped

6 slices bacon, cooked crisp and crumbled

2 hard-cooked eggs, finely chopped

3 ounces blue cheese, crumbled

1 avocado, finely chopped

DRESSING:

1⅓ cups olive oil

⅔ cup white wine vinegar

2 cloves garlic

1 teaspoon salt

½ teaspoon black pepper

1 teaspoon sugar

1 teaspoon dry mustard

1 teaspoon paprika

1 teaspoon Worcestershire sauce

Prepare greens and refrigerate in plastic bags until ready to use. Combine dressing ingredients in a jar. Shake well and refrigerate overnight. Remove garlic and discard. When ready to serve, toss greens and other salad ingredients in a large salad bowl. Shake dressing vigorously and pour half of it over salad. Toss gently. Add more dressing if desired. Serve at once.

Serves 4 to 6
Dressing yield: 2 cups

COLD PASTA AND CHICKEN SALAD

Cold boiled shrimp can be substituted for a great change.

8 ounces vermicelli

1 cup garlic vinaigrette dressing (La Martinique Famous French dressing, if available)

10 fresh sliced mushrooms

1 cup broccoli florets, blanched

10 cherry tomatoes (optional)

2 cups cooked, cubed chicken

⅓ cup fresh basil, chopped, *or* 1½ teaspoons dried

⅓ cup pine nuts, toasted

Cook pasta in boiling water, drain and transfer to a mixing bowl. Add ⅓ cup dressing, toss, let cool, and chill for at least 3 hours. Place remaining dressing in another bowl. Add mushrooms, broccoli, and tomatoes. Stir to coat thoroughly, and chill. When ready to serve, add chicken to the pasta, and toss. Add vegetables, chopped basil, and pine nuts, and toss once more.

Serves 4 to 6

CRANBERRY CHICKEN SALAD

CRANBERRY LAYER:

1 envelope unflavored gelatin
¼ cup cold water
1 tablespoon lemon juice
1 can (16 ounces) whole-berry
  cranberry sauce

1 can (8 ounces) crushed
  pineapple
½ cup broken walnuts

CHICKEN LAYER:

2 envelopes unflavored gelatin
½ cup cold water
6 tablespoons lemon juice
4 cups diced cooked chicken

1 cup chopped celery
4 tablespoons minced parsley
1½ teaspoons salt
1 cup mayonnaise for garnish

CRANBERRY LAYER: Soften gelatin in cold water, then dissolve over hot water. Mix with lemon juice and cranberry sauce. Add pineapple and walnuts and pour into a shallow oblong pan (10 × 6 × 1½). Refrigerate until firm. Then prepare chicken layer.

CHICKEN LAYER: Soften gelatin in cold water, then dissolve over hot water. When cool, add lemon juice, chicken, celery, parsley, and salt. When cranberry layer is firm, pour chicken mixture on top. Return to refrigerator until firm. Unmold on a bed of lettuce and serve with mayonnaise.

Serves 8

CHICKEN-AVOCADO SALAD

2 cups cooked, shredded white
  meat of chicken
1 cup grated carrots
1 can (4 ounces) whole green
  chilies, chopped
1 teaspoon grated onion
2 teaspoons white wine vinegar

2 teaspoons salad oil
Salt to taste
1 cup diced avocado
6 tablespoons mayonnaise
Lettuce leaves and sliced black
  olives for garnish

Combine first seven ingredients. Chill. Before serving, add avocado and mayonnaise. Serve on lettuce leaves and garnish with sliced black olives.

Serves 4 to 6

FLUFF'S CHUTNEY CHICKEN SALAD

1 cup mayonnaise
¼ cup chutney, chopped
1 teaspoon curry powder
2 teaspoons grated lime peel
¼ cup fresh lime juice
½ teaspoon salt
1 can (15 ounces) pineapple
  chunks, drained, or fresh
  equivalent

4 cups diced cooked white
  chicken meat
2 cups diagonally sliced celery
1 cup sliced green onions
½ cup toasted sliced almonds

Combine mayonnaise, chutney, curry powder, lime peel, lime juice, and salt. Chill for several hours. Cut pineapple chunks in half and mix with chicken, celery, green onions, and almonds. Fold in mayonnaise mixture, cover, and chill.

Serves 6 to 8

PAELLA SALAD

1 package (7 ounces) yellow rice, cooked
2 tablespoons tarragon vinegar
⅓ cup oil
1½ teaspoons salt
⅛ teaspoon dry mustard
1 large tomato, chopped
½ cup finely chopped onion

½ green bell pepper, chopped
⅓ cup thinly sliced celery
1 tablespoon chopped pimiento
2 cups bite-size pieces of white chicken meat
1 cup boiled shrimp
1 cup cooked green peas (optional)

Mix rice, vinegar, oil, salt, and mustard, and chill. Add remaining ingredients, toss lightly, and chill well. This is better if made ahead.

Serves 6 to 8

CREAM BORDELAISE SALAD DRESSING/DIP

Tasty on greens or seafood salads.

1 large onion
1 whole lemon, quartered and seeded
2 to 3 garlic cloves
1 quart Hellmann's mayonnaise
⅓ teaspoon marjoram

¾ teaspoon nutmeg
1 teaspoon salad herbs
2 tablespoons sherry
1 tablespoon Worcestershire sauce

Grind onion, 2 lemon quarters, and garlic in blender. Squeeze the juice of the other 2 lemon quarters into blender and add remaining ingredients. Blend and taste. If stronger lemon flavor is desired, add remaining rind. Blend again and chill.

Yield: 5 cups

GREEN GODDESS DRESSING

1 ½ cups Hellmann's mayonnaise
1 cup sour cream
¼ cup chopped parsley
3 tablespoons chopped green
    onions
½ teaspoon salt

1 tablespoon wine vinegar
½ to 1 can (2 ounces) anchovy
    fillets, drained and mashed
⅛ teaspoon pressed garlic
3 drops or more green food
    coloring (optional)

Combine all ingredients in a bowl, cover, and refrigerate. If the anchovy flavor becomes too strong, add more sour cream. This dressing complements any green or vegetable salad. *Note:* This does not keep more than 2 days.

Yield: 2¾ cups

TARRAGON ROQUEFORT DRESSING/DIP

This is a mild dressing, and many people who do not usually care for blue cheese seem to like it.

1 package (8 ounces) cream
    cheese
1 package (4 ounces) Roquefort
    cheese
½ cup milk
¼ cup chopped green onion

1 tablespoon chopped fresh
    parsley
3 tablespoons lemon juice
1 teaspoon tarragon
Dash of Tabasco

Combine ingredients in food processor and blend. To make as a dip, use less milk.

Yield: 2¼ cups

BLUE CHEESE DRESSING

Spicy and rich.

2 onions, finely chopped
5 large sprigs parsley, chopped
1 package (12 ounces) blue
  cheese

1 pint Hellmann's mayonnaise
1 cup half-and-half

Grind onions, parsley, and blue cheese in food processor. Add mayonnaise and half-and-half. Blend.

Yield: 1 ½ quarts

CREAM SALAD DRESSING

½ teaspoon salt
½ teaspoon freshly ground
  white pepper

1 tablespoon lemon juice
⅓ cup heavy cream
2 tablespoons peanut oil

Combine salt, pepper, lemon juice, and cream. Whisk for 20 seconds until foamy and creamy. Beat in peanut oil. This is especially good with Bibb or Boston lettuce.

Yield: Approximately ½ cup

FOOD PROCESSOR MAYONNAISE

1 egg
1 tablespoon fresh lemon juice
½ to 1 teaspoon salt

Dash of paprika
Dash of red pepper
1 ¼ to 1 ½ cups Wesson oil

Place all ingredients except oil in food processor with steel blade and process for 1 minute. With machine on, slowly add oil.

Yield: 2 cups

FRUIT DRESSING

1 package (3 ounces) cream
  cheese
¼ cup orange juice
¼ cup lemon juice
¼ cup crushed pineapple

¼ cup sugar
¼ teaspoon salt
1 thin slice orange peel
¼ cup heavy cream

Blend all ingredients until smooth. This dressing complements any fresh fruit.

Yield: Approximately 1½ cups

LUCY'S FRUIT DRESSING

2 eggs, beaten
2 tablespoons flour
⅝ cup sugar
1 cup pineapple juice

Juice of 1 lemon
Juice of 1 orange
½ cup whipping cream,
  whipped

Combine eggs, flour, sugar, and fruit juices. Cook over medium low heat, stirring constantly, until thickened. Cool. Before serving, fold in whipped cream. Use the dressing over a variety of fresh fruit. It will keep refrigerated up to one week.

Yield: 2 cups

SPINACH SALAD DRESSING

1 hard-cooked egg, chopped
2 tablespoons vinegar
2 tablespoons mayonnaise
2 tablespoons Durkee Famous
  Sauce

1 heaping tablespoon horseradish
Dash of Tabasco
Salt and pepper to taste

Mix all ingredients and serve over spinach salad.

Yield: ¾ cup

SWEET AND SOUR DRESSING

½ cup sugar
½ cup vinegar
2 tablespoons oil
1 tablespoon green onion
1 tablespoon parsley

1 tablespoon chives
1 teaspoon Worcestershire sauce
1 teaspoon prepared mustard
Cracked black pepper
1 ice cube

Place ingredients in a plastic container, shake well, and chill. Serve over spinach salad.

Yield: 1 cup

CAESAR SALAD

3 cloves garlic
½ teaspoon salt
1 teaspoon dry mustard
Cracked black pepper to taste
5 anchovy fillets
½ to 1 teaspoon Worcestershire
  sauce
1 coddled egg
1 tablespoon lemon juice

1 tablespoon red wine garlic
  vinegar
6 tablespoons extra virgin olive
  oil
5 tablespoons freshly grated
  Parmesan cheese
1 to 2 heads romaine lettuce
1½ cups fresh croutons

In a wooden salad bowl, mash garlic and salt into a pulp. Add mustard and pepper. Work in well. Add anchovies, and use two forks to continue mashing. Add Worcestershire sauce, coddled egg, and lemon juice. Mix well. Add vinegar and then oil. Add 1 tablespoon of the Parmesan cheese. Mix well. Add lettuce to bowl, and toss to coat. Add remaining 4 tablespoons Parmesan and croutons. Toss and serve immediately. If you don't want a big production, mix all dressing ingredients except the coddled egg and Parmesan in the food processor. Just before serving, stir in coddled egg and 1 tablespoon Parmesan cheese. Proceed as above.

Serves 3 to 4

GREEN GREEK SALAD

1 large head romaine lettuce
8 ounces fresh spinach
10 cherry tomatoes, halved
1 avocado, sliced

6 tablespoons sesame seeds,
 lightly toasted
1 cup croutons

DRESSING:
1 teaspoon salt
½ teaspoon pepper
1 cup olive oil
1 teaspoon dry mustard

6 tablespoons red wine vinegar
2 tablespoons honey
1 clove garlic

Place lettuce, spinach, tomato halves, and avocado in a salad bowl. Combine salt, pepper, olive oil, mustard, vinegar, honey, and garlic in blender, and blend thoroughly. Pour over salad and garnish with sesame seeds and croutons. Toss lightly.

Serves 12
Dressing yield: 1½ cups

RICH AND CHARLIE'S SALAD

Great with Italian dishes.

1 can (8½ ounces) artichoke
 hearts, drained
1 can (10 ounces) hearts of
 palm, drained
1 head romaine lettuce, broken
 into bite-size pieces
1 head iceberg lettuce, broken
 into bite-size pieces

1 jar (4 ounces) diced pimientos,
 drained
1 large red onion, thinly sliced
½ cup olive oil
⅓ cup tarragon vinegar
½ cup grated Parmesan cheese
Salt and cracked pepper to taste

Cut the artichoke hearts into quarters. Slice the hearts of palm. Drain and toss in a salad bowl with lettuce, pimientos, and onions. Mix olive oil and vinegar, and pour over salad. Sprinkle with cheese, salt, and pepper. Toss.

Serves 6 to 8

THE OLD BALINESE ROOM'S
SALAD AND DRESSING

2 large heads Boston lettuce
2 small avocados, peeled and
  sliced
1½ stalks hearts of celery, sliced
2 medium white onions, thinly
  sliced or equivalent amount of
  chopped green onions

1 large green bell pepper, thinly
  sliced
2 tablespoons chopped celery
  leaves

DRESSING:

1 cup mayonnaise
1½ tablespoons Worcestershire
  sauce
½ cup sour cream or whipped
  cream
1 teaspoon Tabasco
1 teaspoon Beau Monde
  seasoning

½ teaspoon mace
1 teaspoon lemon juice
1 tablespoon capers
1 clove garlic
Freshly cracked pepper for
  garnish

Tear lettuce into bite-size pieces and place in a salad bowl. Add remaining prepared vegetables. Combine dressing ingredients, mashing the garlic so that flavor is released. Remove garlic. Mix dressing well, pour over salad, and toss. Sprinkle with freshly cracked pepper.

Serves 12
Dressing yield: 3 cups

ORANGE-ALMOND SALAD

2 cans (11 ounces each)
  mandarin oranges, drained
2 heads romaine lettuce

1 bunch green onions, chopped
1 package (5 ounces) slivered
  almonds, toasted

DRESSING:

¾ cup sugar
1 teaspoon dry mustard
1 teaspoon salt

⅓ cup cider vinegar
1 cup salad oil
1½ tablespoons poppy seeds

Chill mandarin oranges. Tear lettuce into bite-size pieces, and place in a salad bowl. Add oranges, onions, and almonds. Combine sugar, mustard, salt, and vinegar in blender. With blender on, slowly add oil. Add poppy seeds. Pour dressing over salad and toss lightly. Enough dressing for several salads!

Serves 4 to 6
Dressing yield: 2 cups

SEVEN LAYER SALAD

1 package (10 ounces) fresh
   spinach
1 head iceberg lettuce
1 teaspoon sugar
Salt and pepper to taste
6 hard-cooked eggs, finely
   chopped
½ pound boiled ham, cut in
   julienne strips (optional)

1 package (10 ounces) frozen
   peas, thawed
1 small red Bermuda onion,
   sliced
½ pound Swiss cheese, cut in
   julienne strips
1 cup sour cream
2 cups mayonnaise

Tear spinach and lettuce into bite-size pieces. Arrange spinach on bottom of a deep rectangular dish or straight-sided glass bowl. Sprinkle with ½ teaspoon of the sugar, salt, and pepper. Add layers of eggs, ham, and lettuce. Sprinkle with remaining sugar, salt, and pepper. Add layers of peas, onion slices, and Swiss cheese. Mix sour cream and mayonnaise and spread mixture over salad. Cover dish and refrigerate overnight. Toss before serving.

Serves 10

SALAD NICHOLI

1 head romaine lettuce
1 head red-tip lettuce
1 bag (10 ounces) spinach
10 slices bacon, cooked and
   crumbled

1 yellow onion, slivered
1 carton (16 ounces) cottage
   cheese

DRESSING:

½ cup cider vinegar

¼ cup sugar

1 teaspoon dry mustard

1 teaspoon salt

3 tablespoons chopped onion

⅔ cup vegetable oil

In a salad bowl, combine washed greens, bacon, onion, and cottage cheese. Combine vinegar, sugar, mustard, salt, and onion in blender and mix on high speed. With blender on low speed, slowly add oil. Pour dressing over salad and toss.

Serves 10 to 12

Dressing yield: 1½ cups

BLUEBERRY SALAD

1 package (6 ounces) black raspberry Jell-O

2 cups boiling water

1 can (15 ounces) blueberries

1 can (8 ounces) crushed pineapple

1 package (8 ounces) cream cheese

½ cup sugar

1 cup sour cream

½ teaspoon vanilla

½ cup chopped pecans

Dissolve Jell-O in boiling water and chill until slightly thickened. Drain blueberries and crushed pineapple and reserve juices. Add water to juices, if necessary, to make 1 cup liquid. Combine Jell-O, blueberries, pineapple, and liquid. Pour into a 2-quart flat Pyrex dish that has been sprayed with Pam. Cover and chill until firm. Combine cream cheese, sugar, sour cream and vanilla and spread over molded salad. Sprinkle pecans on top.

Serves 8 to 10

CHEESECAKE SALAD

1 tablespoon unflavored gelatin

½ cup lemon Jell-O

3 tablespoons sugar

1 cup boiling water

¾ cup pineapple juice

3 tablespoons lemon juice

½ teaspoon grated lemon peel

1 tablespoon grated orange peel

1 cup cream cheese, softened

1 cup cottage cheese

¾ cup crushed pineapple

1 cup whipping cream, whipped

Combine gelatin, Jell-O, and sugar. Add boiling water and stir until dissolved. Stir in pineapple juice, lemon juice, lemon peel, and orange peel. Chill until Jell-O begins to thicken. Fold in cream cheese and cottage cheese, then crushed pineapple and whipped cream. Pour into a 2-quart mold that has been sprayed with Pam. Refrigerate overnight.

Serves 10 to 12

MOLDED FRESH CRANBERRY SALAD

12 ounces fresh cranberries
1 cup sugar
2 teaspoons grated orange rind
1 envelope unflavored gelatin
1 cup fresh orange juice
1 package (3 ounces) lemon
   Jell-O

½ cup boiling water
1 can (8 ounces) crushed
   pineapple with juice
½ cup pecan pieces
1 cup minced celery
Mayonnaise and fresh orange
   peel for garnish

Grind or process cranberries to measure 1 cup. Mix in sugar and orange rind. Let stand at room temperature for 2 hours. Soften gelatin in ¼ cup of the orange juice. Then add remaining juice. Dissolve lemon Jell-O in boiling water. Combine cranberry mixture, gelatin, Jell-O, pineapple, pecans, and celery. Pour into a 6-cup mold that has been sprayed with Pam. Refrigerate for several hours to set. Unmold on a bed of lettuce. Garnish with mayonnaise and orange peel.

Serves 6 to 8

MOLDED RASPBERRY SALAD

1 large box (6 ounces) raspberry
   Jell-O
2 cups boiling water
2 jars (16 ounces each)
   applesauce

1 cup sour cream
1 package (10 ounces) frozen
   raspberries, thawed
½ cup pecan pieces

Spray 2-quart mold or individual molds with Pam, or rub lightly with mayonnaise. Dissolve Jell-O in boiling water. Stir in applesauce, sour cream, raspberries, and pecans. Pour into mold and chill. Unmold onto lettuce.

Serves 6 to 8

MOLDED GAZPACHO

2 envelopes unflavored gelatin
2¼ cups tomato or Clamato juice
¼ cup red wine vinegar
Juice of ½ lemon
1 teaspoon salt
¼ teaspoon Tabasco
¼ teaspoon garlic salt
½ teaspoon celery salt
1 teaspoon Worcestershire sauce
1 tablespoon parsley

2 small tomatoes, peeled and chopped
⅓ cup finely chopped green bell pepper
1 medium cucumber, peeled, seeded and chopped
¼ cup finely chopped green onion
¼ cup finely chopped celery
Lettuce, sour cream and lemon juice for garnish

Soften gelatin in ½ cup of the tomato juice. Bring remaining tomato juice to a boil, and pour over gelatin mixture. Stir until dissolved. Add vinegar, lemon juice, salt, Tabasco, garlic salt, celery salt, and Worcestershire. Adjust seasoning to taste. Cool mixture until slightly set. Add vegetables, and pour into individual molds or a 4- to 5-cup mold that has been wiped with mayonnaise. Chill until molded. Unmold on a bed of lettuce and garnish with sour cream thinned with lemon juice. This should be made the day before it is served.

Serves 8

MANGO SALAD

This is great as a dessert.

3 packages (3 ounces each) lemon Jell-O
3 cups boiling water
1 package (8 ounces) cream cheese

1 can (30 ounces) mangoes with juice
Fresh strawberries and mandarin oranges for garnish

SAUCE:

2 eggs, slightly beaten

1½ cups sugar

Juice and rind of 2 lemons

Juice and rind of 2 oranges

Dissolve Jell-O in boiling water. In a blender, combine cream cheese, mangoes and juice, and blend. Stir mixture into Jell-O and pour into a 2-quart mold that has been sprayed with Pam. Refrigerate to set. In a saucepan, combine sauce ingredients. Bring to a boil, and boil for 5 to 7 minutes to thicken. Remove from heat and strain. Discard rinds and refrigerate sauce. Remove from refrigerator to soften, 30 minutes before serving. Unmold salad onto a bed of greens and garnish. Serve with sauce.

Serves 12 to 15

Sauce yield: 2 cups

PEACH BANANA FREEZE

1 can (16 ounces) peach slices,
   drained

2 bananas, sliced

1 can (6 ounces) undiluted
   frozen lemonade, thawed

½ pint whipping cream

1 teaspoon sugar

Mash peaches and bananas until mushy. Stir in lemonade. Whip cream with sugar until thick. Fold into fruit mixture and pour into a 1-quart milk carton. Freeze until firm. When ready to serve, remove from freezer, peel carton to expose the amount of salad needed and slice into individual servings. This salad will keep for weeks in the freezer.

Serves approximately 8

SPINACH SALAD WITH CHUTNEY DRESSING

1 bag (10 ounces) fresh spinach

¼ pound fresh mushrooms,
   sliced

½ to 1 cup sliced water
   chestnuts

6 slices bacon, cooked and
   crumbled

½ cup bean sprouts (optional)

¼ cup thinly sliced red onion

DRESSING:

3 tablespoons wine vinegar
3 tablespoons chutney (Major Grey's preferred)
1 clove garlic, crushed

1 teaspoon Dijon mustard
1 teaspoon sugar
⅓ to ½ cup vegetable oil
Salt and freshly ground pepper to taste

Wash and dry spinach. Mix spinach, mushrooms, water chestnuts, bacon, bean sprouts, and onion together in a large bowl. Combine vinegar, chutney, garlic, mustard, and sugar in blender and mix until smooth. With blender on, slowly add oil until thick and smooth. Taste, season, adjusting chutney and/or oil if necessary. Add salt and pepper. Pour dressing over spinach, and sprinkle with freshly ground pepper.

Serves 4 to 6
Dressing yield: ¾ cup

SPINACH MUSHROOM SALAD

2 garlic cloves, quartered
⅔ cup olive oil
2 cups bread cubes
1 package (10 ounces) fresh spinach
3½ tablespoons fresh lemon juice
1 tablespoon Worcestershire sauce

1 egg
½ teaspoon salt
¼ teaspoon pepper
1 pound fresh mushrooms
½ cup grated Parmesan cheese
¼ cup crumbled blue cheese

Let garlic stand in oil at room temperature overnight. Remove garlic and discard. Toast bread cubes in oven at 300 degrees F. for about 25 minutes or until golden. Cover and set aside. Wash, dry, and chill spinach. Combine lemon juice, Worcestershire sauce, egg, salt, pepper and ½ cup of the oil for dressing. Slice mushrooms into dressing and refrigerate for 1 hour. When ready to assemble, toss croutons with remaining oil. Add cheeses to spinach, pour on mushrooms and dressing, and toss. Sprinkle croutons on top.

Serves 10

WILTED SPINACH SALAD

1 bag (10 ounces) spinach
8 slices bacon
2 teaspoons sugar
3 tablespoons minced onion

1 teaspoon Dijon mustard
6 tablespoons vinegar
Pepper to taste

Wash spinach, dry, and refrigerate. Fry bacon until crisp. Remove from pan, drain, and set aside. Pour off all but ⅓ cup bacon drippings. Stir sugar and onion into remaining hot drippings. Cook until onions are translucent and slightly caramelized. Stir in mustard and vinegar. Season with pepper. Just before serving, put spinach in serving bowl, add crumbled bacon to hot dressing, pour over spinach, and toss well.

Serves 4 to 6

BROCCOLI SALAD DRUARY

DRESSING:
⅓ cup ketchup
¾ cup sugar
¼ cup vinegar
2 tablespoons Worcestershire
   sauce

½ teaspoon salt
1 medium onion, quartered
1 cup salad oil

2 bunches broccoli, blanched and
   chopped
2 cups sliced fresh mushrooms

4 hard-cooked eggs, chopped
2 cans (8 ounces each) sliced
   water chestnuts

Combine dressing ingredients in blender. Reserve half the dressing. Pour remaining dressing over salad ingredients. Turn vegetables gently, cover, and refrigerate. The reserved dressing will keep well refrigerated in a covered jar.

Serves 6 to 8
Dressing yield: 2½ cups

BUFFET SALAD

MARINADE:

⅔ cup vinegar
⅓ cup salad oil
¼ to ½ cup sugar
1 teaspoon salt

1 teaspoon pepper
1 purple onion, finely chopped
1 green bell pepper, finely
    chopped

1 can (15 ounces) minature corn
    on the cob, drained
1 can (15 ounces) small whole
    carrots, drained
1 can (8½ ounces) artichokes,
    drained

2 cans (4 ounces each) whole
    mushrooms, drained
1 jar (4 ounces) pimientos,
    drained and chopped

Combine marinade ingredients and pour over vegetables. Cover and refrigerate for 48 hours. To serve, drain and reserve marinade. Leftovers can be refrigerated in marinade for weeks.

Serves 10 to 12
Dressing yield: 1½ cups

FAMILY POTATO SALAD

8 medium Irish potatoes
15 hard-cooked eggs, coarsely
    chopped
1 large white onion, finely
    chopped
6 stalks celery, finely chopped

1 tablespoon chopped parsley
1 pound bacon, cooked and
    crumbled
1 tablespoon bacon drippings
Mayonnaise to taste
Salt and pepper to taste

Cook potatoes in boiling salted water until just tender. Drain and refrigerate overnight. Peel and cube potatoes and place them in a large bowl. Add remaining ingredients and refrigerate. This salad will keep for 2 or 3 days.

Serves 15 to 20

COLD STUFFED ZUCCHINI

4 zucchini, 4 to 6 inches long
½ onion, finely chopped
3½ ounces vinaigrette dressing

FILLING:

3 tomatoes, skinned and finely
   chopped
½ small green bell pepper,
   seeded and finely chopped
¼ purple onion, finely chopped
1 tablespoon capers

1 teaspoon chopped parsley
1 teaspoon fresh chopped basil *or*
   ⅓ teaspoon dried
2 tablespoons vinaigrette dressing
Salt and pepper to taste

Trim ends of zucchini and cook whole in boiling water until tender, about 5 to 8 minutes. Drain and cut in half lengthwise. Scoop out seeds and lay zucchini cut side up in a shallow dish. Sprinkle onion and vinaigrette over zucchini. Cover with foil and chill for at least 4 hours. Combine tomatoes, green pepper, onion, capers, parsley, and basil. Moisten with vinaigrette. Season with salt and pepper. Just before serving, drain zucchini, scrape off onion, and mound filling into zucchini. Serve on a bed of lettuce.

Serves 8

GREEN VEGETABLE SALAD

1 package (10 ounces) frozen
   baby lima beans
1 package (10 ounces) frozen
   peas
4 to 5 tablespoons wine vinegar
1 cup chopped green onions
2 cups diced celery

1 cup water chestnuts, rinsed and
   diced
¼ cup chopped parsley
2 to 3 tablespoons mayonnaise
   (or more)
Salt and pepper to taste

Slightly undercook lima beans and peas according to package directions. Drain and marinate in vinegar overnight. Drain. Add green onions, celery, chestnuts, parsley, and enough mayonnaise to bind. Season with salt and pepper. This keeps well for several days in the refrigerator. It is a great salad for picnics or casual buffets.

Serves 8 to 10

GOURMET DELIGHT SALAD

DRESSING:

1½ cups salad oil
⅔ cup white vinegar
2½ teaspoons salt

1 teaspoon pepper
2 cloves garlic, pressed
1½ teaspoons sugar

1 pound celery hearts, chopped
2 cans (6 ounces each) pitted
   black olives, drained and sliced
2 jars (5 ounces each) stuffed
   green olives, drained and
   sliced
1 head cauliflower, broken into
   florets

1 pint cherry tomatoes, halved
3 to 4 jars (6 ounces each)
   marinated artichoke hearts,
   drained and halved
1 pound carrots, peeled and
   sliced

Combine oil, vinegar, salt, pepper, garlic, and sugar in a jar, and shake. Refrigerate for 24 hours if possible. In a salad bowl, combine vegetables. Add dressing, toss lightly, and marinate in refrigerator for at least 24 hours.

Serves 18 to 20
Dressing yield: 2¼ cups

NINE-DAY SLAW

1 medium head cabbage, coarsely
   shredded (do not use
   processor or grater!)
4 stalks celery, diced
1 onion, diced
1 green bell pepper, chopped
1 jar (4 ounces) chopped
   pimiento, drained

1 cup sugar
1 cup oil
1 cup vinegar
2 tablespoons salt
1 teaspoon dry mustard
1 teaspoon celery seed

In a large bowl, mix cabbage, celery, onion, pepper, pimiento, and 1 cup (minus 2 tablespoons) of the sugar. Combine oil, vinegar, salt, remaining sugar, mustard, and celery seed in saucepan and bring to a boil, stirring constantly. Pour hot mixture over cabbage, and mix. Cool. Cover and chill for 24 hours. This gets better every day and is still good after nine days, if it lasts that long.

Serves 10 to 12

NUTCRACKER AVOCADO-GRAPEFRUIT SALAD

DRESSING:

¼ cup vinegar
Juice of 1 lemon
¼ cup undiluted frozen orange
    juice
½ teaspoon salt

2 teaspoons grated orange peel
¼ cup sugar
½ teaspoon dry mustard
1 cup salad oil

3 large grapefruits or navel
    oranges, peeled and sectioned
    (2 cups of fruit)

2 large ripe avocados, peeled and
    sliced
1 large Bermuda onion, sliced

Mix dressing ingredients and pour over salad. Cover and refrigerate over-night. Before serving, lightly turn salad and arrange on Boston lettuce. This keeps for several days. Additional fruit may be added to the marinade as needed. Good with rich entrees and casseroles.

Serves 8
Dressing yield: 1⅔ cups

MARINATED TOMATOES

3 to 6 tomatoes, sliced

MARINADE:

⅓ cup tarragon vinegar
⅓ cup chopped onion
1 teaspoon cilantro
⅔ cup olive oil
1 teaspoon salt

½ teaspoon pepper
½ teaspoon marjoram
¼ cup parsley
¼ cup chopped chives

Arrange tomato slices in a shallow glass dish. Combine marinade ingredients and pour over tomatoes. Cover and marinate in refrigerator for at least 5 hours. These are better the second day. More tomatoes can be added to the marinade.

Serves 8 to 10
Marinade yield: 1½ cups

MARINATED VEGETABLE SALAD

4 cups sliced zucchini
2 cups sliced yellow squash
2 cups broccoli florets
1½ cups cauliflower florets

1 cup sliced carrots
1 cup sliced purple onion
1 cup halved cherry tomatoes
8 ounces mushrooms, sliced

MARINADE:
2 cups vegetable oil
1 cup white vinegar
½ cup red wine vinegar
½ cup lemon juice
Salt to taste

1 teaspoon oregano
1 teaspoon dry mustard
1 teaspoon dehydrated onion
2 cloves garlic, pressed

Mix vegetables in a bowl. Combine marinade ingredients and pour over vegetables. Refrigerate for several hours or overnight. Drain and serve.

Serves 15 to 20
Marinade yield: 4 cups

PIQUANT PEA SALAD

1 package (20 ounces) frozen green peas, uncooked or blanched
2 green onions, finely chopped

¼ cup finely chopped green bell pepper
1 cup diced celery
½ cup chopped parsley

MARINADE:
½ cup oil and vinegar French dressing (La Martinique)
½ teaspoon salt
½ teaspoon cracked pepper
¼ teaspoon Salad Supreme
¼ teaspoon seasoned salt

¼ teaspoon garlic salt
¼ teaspoon celery salt
1 ounce blue cheese, crumbled
1 can (8 ounces) sliced water chestnuts, drained (optional)

Mix peas, onions, green pepper, celery, and parsley in a large bowl. Combine marinade ingredients and pour over vegetables. Marinate for 6 to 12 hours before serving. This will keep for up to a week in the refrigerator.

Serves 6 to 8
Marinade yield: ⅔ cup

OVERNIGHT SALAD

1 package (10 ounces) frozen
  green peas
1 can (15 ounces) red kidney
  beans, drained
1 can (16 ounces) green beans,
  drained
1 can (16 ounces) white corn,
  drained

1 cup diced celery
1 medium onion, chopped
½ cup chopped green bell
  pepper
8 ounces fresh mushrooms,
  quartered
8 to 10 cherry tomatoes, halved

DRESSING:

¾ cup white or tarragon vinegar
⅓ to ½ cup sugar
2 tablespoons salad oil

1½ teaspoons salt
2 teaspoons water
½ teaspoon paprika

Combine vegetables in a large salad bowl. Substitute any of your favorites, if desired. In a small bowl, combine dressing ingredients and mix until sugar dissolves. Pour over vegetables and toss. Cover and refrigerate for 6 to 8 hours, stirring occasionally. This salad keeps well in the refrigerator for days. Add more vegetables as desired. Drain before serving.

Serves 10 to 12
Dressing yield: 1 cup

RED, WHITE, AND GREEN SALAD

2 bunches broccoli (5 cups),
  broken into florets
1 cauliflower (2½ cups), broken
  into florets
1 onion, finely chopped
2 cups cherry tomatoes

1 cup mayonnaise
½ cup sour cream
1 tablespoon vinegar
2 tablespoons sugar
Salt and pepper to taste

Combine broccoli, cauliflower, onion, and tomatoes in a salad bowl. Mix remaining ingredients together, pour over salad and toss gently to coat vegetables. Cover and refrigerate for 4 hours or more.

Serves 12
Dressing yield: 1½ cups

RANCH POTATO SALAD

2½ pounds red potatoes
½ cup Italian salad dressing
¾ cup thinly sliced celery
½ cup thinly sliced radishes
¼ cup finely chopped cucumber
¼ cup finely chopped onion

¼ cup finely chopped pimiento
2 hard-cooked eggs, coarsely
  chopped
1 cup mayonnaise
1 green onion, thinly sliced

Cook potatoes, covered, in a small amount of boiling salted water for 35 minutes or until just tender. Drain and peel when cool enough. Cut into ½-inch cubes and place in a large bowl. Add Italian dressing, toss lightly, cover, and refrigerate 1½ to 2 hours. Add celery, radishes, cucumber, onion, pimiento, eggs, and mayonnaise. Toss gently to mix well. Cover and refrigerate for several hours. Sprinkle with green onion before serving.

Serves 6 to 8

SUE'S CELERY SALAD

DRESSING:
⅓ cup white wine vinegar
⅔ cup olive oil
1 teaspoon Dijon mustard

3 cups thinly sliced celery
¼ pound fresh mushrooms,
  sliced
1 cup grated Romano cheese

Combine dressing ingredients. Pour over celery and marinate for 2 hours. About 30 minutes before serving, add sliced mushrooms, and toss. Drain immediately and reserve marinade if desired. Serve salad in individual bowls or lettuce leaves. Sprinkle with cheese.

Serves 6 to 8
Dressing yield: 1 cup

Variation: Add sliced black olives, cherry tomato halves, quartered artichoke hearts, and/or sliced cucumbers.

RICE AND ARTICHOKE SALAD

¾ cup rice
1½ cups chicken broth
½ green bell pepper, finely
   chopped
2 green onions, chopped

⅓ cup sliced green olives
1½ to 2 cans (8½ ounces each)
   artichoke hearts, quartered
½ cup mayonnaise
½ teaspoon curry powder

Cook rice in chicken broth, and cool. Add green pepper, green onions, olives, and artichokes. Mix mayonnaise with curry powder and stir into rice. Refrigerate overnight.

Serves 6 to 8

Variation: Add cold shrimp or cubes of white chicken meat for a luncheon entree.

VEGETABLE SALAD PLATTER

⅛ pound nuts (pine nuts or
   blanched almonds)
1 tablespoon butter
1 tablespoon olive oil
1 pound fresh green vegetables
   (broccoli, asparagus, or green
   beans)

4 ripe tomatoes, sliced
Parsley
¼ cup capers, rinsed and
   drained
¼ cup pitted ripe olives

DRESSING:
2 cloves garlic
½ cup olive oil
¼ cup tarragon white wine
   vinegar

Freshly cracked pepper

Sauté nuts in butter and olive oil until lightly browned. Blanch green vegetables in boiling water for 3 minutes. Rinse with cold water and place in refrigerator for at least 1 hour. Arrange green vegetables, sliced tomatoes, and parsley on a platter. Sprinkle capers, olives and nuts on top. Blend garlic, olive oil, and vinegar in blender until well-mixed. Pour over salad and sprinkle with freshly cracked pepper.

Serves 8
Dressing yield: ¾ cup

CHAPTER XII

SOUPS

The Lyndon B. Johnson Space Center

Since 1963, millions of people around the world who have followed U.S. manned space flights on television have known Houston as the home of Mission Control and the training center for America's astronauts. Spread across 1,620 acres of coastal prairie midway between Houston and Galveston, the National Aeronautics and Space Administration's Lyndon B. Johnson Space Center is the city's link with humanity's newest frontier.

From the nerve center in Building 30, a NASA cardiologist in Houston can monitor the heartbeat of an astronaut aboard a space shuttle a quarter of a million miles away, while a systems engineer can check whether oxygen in the spacecraft is flowing at the proper rate. Tuned in to this drama, television viewers who have never even traveled by jet can participate vicariously in the conquest of space.

Houston accepts the Space Age as a matter of course. For a while, there was a tendency to name everything from sports teams to convention halls Astro-Something. Although that trend has passed, some dub Houston Intercontinental Airport "Interplanetary" in anticipation of the time when the city may have one of the country's first space ports. And there are constant reminders that Houston is still Space City, with former astronauts making their current splashdowns in the local business community.

Preparing and eating food under zero-gravity conditions—and making that food palatable despite limitations in weight and storage space aboard cramped space vehicles—have presented a challenge to NASA from the beginning. Early astronauts had to make do with bite-size cubes and semiliquids in toothpaste-type aluminum tubes. By the time of the Gemini and Apollo missions, however, astronauts were able to select their own menus. Apollo astronaut James Irwin even took his favorite gourmet soups with him to the moon.

Before the Columbia Space Shuttle was ready for its first flight, NASA's culinary engineers had devised a system of convenient square containers that fit snugly into a tray-table or into a microwave oven, where they stay put despite the lack of gravity. After being reconstituted with water and heated, if necessary, the space food is almost indistinguishable from the down-to-earth variety.

Of all foods, soups can be both the most ethereal and the most homey and familiar, whether you're on your way into orbit, setting out for a star-studded evening at the theater, or making a controlled landing at the end of a busy day. The recipes that follow include soups for warm weather and for cool, for company and for quiet suppers for two. Cuban Black Bean Soup, Harborside Seafood Bisque, Cold Crab Soup, Tasty Vegetable Velvet Soup, Cardinal Cup—they're all out of this world.

BROCCOLI CREAM SOUP

1 package (10 ounces) frozen
    chopped broccoli
½ cup chopped onion
1 can (10½ ounces) condensed
    chicken broth
2 tablespoons butter

2 tablespoons flour
2 cups half-and-half
1 teaspoon salt
⅛ teaspoon white pepper
½ teaspoon basil

Combine broccoli, onion, and chicken broth in a 2-quart saucepan. Heat to boiling, reduce heat, and simmer for 5 minutes. Blend until smooth in food processor or blender. Melt butter and blend in flour. Add half-and-half, salt, pepper, basil, and puréed vegetables. Simmer for 1 minute, stirring constantly. This soup is delicious piping hot or well chilled.

Serves 4

CREAM OF PUMPKIN SOUP

¼ cup finely chopped onion
2 tablespoons butter or
    margarine
1 teaspoon curry powder
1 tablespoon flour
2 cans (10½ ounces each)
    chicken broth
1 can (1 pound) pumpkin

1 teaspoon brown sugar
⅛ teaspoon ground nutmeg
¼ teaspoon salt
⅛ teaspoon pepper
1 cup light cream
Minced chives or parsley for
    garnish (optional)

In a 3-quart saucepan, sauté onion in butter over medium heat until limp. Stir in curry and flour, and cook until bubbly. Remove from heat, and gradually stir in chicken broth. Add pumpkin, sugar, nutmeg, salt, and pepper. Cook, stirring, until mixture begins to simmer. Stir in cream, and continue heating, but do not boil. Garnish with a few minced chives or parsley when you serve. You may choose to use canned double-strength condensed chicken broth for a richer soup.

Serves 8

CREAM OF VEGETABLE SOUP

Use only fresh vegetables.

¾ cup diced onion
¾ cup butter
1 ½ cups diced potato
¾ cup peeled and diced tomato
¾ cup peeled and diced carrot
¾ cup diced green beans
¾ cup coarsely chopped broccoli
¾ cup minced leek, white part only

¾ cup minced zucchini
1 clove garlic, minced
1 ½ teaspoons sugar or to taste
1 teaspoon salt or more to taste
Pepper to taste
6 cups chicken stock
½ cup heavy cream
Minced parsley for garnish (optional)

In a 5-quart stockpot, sauté onion in butter until soft. Reduce heat to low. Add all remaining ingredients except stock and cream. Cook until vegetables are soft but not brown, about 20 to 30 minutes. Add stock and bring to a boil. Reduce heat and simmer for 10 minutes. Let cool enough to handle, transfer to food processor or blender in batches, and purée until smooth. Taste and adjust seasonings. Return to stockpot and reheat over medium heat. Stir in cream, and heat thoroughly but do not boil. Garnish with parsley.

Serves 12

CREAM OF TOMATO SOUP

1¼ cups thinly sliced yellow onion
4 tablespoons unsalted butter
1 tablespoon olive oil
3 ripe tomatoes, coarsely chopped
3 tablespoons tomato paste
4 tablespoons all-purpose flour

2½ cups strong homemade chicken stock *or* 2 cans (10½ ounces each) condensed chicken broth
½ teaspoon sugar
Salt
White pepper
1 cup heavy cream

In a heavy 3-quart saucepan, sauté onion in 2 tablespoons of the butter and oil for about 5 minutes. Stir in the tomatoes and tomato paste, and cook for 2 to 3 minutes. Sprinkle with flour and mix well with a wooden spoon. Add the broth, sugar, salt, and white pepper to taste and simmer 15 minutes. Purée in food processor or blender at high speed. Strain into saucepan. Add cream and correct seasonings. Heat through and add remaining 2 tablespoons butter bit by bit.

Serves 6

COLD CRAB SOUP

1 tablespoon dry mustard
1 quart buttermilk
1 tablespoon chopped fresh dill or ½ teaspoon dried dill
1 tablespoon salt
1 tablespoon sugar

1 pound fresh lump crab meat, drained and picked
1 cup shredded cucumber for garnish
Paprika for garnish

Mix mustard with a little buttermilk until blended. Add dill, salt, sugar, and remaining buttermilk. Add crab meat and mix in gently to retain lumps. Chill for several hours. Garnish with cucumber and sprinkle with paprika.

Serves 6

HARBORSIDE SEAFOOD BISQUE

7 tablespoons butter
4 tablespoons flour
2 cups milk
1 pound peeled and deveined shrimp, chopped, *or* a combination of shrimp, scallops, langostinos, crab meat, or non-oily whitefish
4 shallots or white of 4 green onions, chopped

1 teaspoon dry mustard
1 tablespoon Worcestershire sauce
1 tablespoon A.1. steak sauce
1 teaspoon salt
1 teaspoon white pepper
Paprika to taste
3 tablespoons sherry
Fish stock (optional)

Melt 4 tablespoons of the butter over high heat. Add flour, and beat vigorously. Remove from heat, add milk, and beat until smooth. Lower heat, and cook until creamy. In remaining 3 tablespoons butter, sauté seafood with shallots or green onions. Combine with white sauce. Add mustard, Worcestershire sauce, A.1. sauce, salt, white pepper, paprika, and sherry. If too thick, thin with fish stock. Leftovers make a delicious sauce for a soufflé.

Serves 4

STEAK SOUP

½ cup butter
1 cup flour
8 cups water
1 pound ground sirloin or chuck
1 cup chopped celery
1 cup chopped carrots
1 cup chopped onions
1 package (10 ounces) frozen mixed vegetables

1 can (16 ounces) tomatoes
2 tablespoons beef concentrate
½ teaspoon black pepper
Celery salt to taste
Garlic salt to taste
Basil to taste

In a 4-quart saucepan, melt butter and add flour to make a smooth paste. Add water and stir until smooth. Add ground meat, celery, carrots, onions, mixed frozen vegetables, tomatoes, beef concentrate, and black pepper. Bring to a boil, reduce heat, and simmer for 5 to 6 hours, stirring occasionally. Season to taste with celery salt, garlic salt, and basil.

Serves 8

OYSTER AND ARTICHOKE SOUP

½ cup unsalted butter
16 green onions
2 large cloves garlic, minced
3 cans (14 ounces each, 10 to 12 count) artichoke hearts, drained
3 tablespoons flour
4 cans (14½ ounces each) chicken broth

1 teaspoon dried red pepper flakes
1 teaspoon anise seed
1 rounded teaspoon salt
1 tablespoon Worcestershire sauce
1 quart oysters

In a 5-quart heavy enameled pot, melt butter, and sauté thinly sliced green onion bottoms, some tops, and garlic until soft but not brown. Rinse artichoke hearts thoroughly in cold water, and drain. Cut into quarters and add to onions. Sprinkle with flour to coat well. Sauté 3 to 4 minutes, but *do not brown*. Add chicken broth, red pepper flakes, anise seed, salt, and Worcestershire sauce. Simmer for about 15 minutes. While mixture cooks, drain and strain liquor from oysters and reserve. Check oysters for shells, and chop coarsely. Add oysters and reserved liquor to pot. Simmer for about 10 minutes. *Do not boil*. Make this soup at least 8 hours before serving, as flavor improves with age. Refrigerate and reheat when ready to serve. Keeps in refrigerator for 3 days.

Serves 12

TOMATO AND CLAM BISQUE

⅓ cup clarified butter
⅓ cup flour
2 cans (6 ounces each) chopped clams, drained, with liquid reserved
Bottled clam juice, if necessary
2 cups heavy cream
1 can (8 ounces) tomato sauce
1 can (16 ounces) peeled tomatoes, undrained and diced

Pinch of sugar
1 bay leaf
½ teaspoon thyme
Dash of salt
Dash of white pepper
1 teaspoon curry powder (optional)

Melt butter in a 2½-quart saucepan. Stir in flour, and cook slowly, stirring, for 2 to 3 minutes. Combine reserved clam liquid and enough bottled clam juice to make 1 cup liquid. Slowly add to butter-and-flour mixture, increasing heat to medium. Stir constantly for 3 to 4 minutes. Gradually add cream, and continue to stir until well heated. Add tomato sauce, tomatoes, sugar, and seasonings. Simmer, uncovered, slowly for 30 minutes. Remove bay leaf. Add rinsed clams and heat through. This freezes well.

Serves 6 to 8

AVGOLEMONO SOUP
(GREEK EGG AND LEMON SOUP)

2½ cups chicken broth	1 egg
Celery leaves	Juice of 1 lemon
Salt to taste	4 tablespoons cooked rice
Pepper to taste	

Simmer the chicken broth with celery leaves, salt, and pepper until it is reduced to 2 cups. Remove from heat. Strain broth into a 1-quart saucepan. Just before serving, beat egg until frothy. Slowly add lemon juice and ½ cup of reduced chicken broth to egg, beating constantly. Add egg mixture and rice to broth, stirring constantly. Heat almost to boiling point and serve immediately. Soup will curdle if allowed to boil. Best results are achieved when chicken broth is not too hot when egg mixture is added. The Greeks usually pepper their soup furiously before eating, but that is a matter of individual taste.

Serves 2

BORSCH

1 can (1 pound) cut beets with liquid	2 tablespoons sour cream
1 can (10½ ounces) beef bouillon	½ teaspoon salt
3 tablespoons lemon juice	Freshly ground pepper to taste
2 tablespoons chopped onion	Sour cream and chives for garnish

Combine all ingredients except garnish in blender and blend for 2 minutes. Chill and top with sour cream and chives.

Serves 4

HAM AND CORN CHOWDER

6 tablespoons butter or margarine
6 tablespoons flour
1 can (10½ ounces) condensed chicken broth
1 soup can water
1 soup can milk
2 cups diced ham

3 ears corn, kernels cut off, *or* 1 can (1 pound, 1 ounce) yellow corn with liquid
3 medium red potatoes, peeled and diced
8 green onions, chopped
Salt and pepper to taste
2 cups half-and-half

Melt butter in a heavy 4-quart saucepan. Stir in flour, and cook for 2 minutes. Add broth, water, and milk, and stir until slightly thickened. Add ham, corn, potatoes, the white part of the onions (reserve green part), salt, and pepper. Simmer over very low heat until potatoes are cooked through, stirring often. Thin with additional milk or broth if too thick. Add half-and-half and adjust seasoning. Simmer for 30 minutes. Serve hot and garnish with chopped green onion tops.

Serves 10

HEARTY SAUSAGE AND ONION SOUP

2 large or 3 medium onions, thinly sliced
¼ cup butter or margarine
1 tablespoon sugar
2 cans (10½ ounces each) beef broth
1 can (10½ ounces) condensed chicken broth
2 soup cans water
1 soup can white wine (sauterne or chablis)

1 piece (8 inches) smoked sausage, diced
Salt and pepper to taste
6 pieces dried French bread, ½-inch thick and about 5 inches in diameter
6 ounces Muenster cheese, sliced
6 ounces Swiss cheese, sliced
12 tablespoons grated Parmesan cheese

In a 4-quart pan, sauté onions in butter until golden but not brown. Sprinkle with sugar, and cook for 1 minute more. Add broth, water, wine, sausage, and salt and pepper to taste. Cover, and simmer for 1 hour. Ladle into six 2-cup ovenproof soup bowls or individual soufflé dishes. Top each with a bread slice, 1 ounce Muenster, 1 ounce Swiss and 2 tablespoons Parmesan cheese. Put on lower rack of oven and broil until cheese bubbles.

Serves 6

CABBAGE SOUP

¼ cup vegetable oil
4 cups shredded cabbage
1½ cups shredded onion
2 cans (16 ounces each)
   tomatoes
1 cup water
2 tablespoons lemon juice
1 tablespoon salt

2 tablespoons flour
2 tablespoons sugar
1 teaspoon black pepper
¼ teaspoon garlic powder
1 teaspoon caraway seeds
Sour cream for garnish
   (optional)

Heat oil in a 3-quart saucepan. Add cabbage and onion, and sauté, covered, for 15 minutes. Break up tomatoes and stir in with all remaining ingredients except the caraway seeds and sour cream. Bring to a boil, stirring occasionally. Simmer, covered, for 30 minutes. Add caraway seeds and simmer for 30 minutes more. Serve hot or cold. Top with a dollop of sour cream. Freezes well.

Serves 6

CARDINAL CUP

2 cans (10¾ ounces each)
   condensed tomato soup
2 cans (10½ ounces each)
   condensed beef broth
⅓ cup thinly sliced onion
4 whole black peppercorns
½ teaspoon salt

1 tablespoon lemon juice
¼ teaspoon nutmeg
1 cup water
½ cup sherry
1 tablespoon chopped parsley for
   garnish

In a 3½-quart saucepan, combine all ingredients except sherry and parsley. Bring to a boil. Reduce heat and simmer, covered, for 30 minutes. Strain and return to saucepan. Add sherry and reheat, stirring occasionally. Top with parsley and serve. This is delicious hot or cold.

Serves 6

BARLEY AND VEGETABLE SOUP

¾ cup pearl barley
11 cups homemade chicken stock
3 tablespoons butter
1½ cups minced onion
1 cup minced carrot
½ pound mushrooms, thinly
   sliced

½ cup minced celery
Salt and pepper
Sour cream, sliced raw
   mushrooms, and minced
   parsley for garnish

Combine barley and 3 cups of the chicken stock in a 2-quart saucepan. Bring to a boil over moderate heat and simmer for 1 hour and 15 minutes or until liquid is absorbed. Put butter, onion, carrot, mushrooms, and celery in a 5-quart kettle. Cover with a buttered round of wax paper and "sweat" for 5 minutes or until vegetables are softened. Add remaining chicken stock and simmer for 30 minutes. Add barley and simmer for 5 minutes. Season with salt and pepper. Ladle into heated bowls. Add a dollop of sour cream, a few slices of raw mushroom, and minced parsley. Serve with bread sticks. Soup keeps in refrigerator for 2 days.

Serves 8

CAULIFLOWER SOUP

1 large onion, sliced
1 clove garlic, crushed
¼ cup butter
1 medium cauliflower, separated
4½ to 5 cups homemade chicken
   stock

Salt and pepper to taste
Chopped parsley for garnish
   (optional)
Croutons for garnish (optional)

In a 4-quart saucepan, sauté onion and garlic in butter until soft. Add cauliflower and stock. Cover and simmer for 1 hour. Purée in food processor or blender. Season with salt and pepper. Garnish with chopped parsley and croutons.

Serves 10

COLD CARROT SOUP WITH BASIL

1 large yellow onion, finely chopped	2 tablespoons fresh basil or ½ teaspoon dried basil
6 medium carrots, peeled and chopped	1 teaspoon salt
4 tablespoons butter	½ teaspoon white pepper
2 small potatoes, peeled, chopped, and rinsed	6 cups boiling homemade chicken stock
	1 cup heavy cream

Sauté onion and carrots in butter, stirring constantly, until slightly browned. Transfer to a 3-quart soup pot. Stir in potatoes, chopped basil, salt, pepper, and boiling chicken stock. Return to a boil, lower heat, and simmer, partially covered, for 20 minutes. Skim off any butter that rises and forms a skim on the surface. Purée the soup in a food processor or blender. Taste and adjust seasoning. Transfer to a bowl and chill thoroughly. Stir in cream just before serving.

Serves 10

GANGA'S CHEESE SOUP

4 or 5 medium carrots, peeled and shredded	2 green onions, minced
3 cups chicken broth	1 jar (8 ounces) Cheez Whiz
	Salt and pepper to taste

Combine all ingredients in a 2-quart saucepan and simmer for 30 to 40 minutes or until carrots are completely tender. Stir well and serve immediately.

Serves 6

COLD TOMATO SOUP

1 can (46 ounces) tomato juice	Freshly ground black pepper to
4 tablespoons tomato paste	taste
8 green onions, white part only,	Juice of 1 lemon
minced	1 teaspoon sugar or more to taste
2 teaspoons salt or to taste	2 cups sour cream
2 pinches powdered thyme	Chopped parsley for garnish
1 teaspoon curry powder	Parmesan Rounds (see below)

The day before serving, combine all ingredients except sour cream and parsley in blender. Blend and refrigerate. Before serving, add sour cream and blend in blender. Top with chopped parsley. Serve with Parmesan Rounds.

Serves 8 to 10

Variation: For a lower-calorie version, try 2 cups of buttermilk instead of sour cream.

PARMESAN ROUNDS

¼ cup chopped green onion	½ cup grated Parmesan cheese
6 tablespoons mayonnaise	Melba rounds

Preheat oven to 350 degrees F. Mix together all ingredients and spread on melba rounds. Bake until cheese melts.

Yield: 60 rounds

CUBAN BLACK BEAN SOUP

1 pound black or turtle beans	4 medium onions
2 quarts water	2 green bell peppers, seeded
5 large cloves garlic	6 tablespoons olive oil
2 tablespoons salt	2 tablespoons water
1 ½ teaspoons ground cumin	½ teaspoon vinegar
1 ½ teaspoons oregano	3 cups boiled rice

Wash and pick over beans. Cover with cold water and soak overnight. Drain and place in 4-quart pot. Cover with 2 quarts of cold water and bring to a boil. Reduce heat and simmer, partially covered, for 1 to 1½ hours, stirring occasionally, until beans are *very* tender and skins burst. Mash with potato masher, leaving some beans whole. Meanwhile, using mortar and pestle, crush together garlic, salt, cumin, and oregano. In food processor, finely chop 2 of the onions and the bell peppers. Heat 5 tablespoons of the olive oil in heavy 2-quart pan and sauté vegetables and garlic mixture over medium heat for 5 minutes. Add 2 tablespoons water and simmer until tender. Do not brown. Add vegetables to cooked and mashed beans and simmer, covered, for 30 minutes or until flavors are well blended. Stir occasionally. Marinate 2 coarsely chopped onions in 1 tablespoon olive oil and vinegar. Serve hot soup in individual bowls with marinated onions and rice. Freezes well.

Serves 10 as an appetizer or
6 as main course

FRESH MUSHROOM BISQUE

½ to ¾ pound fresh
  mushrooms, sliced
1 clove garlic, minced
½ cup finely chopped onion
½ cup butter
2 tablespoons fresh lemon juice
4 tablespoons flour

4 cups chicken broth or
  consommé
2 teaspoons salt
¼ teaspoon black pepper
2 cups half-and-half
Chopped fresh parsley for
  garnish

In a 2-quart saucepan, sauté mushrooms, garlic, and onion in butter, stirring constantly, for 5 minutes or until onion is clear and golden. Sprinkle with lemon juice. Blend in flour. Gradually stir in broth, and add salt and pepper. Cook, stirring constantly, until soup is slightly thickened. Stir in half-and-half. Heat thoroughly. Serve with chopped parsley for garnish.

Serves 4

GAZPACHO

1 cup finely chopped, peeled
   tomatoes
½ cup finely chopped, seeded
   green bell pepper
½ cup finely chopped celery
½ cup finely chopped, peeled
   cucumber
½ cup finely chopped green
   onions
¼ cup finely chopped parsley

1 clove garlic, pressed
2 to 3 tablespoons wine vinegar
2 tablespoons olive oil
1 teaspoon salt
¼ teaspoon pepper
½ teaspoon Worcestershire
   sauce
1 can (46 ounces) V-8 vegetable
   juice
1 cup sour cream for garnish

Combine all ingredients except sour cream and chill well. Top with sour
cream mixed with a hint of garlic, if desired.

Serves 8 to 10

PURÉE OF CARROT SOUP

This soup is easy to prepare, healthy, low-calorie, and elegant.

2 medium onions, chopped
2 tablespoons butter
1 tablespoon vegetable oil
1 pound carrots, peeled and
   thinly sliced

1 quart homemade chicken stock
   (or more)
Salt and pepper to taste
Parsley for garnish
Croutons for garnish

In a 3-quart saucepan, sauté onions in butter and oil until golden. Add carrots and chicken stock. Simmer gently until carrots are soft. Purée in food
processor or blender. Return purée to saucepan, season with salt and
pepper, and add more broth to reach desired consistency. Serve hot with
parsley or croutons for garnish.

Serves 6 to 8

RED BELL PEPPER SOUP

2 cups chopped red bell pepper
  (approximately 2 large
  peppers)
1 cup chopped leeks or green
  onion, white part only

4 tablespoons butter
¾ cup chicken stock
2 cups buttermilk
Salt
White pepper

In a covered heavy 2-quart skillet, sauté peppers and leeks in butter over low heat for 15 minutes or until soft but not brown. Add chicken stock, bring to a boil, and simmer, partially covered, for 30 minutes. Purée in food processor or blender until smooth. Cool. Add buttermilk and chill until very cold. Season to taste with salt and pepper.

Serves 4

SUMMER GARDEN VEGETABLE SOUP

2 cans (10½ ounces each)
  condensed chicken broth
1 soup can of water
2 medium zucchini, sliced
2 medium yellow squash, sliced
2 medium carrots, peeled and
  sliced
½ pound green beans, cut in
  1-inch pieces

1 rib celery, chopped
1 can (12 ounces) V-8 vegetable
  juice
1 teaspoon basil
1 teaspoon chopped green onion
Salt to taste
Dash of pepper

In a 2-quart saucepan, bring chicken broth and water to a boil. Add vegetables and return to boiling. Cover, reduce heat, and simmer for 20 minutes. Add V-8 juice, basil, green onion, salt, and pepper, and simmer for 10 minutes.

Serves 4 to 6

SQUASH SOUP

1 small butternut squash (1 to
  1¼ pounds)
1 tart apple, cored
1 medium onion, chopped
3 tablespoons raw rice
1 teaspoon sugar

Pinch of curry powder
4 cups chicken stock
¼ cup cream
Milk to stretch
1 roll (6 ounces) jalapeño cheese
Salt to taste

Peel and cube squash and apple. Place in a 3-quart saucepan with the onion, rice, sugar, curry powder, and chicken stock. Simmer for 30 to 45 minutes. Purée in food processor or blender. Return to pan. Just before serving, heat and add cream, milk, and cheese. Stir until cheese has melted and season with salt. Also good cold! This freezes well.

Serves 8

SWEET POTATO SOUP

1 or 2 sweet potatoes or yams
  (12 ounces)
3 cans (10½ ounces, each)
  condensed chicken broth or 1
  quart chicken or beef stock

½ cup heavy cream
½ teaspoon freshly ground
  pepper
½ cup grated Swiss cheese

Preheat oven to 350 degrees F. Bake potatoes for 1 to 1½ hours or until soft. Peel and blend in blender with some of the stock until very smooth. Blend in remaining stock and cream. Pour soup into a 3-quart saucepan and cook over low heat. When hot, add pepper. Just before serving, add cheese to hot soup. Stir until cheese is completely melted, and serve.

Serves 6 to 8

TASTY VEGETABLE VELVET SOUP

1 small onion, chopped
3 tablespoons butter
2 cups homemade chicken broth
½ cup peeled cooked potatoes
½ teaspoon celery salt
Salt
White pepper

1 package (10 ounces) frozen
   seasoned Japanese or Chinese
   vegetables *or* be inventive and
   clean out your refrigerator
   and use leftover vegetables
Half-and-half (optional)

Combine onion, butter, and ½ cup of the chicken broth in a 2½-quart saucepan. Cook until liquid evaporates. Add potatoes to onion mixture. Add seasonings, remaining 1½ cups chicken broth and frozen vegetables. Cook for 10 to 15 minutes. Strain and reserve broth, purée vegetable mixture in food processor or blender. When mixture is smooth, return to saucepan along with reserved broth. Taste and correct seasonings. Thin with half-and-half if desired. This is a very tasty basic soup that could have many variations.

Serves 6 to 8

FOUR SEASONS' WATERCRESS VICHYSSOISE

2 leeks, white part only, sliced
   very thin
1 small onion, sliced
1 tablespoon butter
1 cup finely chopped watercress
   leaves (no stems)
2½ medium potatoes, peeled and
   sliced

2 cups homemade chicken stock
½ teaspoon salt
1 cup milk
1 cup light cream
½ cup heavy cream

In a 3-quart saucepan, sauté leeks and onion in butter until limp. Add watercress, potatoes, chicken stock, and salt. Simmer for 35 to 40 minutes. Remove from heat and purée in blender. Return to saucepan and add milk and light cream. Correct seasoning. Bring to a boil. Cool and chill. When cold, blend in heavy cream.

Serves 4

ZUCCHINI SOUP

3 pounds slender zucchini
¼ pound whole slab bacon
1 can (10½ ounces) consommé
3½ cups water
1 teaspoon salt

¼ teaspoon white pepper
Garlic salt if desired
Sour cream and chopped chives
 for garnish

Scrub zucchini and trim ends. Cut into chunks. Cut bacon into 4 or 5 pieces, leaving rind on. Cook all ingredients in a 3-quart saucepan for 1 hour or until zucchini is tender. Remove bacon and blend until smooth in food processor or blender. Serve hot or cold. When served cold, garnish with sour cream and chopped chives. Soup freezes well.

Serves 8

CHAPTER XIII

EGGS AND CHEESE

The Oilfields:

Onshore and Off

Oil and Texas have been linked for even longer than most people realize. Spanish *conquistador* Luis de Moscos made the first petroleum discovery east of what is now Houston at Sabine Pass in 1543. He used the sticky seepage from oil springs to caulk his hand-built boats. In 1866, Lynis T. Barnett sunk an oil well near Melrose but found there was no market for his product.

By the turn of the century, however, the world had developed enough uses for the smelly black substance to consider it valuable. In 1895, the Corsicana Field south of Dallas began producing; and in 1901, Spindletop, a tremendous gusher that lives on in legend, blew in east of Houston. From that point on, the city has been surrounded by fields of derricks pumping black gold.

As the refineries sprang up along the Ship Channel and offshore platforms floated out in the Gulf, the romantic images of the Texas rancher and the cowboy began to be supplanted by equally romanticized versions of the wildcatter—the seat-of-the-pants entrepreneur who drills wells—and the roughneck—the hard-working, hard-fighting, hard-playing man who works them. It wasn't surprising. The old Houston heroes and the new had a lot in common. They embodied independence, optimism, and energy, an ability to cooperate toward a goal but resist being pushed around.

Like the range, the oil patch has its own folklore. In the early days, wildcatters, who often worked as much from instinct as from a solid grounding in geology, would use divining rods, which they called "wiggle sticks," and employ "oil witches." One woman claimed to have aided numerous discoveries by dancing on suspected oil-bearing land until her petticoat fell off. Another oil witch, an apparently pious and straightforward minister, insisted that he suffered piercing headaches every time he walked over an underground pool of petroleum.

With one drill bit called a "Mother Hubbard," a valve assembly dubbed a "Christmas tree," a shovel an "idiot stick," and job titles like "roughneck" and "cherry-picker," it can be pretty hard to figure out an oilfield conversation without a glossary. But whether you understand petroleum jargon or not, there's an unpolished zest and excitement about the business that comes across, despite the grease and grime, discomfort and dangers.

Onshore and off, oil workers are hearty eaters. The technology of the oil patch has changed but not its appetites. Oilfield caterers and offshore platform cooks turn out spreads that would boggle Paul Bunyan. Along with the bread and bacon and barbecue, eggs and cheese are important elements —for breakfast and for side dishes.

The recipes that follow don't assume that you're feeding a drilling crew; you'd have to multiply the quantities twenty times or so to do that. But some of them are substantial enough to satisfy the hungriest roughneck—or teenage track star. Others are almost ethereal, perfect for friends who watch their weight as carefully as a drilling operator watches a pressure gauge. Try the full range, from Country-Style Eggs to Eggs à la Abney to Longneck Jalapeño Quiche, Spinach Quiche Kinkaid, and Filled Soufflé Roll—and be prepared for gushers of compliments.

BUFFET CHEESE DISH

¼ cup melted butter
10 eggs, beaten
½ cup flour
1 teaspoon baking powder
2 cans (3 ounces each) chopped
    green chilies

1 pint cottage cheese
1 pound grated Monterey Jack
    cheese
1 teaspoon salt

Preheat oven to 400 degrees F. Combine ingredients and pour into a greased 10 × 12 × 2-inch baking dish. Bake for 15 minutes, reduce oven temperature to 350 degrees F., and continue cooking for 35 minutes.

Serves 10

COUNTRY-STYLE EGGS

8 slices bacon
4 cups cooked cubed potatoes
½ cup chopped green bell
  pepper
2½ tablespoons chopped onion

Salt and pepper to taste
6 eggs
1 cup shredded Cheddar cheese

Cook bacon until crisp, remove from the skillet, and crumble. Pour off all but 2 to 3 tablespoons drippings. Add potatoes, green pepper, and onion to the skillet, and cook until lightly browned. Season with salt and pepper. Make six wells in mixture. Break 6 eggs into wells, keeping eggs separate as when cooking fried eggs. Cover and cook until eggs are almost done. Then sprinkle with shredded cheese and crisp bacon, cover, and heat until cheese is melted.

Serves 6

EGGS À LA ABNEY

A terrific dish for a crowd.

12 pieces bacon
2 or 3 large green onion tops, thinly
  sliced

12 eggs
Salt and pepper
Grated sharp Cheddar cheese

Preheat oven to 350 degrees F. Cook bacon until slightly done. Curl bacon slices around inside edges of Teflon muffin pan. Place a small amount of bacon drippings in each muffin cup. Sprinkle a few green onion tops in the bottom of each muffin cup. Crack eggs one at a time into a tea cup. Be careful not to break the yolk. Then pour gently into muffin cup. Lightly salt and pepper the eggs and top with grated cheese. Bake for about 10 to 15 minutes, just until eggs are set. Do not cook too long because eggs continue to cook slightly in pan after removing from the oven. Eggs will easily slide out of the muffin pan with the help of a spoon. If you are very careful, they will stay whole. You can cook two muffin pans at once with a little adjustment in the cooking time. These can be prepared ahead of time and stored in the refrigerator until ready to cook.

Serves 6 to 12

FRIED EGGS WITH GARLIC, LEMON, AND MINT

2 cloves garlic   6 eggs
Salt   Dried crushed mint
Juice of ½ lemon or more
4 tablespoons butter or
   margarine

Crush the garlic with salt and mix well with lemon juice. Melt butter in a large frying pan or two small pans. Add garlic-lemon mixture. As garlic begins to color, slide in the eggs, previously broken into a bowl, and fry gently. Crush dried mint and sprinkle over eggs. Cover pan briefly to set yolks. When eggs are set, sprinkle lightly with salt and serve immediately.

Serves 3

MUSHROOM-STUFFED EGGS
WITH MORNAY SAUCE

STUFFING:
1 pound white mushrooms,   4 tablespoons mixed chopped
   cleaned and stemmed   fresh parsley and chervil (may
Lemon juice   substitute 2 teaspoons if dried
8 shallots or green onions,   herbs are used)
   minced   2 to 6 tablespoons heavy cream
4 tablespoons butter   Salt to taste
12 hard-cooked eggs   Freshly ground black pepper

SAUCE:
4 tablespoons butter   Salt
6 tablespoons flour   Freshly ground black pepper
4 cups milk   Freshly grated nutmeg
½ cup heavy cream
½ cup grated Swiss cheese
   (Jarlsberg or Gruyère)

FOR ASSEMBLY:
4 tablespoons stale whole wheat   ½ cup grated Swiss cheese
   bread crumbs   Butter (cold)
3 tablespoons melted butter

STUFFING: Mince mushrooms in food processor and sprinkle with a few drops of lemon juice to keep them white. Cook shallots in butter until limp, but not colored. Add mushrooms and sauté, stirring, until liquid has evaporated and mushrooms are dry. Halve eggs lengthwise, remove yolks, and mash in processor. Transfer to a bowl and add mushrooms, parsley, and chervil, working the mixture into a paste. Stir in cream by spoonfuls, being careful not to let mixture become runny. Season with salt and pepper. Mound mixture into egg whites. Set aside.

SAUCE: Melt butter over low heat. Stir in flour, and cook, stirring, for several seconds. Remove from heat and add milk. Return to heat and whisk vigorously until sauce is smooth. Bring to a boil and simmer 2 minutes. Stir in cream. Add ½ cup cheese and season well with salt, pepper, and nutmeg.

ASSEMBLY: Spread a film of the sauce in a shallow 3-quart baking-serving dish. Place eggs in dish in a single layer and coat with remaining sauce. Combine the bread crumbs, melted butter, and cheese, and sprinkle over eggs. Dot with tiny pieces of butter. Place dish under broiler for five minutes or until brown. The dish can be prepared a day ahead. If prepared ahead, heat in a preheated 375 degree F. oven for 15 minutes before browning under broiler.

Serves 8 to 10

BROCCOLI QUICHE

2 frozen pie shells
1 pound ground spicy sausage
 (may also use smoked)
1 package (10 ounces) cut
 frozen broccoli
1 cup heavy cream

1 package (8 ounces) Velveeta
 cheese, grated
1 cup grated Cheddar cheese
4 eggs, well-beaten
1 cup grated mozzarella cheese

Preheat oven to 350 degrees F. Bake frozen pie shells for 8 to 10 minutes. Cool. Cook sausage and drain. Cook broccoli and drain. Heat cream in a double boiler and stir in Velveeta and Cheddar cheeses. Let mixture cool. Add beaten eggs. Stir until mixed. Layer sausage and broccoli in pie shells. Pour cheese mixture over this. Sprinkle mozzarella on top. Bake for 30 to 45 minutes until brown.

Serves 12 to 16

LUCY'S COMPANY HAM, CHEESE, AND EGGS

14 to 15 slices white sandwich
  bread
1 pound chopped ham (boiled or
  baked)
1 cup grated sharp Cheddar
  cheese
1 cup grated Monterey Jack
  cheese
2 cans (3 ounces each) chopped
  green chilies

7 eggs
½ tablespoon dry mustard
1 teaspoon salt
3 cups milk
1 cup crushed cornflakes, or
  enough to cover
¼ cup melted butter

Preheat oven to 350 degrees F. Remove crusts from bread and cut slices in half. Place half the bread in a buttered Pyrex dish. Layer with ham, Cheddar cheese, Monterey Jack cheese, and green chilies. Cover with remaining bread. Beat eggs with dry mustard, salt, and milk. Pour over casserole and let stand in refrigerator 12 hours or overnight. Before baking, cover with cornflakes and drizzle with butter. Bake for 30 to 40 minutes.

Serves 8 to 12

CRUSTLESS QUICHE LORRAINE

10 slices crisp bacon, crumbled
1 cup grated Swiss or mozzarella
  cheese
¼ cup minced onion
3 jalapeño peppers, seeded and
  chopped *or* 1 can (4 ounces)
  whole green chilies

4 eggs
1 can (13 ounces) evaporated
  milk
½ teaspoon salt
¼ teaspoon sugar
⅛ teaspoon cayenne pepper or
  nutmeg

Preheat oven to 350 degrees F. Sprinkle bacon, cheese, onion, and jalapeños in a 9-inch glass pie plate. Beat eggs, milk, salt, sugar, and cayenne pepper or nutmeg until well blended. Pour over bacon mixture. Bake for 40 minutes or until firm. Allow to stand 10 minutes before cutting. This can be cooked for 9 minutes in the microwave oven, turning every 3 minutes.

Serves 6

EGGS PARMESAN

2 tablespoons butter
1 ounce sherry
2 eggs

Salt to taste
Freshly ground pepper to taste
2 tablespoons Parmesan cheese

Lightly brown the butter in a skillet. As it begins to take on color, add sherry. When the liquid begins to bubble, break the eggs into it. As the whites begin to set, season with salt and pepper. Remove the skillet from the fire and sprinkle Parmesan cheese over eggs. Run the skillet under the broiler. As soon as Parmesan browns, serve. Pour sauce over eggs. Good with English muffins.

Serves 2

LONGNECK JALAPEÑO QUICHE

1 10-inch quiche shell, unbaked
¼ cup chopped onions
2 tablespoons butter
1 tomato, sliced
5 eggs
1 cup cream
1 teaspoon salt

1 teaspoon pepper
1½ cups shredded Monterey
  Jack cheese
¼ cup chopped jalapeño
  peppers
Cherry tomatoes and parsley for
  garnish

Preheat oven to 350 degrees F. Place a well-greased longneck mold on a greased cookie sheet. Gently lay quiche shell in the mold and press against the sides. Line shell with foil, fill with beans or pie weights and bake for 15 minutes. Cool; remove foil and weights. Sauté onions in butter until golden. Spread onions and tomato slices in bottom of shell. Beat together eggs, cream, salt, pepper, and cheese. If you are brave, add the jalapeño peppers. Pour mixture into shell. If faint of heart or stomach, sprinkle desired amount of jalapeño peppers on top of quiche. Cover the neck of the form with foil and bake for 40 to 50 minutes or until quiche is set. Gently remove quiche from the form with two spatulas. Place on a serving platter and garnish with cherry tomatoes and parsley.

Serves 6

SALMON AND FRESH MUSHROOM QUICHE

1 9-inch pie shell
2 tablespoons butter
3 or 4 green onions, chopped
¼ pound fresh mushrooms,
 thickly sliced
4 eggs
1 cup half-and-half

1 teaspoon dillweed
Freshly ground pepper
1 cup boned salmon, fresh or
 canned
¾ cup grated Monterey Jack
 cheese

Preheat oven to 400 degrees F. Bake pie shell for 15 minutes; cool. Reduce oven temperature to 375 degrees F. Sauté onions and mushrooms in butter. Beat together eggs, half-and-half, and seasonings. Place mushroom mixture and chunks of salmon in baked pie shell, sprinkle with cheese, and pour egg mixture on top. Bake at 375 degrees F. for 35 to 40 minutes or until center is firm and top is browned.

Serves 6

SAUSAGE CHEESE PIE

½ pound sausage, cut into
 ¼-inch slices
1 8-inch pie shell, partially baked
½ pound grated Cheddar cheese
3 eggs, slightly beaten

½ cup milk
2 tablespoons bourbon
1 tablespoon lemon juice
½ teaspoon salt
⅛ teaspoon pepper

Preheat oven to 375 degrees F. Cook sausage slices until browned. Drain well and spread over bottom of pie shell. Cover with grated cheese. Beat eggs with milk, bourbon, lemon juice, salt, and pepper, and pour into pie shell. Bake for 40 to 50 minutes or until a knife inserted in the center comes out clean.

Serves 6 as a main dish or
12 for hors d'oeuvres

SPINACH QUICHE KINKAID

1 package (10 ounces) frozen
chopped spinach
Pastry for 9-inch shell
¼ cup grated Parmesan cheese
3 eggs, beaten
1 cup cottage cheese
1 cup heavy cream
2 tablespoons dehydrated onion

1½ teaspoons salt
½ teaspoon pepper
1 teaspoon caraway seeds
¼ teaspoon nutmeg
½ teaspoon Worcestershire
sauce
2 to 3 drops Tabasco sauce
2 tablespoons butter

Preheat oven to 400 degrees F. Cook spinach and drain well. Line a 9-inch pie pan with pastry and cook for 8 minutes. Cool. Reduce oven temperature to 350 degrees F. Sprinkle Parmesan cheese in bottom of shell. Combine all remaining ingredients except butter, and pour over cheese. Brown butter and pour over top. Bake at 350 degrees F. for 30 to 45 minutes or until knife comes out clean.

Serves 6 to 8

HOT FRUIT CASSEROLE

Great with any quiche or egg dish, this is also delicious with pork or ham.

3 cups peach halves
3 cups pear halves
3 cups sliced or chunk pineapple
2 to 3 sliced firm bananas

⅓ cup butter or margarine
¾ cup brown sugar
1 teaspoon ground ginger

Preheat oven to 325 degrees F. Drain fruit well and arrange in casserole or oven dish. Mix butter, sugar, and ginger. Stir over low heat until butter is melted. Pour over fruit. Bake for 30 minutes or until hot and bubbly.

Serves 8 to 10

FILLED SOUFFLÉ ROLL

4 tablespoons butter
½ cup flour
2 cups milk
½ teaspoon salt

Dash white pepper
5 eggs, separated
¼ cup or more grated Parmesan
    cheese

Preheat oven to 400 degrees F. Line a jelly-roll pan with foil that has been *generously* buttered and floured. Melt butter in a saucepan; blend in flour. Stir and cook over medium heat until foamy, about 1 minute. Slowly stir in milk. Cook, stirring constantly, until sauce is thick. Add salt and pepper. Beat egg yolks until fluffy, and add a little of the hot sauce. Add the heated yolks to the saucepan and cook for 1 minute, stirring constantly. Do not boil sauce at any time. Remove from heat, cover, and let cool. Beat egg whites till stiff peaks form. Fold carefully into the sauce. Pour soufflé mixture onto prepared jelly-roll pan. Smooth top evenly and sprinkle liberally with Parmesan cheese. Bake for 20 to 30 minutes until soufflé is puffed and brown. There may be "bubbles" that puff higher in one area than another—no matter. When soufflé is done, turn out immediately on a clean smooth towel. If it cools too much, the soufflé will crack when rolled. Spread with filling of your choice and, with the aid of the towel, roll into a long cylinder. Serve immediately or slide onto plastic wrap, seal carefully, and refrigerate to serve later. This soufflé can be served hot, cold, or at room temperature.

Serves: 6 for brunch
10 for appetizers

FILLINGS

These can be made ahead and kept warm until ready to serve. All fillings should be very *spicy as the soufflé is bland.*

SPINACH/BACON FILLING:
1 package (10 ounces) chopped
    frozen spinach
¼ cup cooked bacon pieces
1 package (3 ounces) cream
    cheese with chives

¼ cup mayonnaise
Salt and pepper to taste

Cook spinach, drain, and heat in a small pan along with bacon pieces, cream cheese, and mayonnaise. Add salt and pepper to taste. This makes a particularly attractive filling.

CRAB CURRY FILLING:

2 tablespoons butter
1 package (6 ounces) frozen
 crab, drained
¼ cup chopped chives or tops of
 green onions
3 tablespoons white wine

1 package (3 ounces) cream
 cheese
Dash or two Tabasco
¼ to ½ teaspoon curry
¼ to ½ teaspoon dry mustard

Melt butter in skillet and add crab and chives. Cook until chives are limp. Add wine, then cream cheese and seasonings. Use ¼ teaspoon curry and mustard if you like a mild filling and ½ teaspoon of both if you like a tastier filling. Spread evenly on soufflé and roll up.

SALMON/DILL FILLING:

2 tablespoons minced green
 onions
2 tablespoons butter

1 package (3 ounces) smoked
 salmon
½ teaspoon dill

Sauté onions in butter, add salmon and dill, and spread over warm soufflé.

Serves 4 to 6

CHAPTER XIV

VEGETABLES

Market Square

Surrounding a square block of green in the shadow of Houston's soaring office towers are some of the city's oldest and quaintest commercial structures—former shops and warehouses dating back before the Civil War. Today, they house trendy little restaurants and wine bars, and the patch of green serves as a setting for weekday brown-bag lunches and outdoor concerts, especially during the citywide Houston Festival each spring.

Throughout the nineteenth century, Market Square was one of the most important commercial centers in Texas. Much of the economic fate of the area rested on what transpired at the nearby Cotton Exchange, which is still standing. As early as 1837, buckskinned hunters bearing wild game from the forests, German farmers with wagonloads of produce, hucksters hawking homespun and calico, politicians making speeches, shrewd pioneer women in poke bonnets, and Indians and trappers bartering pelts for blankets and supplies turned Market Square into a perpetual county fair.

By 1890, the scene had become even more eclectic, especially on Saturday evenings. An article appearing that year in *Harper's Magazine* described Chinese peddlers, Italian hunters, French butchers, Black food vendors, plus a liberal sprinkling of Irish, Mongolian, Dutch, German, Spanish, and American buyers and sellers "laughing, teasing, talking, quarreling, gesticulating, bargaining, staring, keeping appointments and making new ones, being proper or improper, polite or rude as the case may be."

To people arriving from the North, the produce displayed at Market Square strained the imagination. One Southern Pacific Railroad brochure called the Houston area "the cradle of agricultural and horticultural development" and went on to say, "Cold facts will appear distorted; so we are forced to 'tinge the coloring' as light as possible that the skeptic may not be incredulous." Nonetheless, that allegedly light tingeing included accounts of plump red strawberries for sale in Market Square on November 20, 1902, and tales of Texas watermelons weighing as much as eighty pounds, not to mention tomatoes, beans, cucumbers, squash, and other produce, all of a size and flavor to put California to shame.

Although the admittedly delicious fruits and vegetables produced in

South and East Texas now appear in modern supermarkets and roadside stands rather than on carts and wagons around Market Square, Houston cooks still make ample use of this seasonless bounty and many take pride in growing their own vegetables. With the help of a cold frame or a sunny spot sheltered by a wall to the north, some gardeners keep harvesting peppers and broccoli even in December, and techniques for bringing out the flavor of one's crop form a year-round topic of conversation.

This chapter harks back to the cultural and horticultural medley that was Market Square at the turn of the century. Broad Oaks Broccoli Soufflé, Zesty Carrots, Cauliflower with Avocado Sauce, Herbed Green Beans, Cheese Grits, Avocado Pilaf, Red Beans and Rice—all have a touch of the cosmopolitan city, as well as the flavor of the farm.

CHRISTMAS SQUASH

3 medium-large acorn squash	1 teaspoon vanilla
2 eggs, slightly beaten	1 cup butter, softened
1 to 1½ cups sugar	½ teaspoon baking powder
2 tablespoons flour	Nutmeg to taste

Preheat oven to 350 degrees F. Cut each squash into 4 pieces, remove seeds, and boil in water until tender. Peel off skins and place squash in large mixing bowl. Mash with fork and add all remaining ingredients except nutmeg. Pour into 3-quart casserole and bake for 30 minutes or until slightly brown around edges and no longer runny. Sprinkle nutmeg on top and serve.

Serves 8 to 10

STUFFED ACORN SQUASH

2 medium acorn squash	4 tablespoons chopped pecans
8 to 10 fresh medium mushrooms, sliced	4 tablespoons sour cream
1 tablespoon butter	4 tablespoons grated sharp Cheddar cheese
3 to 4 green onions, chopped	

Preheat oven to 350 degrees F. Cut squash in half lengthwise and remove seeds. Put squash, cut side down, in shallow pan of water and steam for 45 to 60 minutes until tender. Sauté mushrooms in butter and mix with onions, pecans, and sour cream. Fill squash cavities with mushroom mixture and sprinkle with cheese. Bake for 10 minutes or until cheese melts.

Serves 4

BROAD OAKS BROCCOLI SOUFFLÉ

2 cups cooked chopped broccoli	½ teaspoon salt
½ cup mayonnaise	2 to 3 drops Tabasco
1 tablespoon butter, melted	Pinch of pepper
1 tablespoon flour	Cherry tomatoes (optional)
3 eggs	Sour Cream Dressing (below)
1 cup light cream	

Preheat oven to 375 degrees F. Mix together broccoli, mayonnaise, and butter. Sprinkle flour on top of mixture. Beat eggs until light and add to broccoli. Add cream, salt, Tabasco, pepper, and mix well. Pour into greased 1-quart mold and bake in pan of water for 55 minutes or until knife comes out clean. Let sit for 5 minutes and turn out onto warm platter. If using ring mold, fill with cherry tomatoes. This can be prepared several days before it is baked. It is delicious served cold with Sour Cream Dressing.

Serves 6 to 8

SOUR CREAM DRESSING

2 tablespoons minced green onion	2 tablespoons white wine vinegar
1 tablespoon anchovy paste	⅛ teaspoon crushed tarragon
2 tablespoons lemon juice	1 cup sour cream
	½ cup mayonnaise

Mix all ingredients together, cover, and chill.

Yield: 2 cups

RED CABBAGE

2 tablespoons butter
2 onions, cut in quarters
4 whole cloves
2 cooking apples, unpeeled,
   cored, and cut in eighths

½ cup red wine vinegar
1 cup water
2 tablespoons sugar
Salt to taste
1 head red cabbage, quartered

Combine all ingredients. Simmer for 3 to 4 hours. Drain and serve.

Serves 6 to 8

CARROTS AND ZUCCHINI

2 tablespoons butter
2 tablespoons vegetable oil
6 medium zucchini, cut in strips
6 medium young carrots, peeled
   and cut in strips

Salt and freshly ground pepper
   or
Salt and sugar
   or
Salt and Parmesan cheese

Heat butter and oil in large skillet over high heat. Add vegetables and stir-fry until tender but still crisp. Sprinkle with your choice of salt and seasoning.

Serves 6

CARROTS IN A RING

½ cup Crisco
¾ cup brown sugar or to taste
2 eggs
2½ cups finely grated fresh
   carrots

Juice of 1 lemon
½ cup flour
1 teaspoon baking powder
½ teaspoon salt
1 tablespoon cold water

Preheat oven to 350 degrees F. Cream Crisco and brown sugar. Add eggs and mix well. Add carrots and lemon juice. Sift together flour, baking powder, and salt, and add to carrot mixture. Stir in water and pour into a buttered 10-cup ring mold or casserole. Bake for 10 minutes. Reduce heat to 325 degrees F. and cook for 20 to 30 minutes more or until set. Unmold and fill with parsley or stir-fried peas.

Serves 10 to 12

CARROTS PARMESAN

6 to 7 large carrots, sliced
½ pint heavy cream
½ cup grated Parmesan cheese
1 small onion, grated

1½ teaspoons seasoned salt
Salt to taste
¼ teaspoon pepper
¼ to ½ cup pecan halves

Preheat oven to 350 degrees F. Cook carrots in salted water for 15 minutes or until tender. Drain and blend in food processor. Add all remaining ingredients except pecans. Mix thoroughly and pour into buttered 2½-quart casserole. Arrange pecan halves on top and bake for 35 to 40 minutes or until hot and lightly browned.

Serves 4

SLICED CARROTS AND MUSHROOMS

1 bunch young carrots
3 tablespoons butter
1 tablespoon olive oil
1 small onion, finely chopped
½ clove garlic, finely chopped

6 fresh mushrooms (or more),
   sliced
Salt and pepper to taste
Pinch of rosemary
4 to 5 tablespoons cream

Scrape carrots and slice diagonally. Melt butter in saucepan. Add oil, onion, and garlic, and sauté for 1 minute. Add carrots and cook until they are almost tender. Add mushrooms and seasonings, cover, and cook over low heat for 10 minutes or until just tender. Stir in cream and adjust seasoning.

Serves 4

ZESTY CARROTS

6 to 8 carrots, peeled
¼ cup carrot liquid, reserved
2 tablespoons grated onion
2 tablespoons horseradish
½ cup mayonnaise
½ teaspoon salt

¼ teaspoon pepper
¼ cup bread crumbs
1 tablespoon butter, melted
Dash of paprika
Parsley for garnish

Preheat oven to 375 degrees F. Cut carrots into strips and cook. Drain and reserve ¼ cup cooking liquid. Arrange carrots in a shallow 1½-quart casserole. Mix reserved liquid, onion, horseradish, mayonnaise, salt, and pepper, and pour over carrots. Top with mixture of bread crumbs, butter, and paprika. Bake for 15 to 20 minutes. Garnish with parsley.

Serves 4 to 6

CAULIFLOWER WITH AVOCADO SAUCE

1 cauliflower
1½ teaspoons salt
2 fresh serrano chilies, seeded
   and chopped
3 sprigs cilantro, leaves only
2 tablespoons finely chopped
   onion

1 large tomato, skinned and
   chopped
2 avocados, peeled and chopped
2 ounces Mexican cheese or
   Monterey Jack cheese, grated

Bring 7 to 8 quarts of water to a boil. Add whole cauliflower and 1 teaspoon of the salt. Cook until just tender, about 10 minutes. Drain. Meanwhile, combine chilies, cilantro, onion, ½ teaspoon salt, tomato, and avocados in food processor. Blend until well mixed but not puréed. Pour over hot cauliflower and sprinkle with cheese.

Serves 6

ESCALLOPED CELERY

4 cups coarsely chopped celery
¼ cup slivered blanched
 almonds
1 can (6 ounces) water
 chestnuts, slivered
½ cup canned mushroom pieces

4 tablespoons butter
3 tablespoons flour
½ cup half-and-half
1 cup chicken broth
½ cup dried bread crumbs
½ cup grated Parmesan cheese

Preheat oven to 375 degrees F. Boil celery no longer than 5 minutes. Drain, and add almonds, chestnuts, and mushroom pieces. In saucepan, melt butter, add flour, and cook until it bubbles. Add cream and chicken broth, and cook until thicker. Blend celery mixture into sauce. Pour into ovenproof casserole and top with bread crumbs. Sprinkle cheese on top and bake until hot and bubbly. Leftovers make a delicious stuffing for mushroom caps.

Serves 8

BABY DOLL'S WHITE CORN

10 ears white corn (do not
 substitute)
3 cups heavy cream
½ cup butter

Cut corn off cobs and put in top of double boiler. Cover with cream, add butter, and cook for 3 hours. Will freeze.

Serves 8 to 10

CORN CASSEROLE

6 tablespoons butter
2 tablespoons flour
2 cups cream or half-and-half
2 cans (1 pound each) whole corn,
 drained
Salt and pepper to taste

1 cup grated Gruyère or Swiss
 cheese, divided in thirds
1 can (7½ ounces) pitted ripe
 olives, drained and sliced
Finely chopped parsley for
 garnish

Preheat oven to 350 degrees F. In saucepan, combine 2 tablespoons butter and flour. Cook over medium heat stirring constantly for about 5 minutes. Slowly add cream and continue to cook until thickened. Set aside. In buttered, shallow 2-quart casserole, layer half the corn, sprinkle with salt and pepper, dot with 2 tablespoons butter, sprinkle with ⅓ cup grated cheese and half the olives. Repeat layers. Pour cream sauce over all and top with remaining cheese. Bake for 25 minutes and garnish with parsley.

Serves 4 to 6

CURRIED CORN PUDDING

½ cup chopped onion
½ cup chopped green bell
  pepper
3 tablespoons butter
1 tablespoon curry powder
  (optional)
3 cups cooked corn or 3 cans (16
  ounces each) whole corn,
  drained

2 cups light cream
3 eggs, slightly beaten
1 teaspoon salt
½ teaspoon sugar
Parsley for garnish

Preheat oven to 350 degrees F. Sauté onion and green bell pepper in butter until soft. Stir in curry powder and transfer to a bowl. Add remaining ingredients and blend thoroughly. Pour into buttered soufflé dish and bake for 45 minutes. Garnish with parsley.

Serves 8

EGGPLANT CASSEROLE FOR EGGPLANT HATERS

2 medium-large eggplants, peeled
  and cubed
1 cup eggplant stock, reserved
3 slices stale bread
2 eggs, beaten
½ cup milk
1 can (10½ ounces) cream of
  mushroom soup

1 tablespoon minced onion
½ teaspoon celery seed
Ground black pepper
1 teaspoon salt
2 tablespoons butter
½ pound Cheddar cheese, grated

Preheat oven to 325 degrees F. Cover eggplant with boiling, salted water and simmer for 5 minutes. Drain, reserving 1 cup stock, and set aside. Crumble bread in large mixing bowl. Add eggs, milk, soup, onion, and seasonings. Mix well, so that there are no lumps of bread. Add stock from eggplant and mix. Layer half the eggplant in a buttered 2-quart casserole. Cover with half the bread mixture, dot with half the butter, and top with half the cheese. Repeat layers. Cover and bake for 1 to 1½ hours.

Serves 10

FRIED EGGPLANT

1 cup flour	1 eggplant, peeled and sliced ¼
1 teaspoon baking powder	to ½ inch thick
1 cup beer	Vegetable oil

Combine flour, baking powder, and beer to make beer batter. Dip eggplant slices in batter and cook in hot oil (about 370 degrees F.) until golden brown. This makes enough batter for one eggplant. This can also be used for okra, zucchini, or mushrooms.

Serves 2 to 4

RATATOUILLE

2 tablespoons oil	½ pound mushrooms, quartered
2 cloves garlic, minced	3 tablespoons minced parsley
1 onion, sliced	1 can (14½ ounces) tomatoes
1 green bell pepper, sliced	Salt to taste
1 eggplant, peeled and cut up	Pepper to taste
2 zucchini, quartered lengthwise and cut in pieces	

In a large heavy saucepan, layer ingredients in the order given. Set casserole on burner that has been heated to high temperature. Reduce to medium, and cook for 10 to 12 minutes or until done. Stir occasionally. This is better if prepared ahead and allowed to sit overnight.

Serves 5 to 6

GREEN BEANS SUPREME

½ cup sliced onion
1 tablespoon parsley
2 tablespoons butter
2 tablespoons flour
1 teaspoon salt
¼ teaspoon pepper
½ teaspoon grated lemon or lime
  peel
1 cup sour cream

2 packages (10 ounces each)
  frozen or 1 pound fresh green
  beans, cooked and drained
½ cup grated Swiss cheese
2 tablespoons butter, melted
  (optional)
½ cup dry bread crumbs
  (optional)

Preheat oven to 275 degrees F. Cook onion and parsley in butter until tender but not brown. Add flour, salt, pepper, lemon peel, and sour cream. Mix well. Stir in beans and heat. Pour into baking dish and top with grated cheese. If desired, combine butter and bread crumbs and sprinkle on top. Bake until heated through.

Serves 6 to 8

GREENS

¼ pound salt pork, diced
2 cups water
2 to 3 pounds turnip greens
2 turnip roots
Salt and pepper to taste
1 tablespoon bacon drippings or
  to taste (optional)

3 slices of crisp bacon (optional)
½ hard-cooked egg, chopped
  (optional)
Vinegar or hot pepper sauce
  (optional)

Cook salt pork in water for 30 minutes in a covered saucepan. Wash greens carefully and add to water and pork. Cook until tender, and add chopped turnip roots. Cook until roots are tender. Add salt and pepper and bacon drippings if desired. Garnish with crisp bacon pieces and hard-cooked egg. Serve with vinegar or hot pepper sauce.

Serves 6

HERBED GREEN BEANS

1 pound fresh green beans *or* 2
    packages (10 ounces each)
    frozen green beans
¼ cup butter
¼ cup finely chopped onion
½ clove garlic, minced

¼ cup chopped celery
½ cup minced parsley
¼ teaspoon rosemary
¼ teaspoon basil
¾ teaspoon salt

Cook and drain beans. While beans are cooking, melt butter and sauté onion, garlic, celery, and parsley. Add herbs and salt. Simmer, covered, for 10 minutes. Just before serving, toss onion mixture and beans together.

Serves 4 to 6

MUSHROOM STRUDEL

1 pound chopped mushrooms
1 clove garlic, crushed
⅓ cup butter, unsalted
2 tablespoons dry sherry
2 tablespoons chopped parsley
¼ teaspoon salt
Pepper to taste

2 tablespoons chopped green
    onion
½ cup sour cream
1 package phyllo pastry leaves
1 cup melted butter
Bread crumbs

Preheat oven to 375 degrees F. Press moisture from mushrooms with a dish towel. Sauté mushrooms and garlic with the ⅓ cup butter for about 3 minutes. Add sherry, parsley, seasonings, and green onion, and cook until most of the liquid has been absorbed. Remove from heat and stir in sour cream.

Assembly: Spread out a clean, slightly damp dish towel. Lay ½ of 1 phyllo leaf on the towel. Brush with melted butter and sprinkle all over with bread crumbs. Repeat with 2 more sheets. Spread ⅙ of the mushroom mixture on the narrower end of dough up to 2 inches from the sides and 2 inches from the edge. Use the towel to lift and roll the filling in the dough. Fold sides in after 1 or 2 rolls and finish rolling up. Brush the seam with butter to seal. Brush the whole strudel with butter. Bake for about 15 to 20 minutes or until golden brown. This can be frozen.

Serves 6

CHEESE GRITS

1½ cups grits
6 cups boiling water
1 pound sharp Cheddar cheese,
   grated
2 teaspoons salt

2 teaspoons savory salt
Dash Tabasco
3 eggs, beaten
¾ cup butter

Preheat oven to 250 degrees F. Cook grits slowly in boiling water until very thick. Add remaining ingredients and bake in a greased casserole for 1 hour.

Serves 8 to 10

HOMINY CASSEROLE

2 cans (15 ounces each) white
   or yellow hominy
1 can (10½ ounces) Cheddar
   cheese soup

1 can (4 ounces) chopped green
   chilies, drained
1 cup sour cream
1 cup grated Cheddar cheese

Preheat oven to 375 degrees F. Mix hominy, soup, chilies, and sour cream. Pour into casserole and bake for 30 minutes. Top with cheese and bake for 10 minutes more.

Serves 6

STUFFED MUSHROOMS

½ pound mushroom pieces,
   including stems from caps
3 tablespoons butter
2 large shallots, finely minced
Salt and pepper to taste
1 package (8 ounces) cream
   cheese

2 tablespoons fresh minced dill
   (less if dried dillweed is used)
2 tablespoons Parmesan cheese
12 to 16 large mushroom caps
2 tablespoons oil

Preheat broiler. Chop mushroom pieces. Sauté in butter with shallots until juice evaporates. Season with salt and pepper. Combine cream cheese, dill, Parmesan cheese, and mushroom mixture. Mix until well blended. Wipe outsides of mushroom caps lightly with oil. Stuff with cheese mixture and broil for 3 to 5 minutes. If you prefer a softer mushroom, bake at 350 degrees F. for 10 to 15 minutes.

Serves 4 to 6

JALAPEÑO POTATOES

8 medium boiling potatoes (about 4 pounds)	2 tablespoons flour
Salt and pepper to taste	2 cups milk
1 green bell pepper, chopped	1 roll (6 ounces) jalapeño cheese
8 green onions, chopped	1 roll (6 ounces) garlic cheese
1 cup butter melted	1 jar (4 ounces) pimientos, drained

Preheat oven to 350 degrees F. Boil potatoes in their jackets until just tender. Peel and slice. In a flat buttered 3-quart casserole, layer potato slices and season with salt and pepper. Sauté bell peppers and onions in ½ cup butter until tender. In saucepan, combine flour and ½ cup butter and stir until bubbly. Add milk and cheeses and stir over medium heat until cheese melts. Add onion mixture and pimientos and blend well. Pour over potatoes and bake for 45 minutes. This is best when assembled the day before.

Serves 12

HOT POTATO SALAD

6 to 8 medium potatoes, boiled and diced	Salt and pepper to taste
½ pound Velveeta cheese, cut up	2 strips uncooked bacon, cut in pieces
1 medium onion, chopped	Stuffed green olives, sliced (optional)
½ teaspoon dry mustard	Mushrooms, sliced (optional)
1 cup mayonnaise	

Preheat oven to 350 degrees F. Mix together potatoes, cheese, onion, mustard, mayonnaise, salt, and pepper, and put in a casserole. Top with bacon, olives, and mushrooms. Bake for 30 minutes. This may be prepared the day before and baked before serving.

Serves 6 to 8

POTATO PIE

1 pound cottage cheese
2 cups cooked mashed potatoes
½ cup sour cream
2 eggs
⅔ cup sliced green onions (tops only)

1 teaspoon salt
⅛ teaspoon cayenne
4 tablespoons freshly grated Parmesan cheese
1 10-inch unbaked pastry shell

Preheat oven to 425 degrees F. Blend cottage cheese in food processor until smooth. Add mashed potatoes and blend. Add sour cream, eggs, onions, salt, cayenne, and 3 tablespoons of the cheese, and blend thoroughly. Spoon into pastry shell and sprinkle with remaining cheese. Bake for 50 minutes until golden.

Serves 6 to 8

ROBERT'S AVOCADO PILAF

An excellent accompaniment to lamb.

8 tablespoons butter
4 tablespoons finely chopped onion
1 cup uncooked rice
4 tablespoons dry white wine
3 cups beef stock
Salt to taste
1¼ cups sliced fresh mushroom caps

½ teaspoon finely chopped garlic
2 tomatoes, peeled, seeded, and diced
¼ teaspoon dried oregano
Freshly ground black pepper
1 avocado
Lemon juice

Preheat oven to 400 degrees F. Melt half the butter in a heavy casserole. Add onion, and sauté for one minute. Add rice, and cook, stirring, over moderate heat for another minute. Pour in the wine and stock. Season to taste with salt and bring to a boil. Cover tightly and transfer to the oven. Bake for 18 minutes, stirring once with a fork halfway through the cooking time. Sauté mushrooms in 2 tablespoons of the butter for 3 minutes. Add garlic, tomatoes, and oregano. Season to taste with salt and pepper. Simmer for 5 minutes. Peel and dice avocado. Brush the pieces with lemon juice and add to the mushroom mixture. Toss rice gently with mushrooms and avocado and remaining 2 tablespoons of butter. Serve hot.

Serves 10 to 12

GREEN RICE

1 cup uncooked rice
1 cup sour cream
¼ cup salad oil
2 cloves garlic, crushed
¾ cup chopped fresh parsley
½ cup chopped onion
1 can (4 ounces) chopped green chilies, drained

½ teaspoon chili powder
1 teaspoon cumin powder
1 jalapeño pepper, seeded and chopped (optional)
2 cups grated sharp Cheddar cheese
1 cup grated Monterey Jack cheese

Preheat oven to 275 degrees F. Cook rice according to package directions. Add remaining ingredients, reserving a little Monterey Jack cheese for the top. Pour into a casserole and bake uncovered for 45 minutes or until hot.

Serves 10

RICE ORIENTAL

⅓ cup finely chopped onion
1 tablespoon butter
1 cup raw rice (Texmati or Nutty rice preferred)
2 teaspoons white raisins

½ cup blanched almonds
1½ cups chicken broth
Salt and freshly ground pepper to taste

Sauté onion in butter. Add rice, raisins, and almonds, and stir. Add broth, salt, and pepper, and bring to a boil. Simmer, covered, for 20 minutes until the rice is tender and liquid is absorbed. Doubles easily.

Serves 4

RICE PILAF

3 tablespoons butter	½ teaspoon white pepper
1 medium onion, chopped	Salt to taste
1 cup unconverted rice	4 tablespoons grated Parmesan
1 teaspoon saffron pistils	cheese
1 cup chicken broth	Toasted almonds
½ cup dry white wine	

Melt 2 tablespoons of the butter in a heavy pot and add onions. Cook and stir over a low heat for 5 minutes. Do not allow onion to brown. Add rice, and stir to coat with butter. Add saffron, broth, wine, pepper, and salt. Bring to a boil, stirring to avoid scorching. Reduce heat to low, cover, and cook slowly for about 25 minutes. Five minutes before serving, stir in cheese and remaining tablespoon of butter. Pack into well-buttered mold(s). Unmold onto a serving platter or individual plates. Sprinkle with toasted almonds.

Serves 4 to 5

RICE RING FILLED WITH MUSHROOMS

4½ cups water	1 teaspoon garlic salt
2 packages (6 ounces each) long-grain and wild rice	2 tablespoons cornstarch
	⅓ cup water
6 tablespoons butter or margarine	1 can (8 ounces) sliced water chestnuts, drained
1 pound fresh mushrooms, halved or quartered	1 jar (4 ounces) diced pimientos, drained
2 cups frozen small whole onions, thawed	Cherry tomatoes for garnish (optional)
⅓ cup dry sherry	Parsley for garnish (optional)

Combine water, rice, seasonings from package, and 2 tablespoons of the butter in a large saucepan. Bring to a boil, cover tightly, and cook over low heat until liquid is absorbed, about 25 minutes. While rice cooks, sauté mushrooms in remaining 4 tablespoons butter for 5 minutes, stirring occasionally. Stir in onions, sherry, and garlic salt. Bring to a boil, reduce heat, cover, and simmer for 5 minutes. Dissolve cornstarch in cold water and stir into mushroom mixture. Add water chestnuts, and cook, stirring constantly, until thick and glossy. Stir pimientos into rice. Spoon rice into a 6-cup ring mold and let stand for 2 to 3 minutes. Unmold onto a warm serving plate and fill center with mushroom mixture. Garnish with cherry tomatoes and parsley.

Serves 10 to 12

SKILLET RICE DRESSING

STOCK:

Heart, liver, neck, and gizzards
    from a turkey, hen or chicken
4 cups water
Tops and leaves from 1 bunch of
    celery

1½ cups chopped celery
1 large onion, quartered
1 bay leaf
Salt and pepper

DRESSING:

2 cups uncooked rice
4 cups water
1½ cups chopped onion
1½ cups chopped celery
¼ cup chopped fresh parsley
½ cup butter

Salt to taste
¼ teaspoon Lawry's Seasoned
    Pepper
1 cup cornbread crumbs
½ cup chopped pecans

STOCK: Cover the giblets with about 4 cups of water. Add the next five ingredients and simmer 1 to 1½ hours. Strain the stock, removing solids. Discard the vegetables. Chop the livers, gizzards, and heart, and remove the meat from the neck bone. Reserve for later use. Stock may be refrigerated overnight and the fat can then be removed from the top, along with lots of extra calories.

DRESSING: Cook the rice in 4 cups of boiling water. In a large heavy skillet, sauté the onion, celery, and parsley in the butter for 5 minutes. Add the rice and enough stock to make very moist, about 1½ cups. Add the reserved giblets if desired, and the salt and pepper. Stir and cook slowly, uncovered, until all of the stock is absorbed. Add more stock, about another 1½ cups, and continue cooking until most of the liquid is gone. Be sure to stir occasionally with a 2- to 3-tine fork to fluff and prevent scorching. Five minutes before serving, add the cornbread and pecans. Does not freeze.

Serves 6 to 8

WILD RICE EN CONSOMMÉ

¼ cup chopped onions
½ cup sliced fresh mushrooms
½ cup butter
2 cups wild rice
1 teaspoon salt

2 cups consommé
2 cups water
¾ cup chopped pimientos
½ cup chopped fresh parsley

In a 3-quart saucepan, briefly sauté onions and mushrooms in butter. Stir in the rice and salt. Add consommé and water. Simmer, covered, for 1 hour. Remove from heat and let rest, covered, for 15 minutes. Add pimientos and parsley, and serve. To be more economical, use 2 boxes Uncle Ben's Long Grain and Wild Rice. Do not use the seasoning packets; save them to jazz up white or brown rice at a later date!

Serves 8

HOPPING JOHN RELISH

1 tomato, chopped
½ onion, chopped
Oil and vinegar Italian dressing

Combine tomato and onion. Marinate in a little Italian dressing in the refrigerator while beans cook. Serve in a side dish for each person to use as topping. Serve with Red Beans and Rice.

Yield: 1 cup

RED BEANS AND RICE

1 bag (16 ounces) red kidney
    beans
2 large onions, chopped
3 celery stalks with leaves,
    chopped
1 green bell pepper, chopped
3 garlic cloves, chopped
2 bay leaves
1 ham bone, hock, *or* leftover
    ham pieces (about 2 cups of
    large pieces *or* 2 cups sliced
    sausage)

4 teaspoons salt
1½ teaspoons black pepper
½ teaspoon red pepper
1 teaspoon Tabasco
2 tablespoons Worcestershire
    sauce
Hopping John Relish (above)

Cover beans with water and soak overnight in the refrigerator; add more water if needed to keep beans covered. Drain the beans and put them in an iron Dutch oven or a heavy pot. Add the remaining ingredients and enough water to cover by about 2 inches. Cook slowly for about 2 hours, stirring occasionally. Adjust seasoning to your taste. Mash some of the beans to make gravy thicker and richer. Serve over rice with Hopping John Relish and cornbread. Freezes well.

Serves 8

SNOWPEAS AND MUSHROOMS

1 tablespoon butter or margarine
¾ pound fresh mushrooms,
    sliced
2 green onions, thinly sliced

1 can (8 ounces) sliced water
    chestnuts, drained
¾ pound fresh snowpeas
Pinch of ginger (optional)

In a heavy skillet, melt butter over medium heat. Sauté mushrooms, green onions, and water chestnuts until slightly tender. Add snowpeas, and continue to sauté mixture until peas turn bright green and are barely tender. Sprinkle with ginger if desired. *Be very careful not to overcook peas.* For a delicious entree, add 1½ pounds of raw, cleaned, and deveined shrimp when sautéing mushrooms, etc.

Serves 6 to 8 as a vegetable
or 4 as an entree

SPINACH CROQUETTES

2 pounds fresh spinach or 3
   packages (10 ounces each)
   frozen chopped spinach
6 ounces mozzarella cheese
6 ounces ham, cubed

2 eggs
Pepper to taste
Very fine cracker crumbs
Fat or oil

Wash and dry spinach. Cook spinach until wilted, drain thoroughly, and chop. Combine with cheese, ham, 1 of the eggs, and pepper. Form into croquettes and dip in 1 beaten egg. Roll in cracker crumbs and fry.

Serves 4

TOMATOES A QUESO

4 medium onions, thinly sliced
3 tablespoons butter
6 to 8 large tomatoes, thickly
   sliced
1 cup grated sharp Cheddar
   cheese
½ cup grated Monterey Jack
   cheese

1 cup fresh bread crumbs
Salt
1 teaspoon paprika
2 eggs, beaten
1 cup sour cream
Lawry's Seasoned Salt

Preheat oven to 375 degrees F. Sauté onions in butter for 5 minutes. Do not brown. In a greased deep 2-quart casserole, arrange a layer of tomatoes. Sprinkle with half of each kind of cheese and half of bread crumbs, onion, salt, and paprika. Repeat. Combine eggs and sour cream and pour over tomatoes. Sprinkle with Lawry's Seasoned Salt and paprika to add color. Bake, covered, for 30 minutes. Uncover and continue baking for 15 minutes more until brown. This can be assembled without the sour cream sauce the day before. Cover with sauce just before baking.

Serves 8 to 10

SPINACH STUFFED SQUASH

6 medium zucchini or baby
    yellow squash
1 cup fine soft bread crumbs
½ to ¾ cup cooked, drained,
    chopped spinach
½ cup grated Parmesan cheese
1 tablespoon minced onion

2 eggs, slightly beaten
2 tablespoons oil
¼ teaspoon thyme
Salt and pepper
Garlic salt to taste
Paprika

Preheat oven to 350 degrees F. Wash squash, cut off ends, and parboil in boiling salted water for 15 minutes. Drain and let cool. Cut in half lengthwise and scoop out pulp. Drain pulp thoroughly and mash. Combine pulp with next 8 ingredients, setting aside part of the cheese. Fill shells with this mixture. Place in greased shallow baking dish. Sprinkle tops with cheese, garlic salt, and paprika. Bake for 30 minutes.

Serves 10 to 12

YELLOW SQUASH CASSEROLE

4 to 5 pounds yellow squash,
    sliced
1 onion, chopped
1 teaspoon sugar
Salt and pepper to taste
1 cup water

3 packages (8 ounces each)
    cream cheese
4 tablespoons butter
Buttered bread crumbs for
    topping

Preheat oven to 350 degrees F. Combine squash, onion, sugar, salt, pepper, and water in large covered saucepan, and cook until vegetables are tender. Drain vegetables, reserving liquid. Mash well and drain again. Cream cheese with a little reserved liquid until it is the consistency of whipped cream. Add butter to squash and stir until melted. Pour squash into buttered shallow 3-quart casserole and cover with cream cheese mixture. Mix lightly with fork. Cover with bread crumbs and bake for 30 minutes until bubbly.

Serves 10 to 12

TOMATOES AND ARTICHOKES AU GRATIN

½ cup chopped onion
2 tablespoons shallots
½ cup butter
1 can (2 pounds, 3 ounces)
   whole tomatoes, drained
1 can (14 ounces) artichoke
   hearts, drained and quartered

½ teaspoon basil
1 tablespoon sugar
Salt and pepper to taste
Parmesan cheese

Preheat oven to 325 degrees F. Sauté onions and shallots in butter. Add tomatoes, artichokes, and basil, and heat, stirring, for 2 to 3 minutes. Season with sugar, salt, and pepper. Pour into a casserole and top with cheese. Bake until bubbly.

Serves 6

TOMATOES, DEVILED AND BROILED

3 large tomatoes, peeled and
   halved
Salt
6 tablespoons butter, softened
5 teaspoons Worcestershire sauce

1½ teaspoons vinegar pepper
   sauce
1 teaspoon dry mustard
1 teaspoon minced parsley
1 teaspoon grated onion

Sprinkle tomato halves with salt and place in an 8-inch-square Pyrex dish. Cream together all other ingredients. Spread mixture on tomatoes and broil 4 inches from the element, basting twice, for about 8 minutes.

Serves 6

TOMATO PIE

1 9-inch pie crust, unbaked
5 tomatoes, sliced
Salt and pepper to taste
½ teaspoon oregano
1 cup chopped green onions

2 cups grated, sharp Cheddar
   cheese
1 cup mayonnaise
½ cup freshly grated Parmesan
   cheese

Preheat oven to 400 degrees F. Prick pie crust and bake for 10 minutes. Remove from oven. Reduce oven temperature to 325 degrees F. Cover bottom of pie crust with two layers of tomato slices. Sprinkle with salt and pepper and half the oregano and onions. Repeat layers. Combine Cheddar cheese and mayonnaise and spread over pie. Top with Parmesan. Bake for 45 minutes.

Serves 6 to 8

MIXED VEGETABLE CASSEROLE

1 large package (20 ounces) frozen mixed vegetables *or* 1 package (10 ounces) peas plus 1 package (10 ounces) green beans
1 cup chopped celery

1 cup grated Cheddar cheese
1 cup mayonnaise
1 medium onion, chopped
½ cup margarine, melted
34 Ritz crackers, crumbled

Preheat oven to 350 degrees F. Cook vegetables and celery until tender, drain, and place in a greased casserole. Combine cheese, mayonnaise, and onion. Mix thoroughly and spread over vegetables. Combine margarine and crackers, and sprinkle over top. Bake for 30 minutes.

Serves 6 to 8

LANA'S YAMS

4 pounds unpeeled fresh yams *or* 3 cans (1 pound, 1 ounce, each) sweet potatoes
1 can (1 pound, 4 ounces) pie-sliced apples, drained
1 cup milk
¼ cup butter or margarine, melted

⅓ cup brown sugar
¼ cup molasses
3 eggs, slightly beaten
½ teaspoon cinnamon
½ teaspoon nutmeg
½ teaspoon grated orange rind
⅔ cup dark or golden raisins

Preheat oven to 325 degrees F. Put yams in enough water to cover them. Bring to boil, add lid, and cook about 25 minutes or until tender. Cool and peel. Beat yams and apples with electric mixer, gradually adding milk until smooth. Beat in all remaining ingredients except raisins. Stir in raisins and put in greased 2-quart casserole. Bake, uncovered, for 50 to 60 minutes.

Serves 6 to 8

YAMS WITH MAPLE SAUCE

2 cups brown sugar
4 tablespoons butter
2 cups canned crushed pineapple
½ teaspoon salt

1 teaspoon maple flavoring
1 cup chopped pecans
12 boiled yams, skinned and
halved lengthwise

Preheat oven to 350 degrees F. Boil sugar, butter, pineapple, and salt for 10 to 20 minutes until slightly thickened. Add maple flavoring and nuts. Place a layer of yams in shallow greased baking dish and cover with half the sauce. Repeat layers and bake for 20 to 30 minutes.

Serves 8 to 10

VEGETABLE PASTA SUPPER

1 jar (6 ounces) marinated
artichoke hearts
4 ounces thin noodles
1 small clove garlic, pressed
⅓ cup chopped onions
1 cup fresh sliced mushrooms
2 cups thinly sliced zucchini

½ cup freshly grated Romano
cheese
1 tablespoon butter
2 tablespoons finely chopped
parsley
Additional Romano cheese
(optional)

Have all ingredients at hand for quick cooking. Drain artichokes, reserving marinade and cut hearts into bite-size pieces. Cook noodles according to package directions, until barely tender. While the noodles cook, sauté garlic and onions in 2 tablespoons of the reserved marinade until soft but not brown. Add mushrooms, zucchini, and artichokes. Cook and stir over moderately high heat until tender-crisp, about 1 minute. Do not overcook.

Remove from heat and gently mix in ¼ cup of the cheese. Drain noodles well and toss with remaining marinade, butter, parsley, and remaining cheese. Serve on a heated platter with the vegetables alongside or toss both together. Serve with additional cheese.

Serves 3 to 4

ZUCCHINI CASSEROLE

2 pounds zucchini and/or yellow
  squash, thinly sliced
1 large onion, chopped
6 tablespoons butter
2 eggs

2 cups sour cream
¾ teaspoon seasoned salt
Salt to taste
¼ teaspoon pepper
2 ½ cups grated Parmesan cheese

Preheat oven to 400 degrees F. Cook squash in small amount of boiling water for 6 to 8 minutes or until tender. Drain *well* in colander. Sauté onion in 4 tablespoons of the butter until tender. Combine with squash, and place in a shallow 2-quart casserole. Beat together eggs, sour cream, salts, pepper, and half of the Parmesan. Pour over squash, dot with extra butter, and sprinkle with remaining cheese. Bake for 15 minutes or until set.

Serves 8

ZUCCHINI SQUARES

1 ½ cups sliced raw zucchini,
  unpeeled (about 2 medium
  zucchini)
½ cup Bisquick
2 eggs, well beaten

½ cup Parmesan cheese
½ cup chopped onion
½ cup butter or margarine,
  melted
½ teaspoon oregano

Preheat oven to 350 degrees F. Combine all ingredients and mix thoroughly. Spread mixture in 8 × 8-inch pan or quiche dish and bake for 30 to 45 minutes until golden brown on top. Cut into squares or wedges and serve. This is good when cut into small squares and served as an hors d'oeuvre.

Serves 8

STUFFED ZUCCHINI

3 medium zucchini
¼ cup finely minced onions
1½ tablespoons olive or
  vegetable oil
½ cup ground almonds
½ cup heavy cream
½ to ⅔ cup dry white bread
  crumbs

½ cup grated Swiss cheese
1 egg, beaten
Salt and pepper to taste
¼ teaspoon ground cloves
2 to 3 tablespoons butter, melted

Preheat oven to 400 degrees F. Trim and scrub zucchini. Place in salted boiling water for 10 minutes. Cut lengthwise and hollow out centers. Salt lightly and drain. Chop pulp from centers. Sauté onions in oil until tender. Stir in chopped zucchini and cook until tender. Remove from heat, scrape into bowl, and stir in almonds and cream. Stir in ⅓ cup of the bread crumbs, all but 3 tablespoons of the cheese, and the egg. Mixture should hold its shape. If it doesn't, add more bread crumbs. Add salt, pepper, and cloves. Arrange zucchini halves in well-buttered dish. Stuff with mixture and sprinkle with remaining bread crumbs and cheese. Dribble butter over top and bake in upper third of oven for 25 to 30 minutes until bubbling hot and brown on top.

Serves 4 to 6

CHAPTER XV

DESSERTS

Post Oak

What Fifth Avenue is to New York and Rodeo Drive to Beverly Hills, Post Oak Boulevard is to Houston. This is the place to buy anything from a mink Stetson or a pair of hand-stitched eel-skin cowboy boots to a flawless Ming vase or a chic little cocktail dress by Ungaro or Saint-Laurent. There are shops with terrific bargains and boutiques with window displays aimed at the wives of Texas oil tycoons, Saudi sheiks, and Latin American politicos.

Post Oak also has some of Houston's best and most interesting French, Austrian, and oriental restaurants and many of its most elegant and well-run hotels. Here you can have a late Continental supper or high tea at four; and in almost every shop, salespeople speak several languages. At many Post Oak stores, a third or more of the customers come from Latin America or the Middle East.

One thing that distinguishes Post Oak from its East and West Coast counterparts is the striking post-modernist architecture of Philip Johnson, Cesar Pelli, and I. M. Pei. Another is that you have to get around by car; you can't stroll down the boulevard, window-shopping as you go. The district is a string of shopping centers and malls, each its own separate and tempting world, linked by a broad strip of asphalt. You drive to one self-contained world, survey its wonders, then drive on to the next.

The largest of these malls is the all-but-overwhelming Galleria, inspired by Milan's famous shopping plaza and anchored by two of the state's premier specialty department stores, as well as branches of top stores from New York and Chicago. Linking these giants are scores of smaller shops, along with restaurants, movie theaters, two hotels, a bank, and a central ice-skating rink. In the Galleria and elsewhere along Post Oak Boulevard, the choices are so many and varied that some shoppers have to stop for a cup of coffee at a quiet cafe to clear their heads before approaching the difficult decisions ahead of them. It's one thing to go looking for a pair of simple shoes and to hope to find one or even two to choose from; it's another to be confronted with fifteen or even thirty. And then there are so many other lovely temptations so attractively displayed. "Can all this richness possibly be good for you?" some shoppers wonder as they contemplate their espresso or iced tea. Then they smile slightly and rephrase their thoughts: "Can it really be that bad?"

Desserts are like that, too, whether they're wheeled out on a cart at a posh Post Oak restaurant or collected as recipes in this chapter. You know you should ask for a slice of unadorned cantaloupe, but with marvels like Chocolate Intemperance, Frozen Brandy Alexander Pie, Texas Pecan Balls, Amaretto Mousse, Pecan Pie, Lotus Ice Cream, and Texas Gold Bars there for the taking, what can you do? Choice is hard enough; restraint is impossible.

ALMOND MACAROON CAKE

CAKE:
1 box angel food cake mix

FILLING:
1 cup butter   5 egg yolks
1 box (1 pound) powdered sugar   16 almond macaroons, crumbled
⅔ cup bourbon   1 cup slivered almonds, toasted

FROSTING:
1 pint whipping cream   3 to 4 tablespoons bourbon
½ cup powdered sugar   1 cup slivered almonds, toasted

CAKE: Prepare angel food cake according to package directions and refrigerate overnight. Next day, slice cake into four layers.
FILLING: Cream butter, sugar, and bourbon. Add egg yolks, one at a time, beating after each addition. Fold in macaroons and almonds. Spread mixture between layers. Refrigerate.
FROSTING: Whip cream with sugar, and add bourbon. Spread over cake and sprinkle with almonds. Refrigerate until 30 minutes before serving.

Serves 12 to 16

ANGEL FOOD DELIGHT

CAKE:
1 box angel food cake mix

FILLING:

3 cups chilled whipping cream   Pinch of salt
1½ cups powdered sugar   ⅓ cup toasted almonds
¾ cup cocoa   Whole almonds for garnish

CAKE: Prepare cake according to package directions.
FILLING: Combine all ingredients and whip until fairly thick. After cake has
cooled, slice off the top 2 to 2½ inches with a serrated knife. Set aside.
Make a trench 1½ inches deep in the bottom portion of the cake by cutting 2 concentric circles. Pull out bits of cake from center. Be careful not
to tear sides. Fill the trench with chocolate filling, replace top and cover
cake with remainder of filling. Top can be decorated with whole almonds.
Refrigerate 3 to 4 hours before serving. This must be served cold.

Serves 12 to 16

BUTTER PECAN CAKE

1⅓ cups chopped pecans   2 teaspoons baking powder
1½ cups butter   ½ teaspoon salt
2 cups sugar   1 cup milk
4 eggs   2 teaspoons vanilla
3 cups flour   Butter Pecan Frosting (below)

Preheat oven to 350 degrees F. Toast pecans in ¼ cup of the butter for 20
to 25 minutes in the oven. Stir now and then. Cream remaining 1¼ cups
butter with sugar. Add eggs and beat well. Add dry ingredients alternately
with milk. Add vanilla and pecans. Divide batter evenly in three greased
and floured 9-inch cake pans. Bake for 25 to 30 minutes. When cool,
remove from pan and frost between layers and on top with Butter Pecan
Frosting.

Serves 15 to 18

BUTTER PECAN FROSTING

¼ cup butter, softened
1 box (1 pound) powdered
   sugar, sifted
1 teaspoon vanilla

5 to 7 tablespoons evaporated
   milk or cream
⅔ cup toasted pecans

Combine all ingredients and mix well. Makes enough frosting for a 3-layer 9-inch cake.

CATHY'S ALMOND POUND CAKE

CAKE:
Thinly sliced almonds
½ cup butter
½ cup Crisco
2 cups sugar

6 eggs
2 cups flour, sifted
2 teaspoons almond extract

GLAZE:
1 cup sugar
¼ cup water
2 tablespoons almond extract

CAKE: Preheat oven to 325 degrees F. Generously grease large tube pan. Press almonds onto sides and bottom and set aside. Using mixer, cream together butter, Crisco, and sugar. Add eggs, one at a time, continuing to beat. Gradually add flour and almond extract. Beat at high speed until batter is fluffy. Pour into prepared pan. Bake for 1 hour.
GLAZE: Boil sugar and water for 1 minute. Remove from heat. Add almond extract. Pour over lukewarm cake. Leave cake in pan until it has cooled completely.

Serves 12 to 16

CHOCOLATE ANGEL FOOD CAKE

1 Duncan Hines Angel Food
  cake mix
¼ cup cocoa
¼ cup sugar

½ cup chopped walnuts
¼ cup chopped chocolate chips
White Mountain Icing (below)

Preheat oven and prepare pan according to package directions. Follow instructions for egg-mixture package. Before adding contents of flour package to beaten eggs, sift flour with cocoa and sugar. Then continue as directed. Before pouring batter into tube pan, fold in nuts and chips. Bake the cake at suggested temperature for 30 to 40 minutes until brown and dry on top. Cool, inverted, for 1½ hours. Frost with White Mountain Icing.

Serves 12 to 16

WHITE MOUNTAIN ICING

2 cups sugar
¾ cup water
2 tablespoons white Karo syrup

2 egg whites, beaten 2 minutes
2 tablespoons vanilla

Combine sugar, water, and Karo syrup, and bring to a boil. When mixture reaches 240 degrees, slowly add in a thin stream to fluffy egg whites. Continue beating about 2 minutes or until mixture is of spreading consistency. Add vanilla. Frost cake on top and sides and sprinkle top with a few chocolate chips. Makes enough frosting for top and sides of a large tube cake.

COCONUT POUND CAKE

1 cup margarine
⅔ cup Crisco
3 cups sugar
5 eggs, beaten
3 cups flour

1 teaspoon baking powder
1 cup milk
2 teaspoons coconut flavoring
1 can (3½ ounces) coconut

Preheat oven to 325 degrees F. Mix ingredients in order listed. Pour into a greased and floured 10-inch tube pan or two 9 × 5 × 3-inch loaf pans. Bake for 1 hour and 30 minutes.

Serves 16

COLONIAL HOLIDAY RING

CAKE:
1 cup butter
2 cups sugar
4 eggs, beaten
4 cups self-rising flour
1½ cups buttermilk

1 tablespoon grated orange rind
2 packages (8 ounces each)
    chopped dates
1 cup chopped pecans

ORANGE GLAZE:
2 cups sugar
1 cup orange juice
2 tablespoons grated fresh orange
    rind

¼ cup rum (optional)

CAKE: Preheat oven to 350 degrees F. Cream butter and sugar. Add beaten eggs and mix well. Sift flour and add to creamed mixture alternately with buttermilk. Add orange rind, dates, and pecans. Pour into a greased and floured 10-inch tube pan. Bake for 1 hour and 30 minutes or until it tests done.

GLAZE: Dissolve sugar in orange juice over medium heat. Do not boil. Add orange rind and rum. Remove cake from oven and punch holes all the way through the cake with an ice pick. Pour hot glaze over cake. If cake has not pulled away from the sides and tube, loosen with a knife so the glaze can run down the sides and center. Let cake stand in pan for several hours or overnight. It must be completely cool before removing from pan.

Serves 12 to 14

DOROTHY'S POPPY-SEED CAKE

CAKE:

⅓ cup poppy seeds
1 cup milk
⅔ cup butter
1½ cups sugar

2 cups cake flour
2½ teaspoons baking powder
1 teaspoon vanilla
4 egg whites

CUSTARD:

½ cup sugar
⅓ cup flour
¼ teaspoon salt
2 cups milk or cream, scalded

3 egg yolks
1 teaspoon vanilla
1 cup chopped almonds
1 tablespoon rum or sherry

CAKE: Preheat oven to 350 degrees F. Soak poppy seeds in ¾ cup of the milk for 2 hours. Cream butter and sugar. Sift flour and baking powder and add to butter and sugar. Combine ¼ cup milk and vanilla and add to mixture. Add poppy seeds and mix well. Fold in beaten egg whites. Bake in 2 greased and floured 9-inch layer pans for 20 to 25 minutes.

CUSTARD: Combine sugar, flour, and salt. Add milk. Pour over egg yolks and stir well over low flame until thick. Cool. Add vanilla, chopped almonds, and rum.

Assembly: Spread custard between two cooled cake layers. Ice with your favorite 7-minute icing.

Serves 10 to 12

FRESH APPLE CAKE

2 cups sugar
2 eggs
1¼ cups Wesson oil
1 teaspoon vanilla
1 teaspoon lemon juice

½ teaspoon salt
1½ teaspoons baking soda
3 cups flour
3 apples, peeled and chopped
1 cup nuts (optional)

Preheat oven to 325 degrees F. Grease and flour large tube pan. Combine sugar, eggs, oil, vanilla, lemon juice, salt, and baking soda. Add flour, apples, and nuts. Mix well. Pour into prepared pan. Bake in preheated oven for 1 hour and 15 minutes. Check after 1 hour. Cool on rack.

Serves 12 to 14

FRANKFURTER KRANZ
(GERMAN WREATH CAKE)

CAKE:
1 box Duncan Hines Butter
  Recipe cake mix

BUTTER CREAM FILLING:

¾ cup milk
4½ tablespoons flour

¾ cup butter
1¼ cups sugar

KROHART (NUT TOPPING):
1 teaspoon butter
2 tablespoons sugar
4 tablespoons chopped nuts

CAKE: Prepare cake according to package directions for a 2-layer cake.
BUTTER CREAM FILLING: Combine milk and flour. Cook until thick and let cool completely. Cream butter and gradually add sugar. Add cooled milk mixture. Beat until fluffy.
KROHART: Melt butter with sugar, stirring constantly, until mixture is slightly browned. Add nuts. Pour onto a greased platter or foil to cool. Break into small pieces. When cake has cooled, fill and frost layers with Butter Cream Filling and top with Krohart.

Serves 10 to 12

GRAN'S MAHOGANY CAKE

⅔ cup butter
2 cups sugar
3 egg yolks
4 heaping teaspoons cocoa
4 tablespoons hot water
1 teaspoon nutmeg
½ teaspoon ground cloves

½ teaspoon cinnamon
1 tablespoon vanilla
⅔ cup milk
2 cups flour
3 teaspoons baking powder
4 egg whites
Mocha Frosting (below)

Preheat oven to 350 degrees F. Cream butter and sugar. Add egg yolks. Blend cocoa and hot water and add to sugar mixture. Add spices, vanilla, and milk, and mix well. Add 1 cup of the flour. Combine remaining flour with baking powder, add to mixture, and blend thoroughly. Beat egg whites until they form stiff peaks, and fold into batter. Pour into two greased and floured 9-inch cake pans. Bake for 40 to 45 minutes. Cool, and frost with Mocha Frosting.

Serves 10 to 12

MOCHA FROSTING

1 box (1 pound) powdered
  sugar, sifted
¼ cup butter
1 egg yolk

2 tablespoons cocoa
3 tablespoons hot coffee
1 tablespoon vanilla

Cream sugar and butter. Add egg yolk. Blend cocoa and hot coffee and add to mixture. Add vanilla. Beat until spreadable.

Makes enough to ice a 9-inch 2-layer cake.

LUCY'S ITALIAN CREAM CAKE

½ cup margarine
½ cup vegetable shortening
2 cups sugar
5 eggs, separated
1 teaspoon baking soda
½ teaspoon salt
2 cups flour

1 cup buttermilk
1 teaspoon vanilla
1 can (3½ ounces) Angel Flake
  Coconut
1 cup chopped pecans
Cream Cheese Icing (below)

Preheat oven to 350 degrees F. Cream margarine, shortening, and sugar until light and fluffy. Add egg yolks one at a time; beat well. Sift dry ingredients together and add to creamed mixture alternately with buttermilk. Add vanilla, coconut, and pecans. Beat egg whites until stiff and fold into batter. Pour batter into three greased and floured 8-inch cake pans. Bake for 25 minutes. Invert onto wire racks, remove pans, and let cool. Frost with Cream Cheese Icing. Sprinkle pecans or coconut on top and sides.

Serves 15 to 18

CREAM CHEESE ICING

¼ cup margarine
1 package (8 ounces) cream
  cheese
1 box (1 pound) powdered sugar

1 teaspoon vanilla
Chopped pecans or coconut
  (optional)

Cream margarine and cream cheese until smooth. Add sugar, and beat. Stir in vanilla. Mix in pecans or coconut if desired.

Makes enough to ice an 8-inch 3-layer cake.

TREASURED GINGERBREAD

2 cups flour
1 box (1 pound) dark brown
  sugar
¾ cup margarine, softened
2 teaspoons cinnamon

1 teaspoon baking soda
1 teaspoon nutmeg
½ teaspoon ginger
2 eggs
1 cup buttermilk

Preheat oven to 350 degrees F. Combine flour and sugar. Cut in margarine. Reserve 1 cup of this mixture for topping. Add cinnamon, soda, nutmeg, and ginger to remaining flour mixture. Stir in eggs and buttermilk. (Do not use electric mixer.) Pour batter into ungreased 9 × 13-inch pan. Sprinkle the reserved topping over batter and bake in preheated oven for 45 minutes or until done.

Serves 10 to 12

CHEESECAKE COOKIES

⅓ cup butter or margarine
⅓ cup brown sugar
1 cup flour
½ cup chopped nuts
¼ cup sugar
1 package (8 ounces) cream
  cheese

1 egg
1 tablespoon lemon juice
2 tablespoons milk
½ teaspoon vanilla

Preheat oven to 350 degrees F. Cream butter and brown sugar until light and fluffy. Add flour and nuts; blend until mixture resembles crumbs. Set aside 1 cup of mixture. Press remainder into 8 × 8-inch pan. Bake for 12 to 15 minutes. Let cool. Beat sugar and cream cheese until smooth. Add remaining ingredients and beat well. Spread over crust. Sprinkle reserved crumbs on top, pressing down lightly with fingers. Bake for 25 minutes, cool, and cut into bars. Store in refrigerator.

Yield: 25 to 36 bars

CARAMEL BROWNIES

1 package (14 ounces) caramels
⅔ cup evaporated milk
1 package (17½ ounces) German chocolate cake mix

¾ cup margarine, melted
1 cup chopped pecans
1 cup semi-sweet chocolate chips

Preheat oven to 350 degrees F. Cook caramels and ⅓ cup of the milk in a large saucepan over low heat; stir constantly until caramels are melted. Set aside. Combine cake mix, margarine, remaining milk, and nuts. Stir by hand until it holds together. Press half of the dough into a greased 13 × 9-inch pan. Bake for 6 minutes. Remove from oven and sprinkle with chocolate chips. Spread caramel mixture over chocolate chips. Crumble and press the remaining dough over the top. Return to oven and bake for 15 to 18 minutes. Cool slightly. Refrigerate for 30 minutes to set caramel layer.

Yield: 48 brownies

BLACK-EYED SUSAN COOKIES

COOKIES:
2 cups butter or margarine
6 tablespoons sugar
1 tablespoon almond extract

4 cups flour
1 teaspoon salt

ICING:
1 package (6 ounces) semi-sweet chocolate chips
2 tablespoons butter

3 tablespoons milk
1 cup sifted powdered sugar
Almonds for garnish

COOKIES: Preheat oven to 400 degrees F. Cream butter. Add remaining ingredients and mix well. Roll into small balls and place on ungreased cookie sheet. (This is easier if dough is chilled slightly.) Flatten slightly. Bake for 10 to 12 minutes.

ICING: Combine chocolate chips, butter and milk in pan. Stir over low heat until chocolate is just melted. Remove, and stir in sugar. Beat until smooth, glossy, and easy to spread. If not glossy, stir in a few drops of hot water. Top each cookie with icing and an almond half.

Yield: 125 2-inch cookies

DOUBLE-FROSTED BROWNIES

FIRST LAYER:

2½ ounces unsweetened
  chocolate
½ cup butter
2 eggs
1 cup sugar

½ cup flour
¼ teaspoon salt
1 teaspoon vanilla
½ cup chopped pecans

SECOND LAYER:

½ cup butter
3 tablespoons milk
2 tablespoons vanilla instant
  pudding mix

2¼ to 2½ cups powdered sugar

THIRD LAYER:

1 package (6 ounces) semi-sweet
  chocolate chips

1½ tablespoons butter
3 tablespoons water

FIRST LAYER: Preheat oven to 350 degrees F. Melt chocolate and butter together. Beat eggs, add sugar, and mix well. Stir into chocolate and butter. Mix flour and salt; blend into chocolate mixture. Add vanilla and nuts. Spread in a greased 11 × 7-inch Pyrex dish. Bake for 22 minutes. Let cool.

SECOND LAYER: Cream butter. Combine milk and pudding mix, and add to butter. Gradually stir in powdered sugar. Spread on top of brownie. Refrigerate until firm.

THIRD LAYER: Melt chocolate chips in butter and water over very low heat. When slightly cool, spread over top and refrigerate.

Yield: 35 to 40 brownies

DATE NUT BALLS

¾ cup butter
1 cup sugar
1 package (8 ounces) chopped
  dates

1 cup chopped pecans
1 teaspoon vanilla
2 heaping cups Rice Krispies
Powdered sugar or coconut

If dates are already sugared, reduce sugar by 2 tablespoons. Melt butter in a saucepan. Add sugar and dates. Cook, stirring constantly, until mixture forms a soft ball when dropped in cool water. This takes about 5 minutes. Remove from heat, and add pecans and vanilla. Combine with Rice Krispies, and mix well. Spread mixture on wax paper and allow to cool. Shape into small balls and roll in powdered sugar or coconut. Store in tightly covered tin or freeze.

Yield: 4½ dozen

CHEWY BROWN SUGAR COOKIES

½ cup butter
2 cups brown sugar
2 eggs
1 teaspoon vanilla

1 cup flour
¼ teaspoon salt
1 cup chopped pecans or walnuts

Preheat oven to 350 degrees F. Cream butter and sugar. Add eggs, one at a time, beating well. Add vanilla. Sift flour with salt and add to butter mixture. Add half of the nuts. Spread in a greased but not floured 9 × 13-inch pan. Spread batter fairly thin. Sprinkle with remaining nuts. Bake for 30 minutes. Cut while hot, but leave in pan to cool.

Yield: 48 cookies

GRAPE-NUTS COOKIES

3⅓ sticks margarine
1½ cups sugar
3⅓ cups unsifted all-purpose
  flour

¼ teaspoon salt
1 teaspoon vanilla
½ to ¾ cup Grape-Nuts

Preheat oven to 375 degrees F. Mix all ingredients with electric mixer. Press dough into balls (about 1 teaspoon) and place on an ungreased cookie sheet. Bake for 8 to 10 minutes or until golden brown. Cool.

Yield: 100 2-inch cookies

COWBOY COOKIES

1 cup unsalted butter or
    margarine
½ cup sugar
1½ cups brown sugar
2 eggs
1½ teaspoons vanilla

1¼ cups flour
1 teaspoon baking soda
1 teaspoon salt
3¼ cups oatmeal
1 cup chopped nuts
1 cup chocolate chips

Preheat oven to 350 degrees F. Cream butter and sugars. Add eggs and mix well. Add remaining ingredients. Drop teaspoon-size balls on a well-greased cookie sheet. Bake for 13 to 15 minutes.

Yield: 6 dozen

FUDGE CAKE

This rich finger food is more like a brownie than a cake.

1½ cups margarine
6 squares unsweetened chocolate
3 cups sugar
6 eggs

1½ cups flour
1½ teaspoons baking powder
2 tablespoons vanilla
1 cup pecans

Preheat oven to 350 degrees F. Melt margarine, chocolate, and sugar in double boiler over low heat. Transfer to a large mixing bowl. Drop in eggs and beat well. Add flour and baking powder; beat. Mix in vanilla and nuts. Pour into two greased and floured 7 × 10-inch pans. Bake for 40 to 50 minutes or until cake tests done with a toothpick.

Serves 12 to 16

LEMON DROP COOKIES

This is a chewy cookie with a crunch.

½ cup butter	1½ cups sifted flour
¾ cup sugar	1 teaspoon baking powder
1 egg	¼ teaspoon salt
1 teaspoon lemon peel	½ cup crushed fine lemon drop
1 tablespoon light cream	candy (6½-ounce package)

Preheat oven to 350 degrees F. Cream butter and sugar until very light and fluffy. Add egg; beat well. Blend in lemon peel and cream. Sift together flour, baking powder, and salt. Stir in candy and blend into creamed mixture. Drop by teaspoonfuls onto lightly greased cookie sheet. Bake for 10 minutes or until golden brown. Let cool slightly before removing from pan.

Yield: 3 dozen cookies

LEMON PECAN SLICES

FIRST LAYER:
1 cup all-purpose flour
½ cup butter

SECOND LAYER:

2 eggs, beaten	1 cup chopped pecans
½ cup light brown sugar	2 tablespoons flour
½ cup grated coconut	½ teaspoon baking powder
1 teaspoon vanilla	½ teaspoon salt

THIRD LAYER:
1½ cups powdered sugar
Lemon juice

Preheat oven to 350 degrees F.
FIRST LAYER: Combine flour and butter and spread evenly in a 9 × 13-inch pan. Bake for 12 minutes.
SECOND LAYER: Mix together all ingredients for second layer. Spread mixture over baked layer and bake for 20 minutes. Cool.

THIRD LAYER: Combine powdered sugar with enough lemon juice to reach spreading consistency. Frost cake and cut into squares.

Yield: 24 to 30 squares

MELTING MOMENTS

This dough may be formed into long rolls and frozen. When ready to bake, slice off desired amount and dip in sugar.

½ cup cornstarch
½ cup powdered sugar
1 cup flour, sifted

¾ cup butter or margarine,
   softened
Granulated sugar

Preheat oven to 350 degrees F. Mix cornstarch, powdered sugar, and flour. Blend in butter. Refrigerate for one hour. Form into 1-inch balls and roll in sugar, coating well. Place on an ungreased cookie sheet. Flatten with a cookie stamp or the bottom of a glass. Bake for 15 to 20 minutes.

Yield: 3 dozen

ORANGE SLICE COOKIES

When stored in an airtight container, these will be chewier the second day.

2 cups (12-ounce package)
   candied orange slices
1 cup sugar
1 cup brown sugar, packed
1 cup shortening
2 eggs
1 teaspoon vanilla

2 cups all-purpose flour
1 teaspoon baking powder
1 teaspoon baking soda
½ teaspoon salt
2 cups quick-cooking rolled oats
1 cup flaked coconut
Extra sugar

Preheat oven to 350 degrees F. Snip candied orange slices into small pieces using kitchen scissors that have been dipped in hot water. Set aside. Cream together sugars and shortening until fluffy. Add eggs and vanilla. Beat well. Combine flour, baking powder, baking soda, and salt. Stir gradually into creamed mixture. Add oats, candied orange pieces, and coconut. Mix thoroughly. Shape into 1-inch balls, roll in sugar, and place on greased cookie sheet about 2 inches apart. Bake for 10 to 12 minutes or until lightly browned. Remove and cool on wire rack.

Yield: 6 dozen

PARTY COOKIES

1 cup butter
1 cup brown sugar
1 egg yolk
2 cups flour

1 teaspoon vanilla
5 or 6 (1 ounce each)
  milk-chocolate bars
1 cup nuts, chopped

Preheat oven to 350 degrees F. Cream butter and sugar. Add egg yolk, flour, and vanilla. Spread about ¼ inch thick on greased 10 × 15-inch jelly-roll pan. Bake for 20 to 25 minutes. Remove from oven and cover with chocolate bars. Spread chocolate over dough as it melts. Sprinkle with nuts. Cut while warm.

Yield: 72 squares

PEANUT BUTTER SOMBREROS

1 ¾ cups flour
½ teaspoon salt
½ cup peanut butter
2 tablespoons milk
½ cup brown sugar, packed
½ cup sugar
1 teaspoon baking soda

1 egg
1 teaspoon vanilla
½ cup shortening
Extra sugar
4 dozen chocolate kisses,
  unwrapped and chilled

Preheat oven to 375 degrees F. Combine all ingredients except extra sugar and chocolate kisses. Beat at slow speed with electric mixer until mixed. Shape into small balls and roll in extra sugar. Bake on ungreased cookie sheet for 10 to 12 minutes. Remove from oven and immediately press a chocolate kiss into center of each cookie. Remove to wire rack and cool.

Yield: 4 dozen cookies

SAND TARTS

1 cup butter
¼ cup powdered sugar
2 teaspoons vanilla

1 tablespoon water
2 cups flour
1 cup coarsely chopped nuts

Preheat oven to 300 degrees F. Cream butter and sugar. Add vanilla and water. Gradually add flour, mixing thoroughly. Add nuts. Mix. Shape into small rolls about 1½ inches long. Bake on ungreased cookie sheet for 20 minutes or until light brown. While still hot, roll in powdered sugar.

Yield: About 3 dozen cookies

SUPER CRUNCH COOKIES

1 cup unsalted butter
1 cup sugar
1 cup brown sugar, packed
1 egg
1 cup salad oil
1 cup rolled oats
1 cup crushed cornflakes

½ cup shredded coconut
½ cup chopped pecans or
   walnuts
3½ cups all-purpose flour, sifted
1 teaspoon baking soda
1 teaspoon salt
1 teaspoon vanilla

Preheat oven to 325 degrees F. Cream butter and sugars until fluffy. Add egg and salad oil. Mix. Add oats, cornflakes, coconut, and nuts. Mix well. Blend in remaining ingredients. Form into small balls, place on an ungreased cookie sheet, and flatten with a fork dipped in water. Bake for 12 minutes. Cool slightly before removing to wire rack.

Yield: 6 to 9 dozen cookies

TEXAS GOLD BARS

1 package yellow cake mix
   (plain, without pudding)
1 egg, slightly beaten
½ cup margarine, melted
1 tablespoon vanilla

1 package (8 ounces) cream
   cheese
1 pound powdered sugar
2 eggs, slightly beaten

Preheat oven to 325 degrees F. Combine cake mix, 1 egg, and melted margarine. Press into an ungreased 9 × 13-inch Pyrex pan. (Do not use a metal pan.) Mix remaining ingredients and spread over top. Bake for 50 minutes. Let cool slightly before cutting into bars.

Yield: 48 bars

TOFFEE CHOCOLATE SQUARES

24 double graham crackers
1 cup butter
1 cup dark brown sugar

12 ounces milk chocolate chips
1 cup finely chopped pecans

Preheat oven to 400 degrees F. Line a 10 × 15-inch jelly-roll pan with foil. Separate graham crackers and place side by side to cover foil. Combine butter and sugar, and simmer for 3 minutes or until mixture starts to thicken. Pour hot mixture quickly over graham crackers. Bake for 5 minutes. Remove from oven and sprinkle on chocolate chips, spreading to cover evenly as chips melt. Sprinkle with pecans. Cool and cut into squares.

Yield: About 75 squares

TRULY DIFFERENT CHOCOLATE CUPCAKES

These cupcakes taste even better than brownies and don't have to be frosted.

4 squares semi-sweet chocolate
1 cup margarine
¼ teaspoon butter flavoring
1½ cups chopped nuts

1¾ cups sugar
1 cup flour
4 extra-large eggs
1 teaspoon vanilla

Preheat oven to 325 degrees F. Melt chocolate and margarine in a heavy pan. Add butter flavoring and nuts. Stir until blended. In a large bowl, combine sugar, flour, eggs, and vanilla. Mix until well blended. *Do not beat.* Add chocolate mixture and stir until blended thoroughly. Spoon batter into muffin pans lined with paper baking cups. Fill each cup half full. Bake in preheated oven for 35 minutes or until done.

Yield: 24 cupcakes

CREAMY MILK CHOCOLATE FROSTING

¼ cup Crisco, melted
⅓ cup cocoa
¼ teaspoon salt
⅓ cup milk

1½ teaspoons vanilla
1 box (1 pound) powdered
    sugar, sifted

Combine Crisco, cocoa, and salt. Stir in milk and vanilla. Mix in sugar in three parts. Stir until smooth and creamy. If frosting becomes too thin, add more sugar; if too thick, add more milk. This makes enough frosting for two 9-inch layers or one 9 × 13-inch sheet cake.

CISSY'S CINNAMON ICE CREAM

3½ cups sugar
¾ cup water
2 tablespoons cinnamon
4 eggs
6 cups milk, scalded

Dash salt
3 cups half-and-half
1 cup heavy cream
4 teaspoons vanilla

Mix 2 cups of the sugar, water, and cinnamon. Set aside. In heavy saucepan, beat eggs and 1½ cups sugar until well mixed. Add milk and salt. Stir over low heat until custard coats a spoon. Remove from heat and stir in cinnamon syrup. Cool *completely*. Add half-and-half, heavy cream, and vanilla. Freeze in ice cream freezer. Serve with hot apple pie.

Yield: 5 quarts

CRANBERRY ICE CREAM

A tart ice cream to be served with the meal but also good as a dessert.

1 pint fresh cranberries
Water
1 cup sugar

Juice of 1 lemon
1½ cups whipping cream,
    whipped

Cover cranberries with water and cook until skins pop open. Strain immediately and add sugar to hot juice. When cool, add lemon juice and whipped cream. Freeze in small portions in individual glasses or in ice cream freezer.

Serves 8 to 10

ENGLISH TOFFEE ICE CREAM

4 bars (1 ounce each)
   chocolate-covered toffee
1 can (14 ounces) sweetened
   condensed milk

½ cup strong coffee, cooled
2 cups whipping cream
1 ½ teaspoons vanilla

Place toffee bars between two pieces of wax paper and crush with rolling pin. Set aside. Combine condensed milk, coffee, whipping cream, and vanilla. Chill well. Whip mixture until consistency of custard, 5 to 10 minutes. Fold in crushed toffee. Spoon into refrigerator trays or shallow Pyrex dish, and freeze. After 1 hour, stir to redistribute toffee.

Serves 6 to 8

LOTUS ICE CREAM

Juice of 4 lemons
1 tablespoon grated lemon rind
2 cups sugar
Boiling water
3 eggs

2 cups milk, scalded and cooled
1 teaspoon almond extract
¼ cup finely ground almonds
1 quart heavy cream

Combine juice, rind, and 1 cup of the sugar. Add enough boiling water to cover. Stir until sugar is dissolved, and set aside. Beat remaining cup of sugar with eggs until light. Slowly add scalded milk, and cook in double boiler until thick and smooth. Strain into another bowl and cool. Stir in almond extract and ground almonds. Add lemon mixture and blend thoroughly. Add cream and freeze in ice cream freezer.

Yield: 2 quarts

PEACH SHERBET

Juice of 3 oranges (1½ cups)
Juice of 3 lemons (9
  tablespoons)
3 cups sugar

4 peaches, puréed
2 pints half-and-half
About 3 cups milk to make ¾
  gallon of sherbet mix

Mix all ingredients together and freeze in ice cream freezer.

Yield: 1 gallon

PEPPERMINT ICE CREAM

6 eggs, beaten until frothy
1 can (14 ounces) Eagle Brand
  milk
1½ cups sugar

4 pints half-and-half
1 teaspoon vanilla
1½ cups crushed peppermint
  pieces or sticks

Mix together all ingredients except peppermint. Freeze in ice cream freezer until half frozen. Add peppermint and continue to freeze until hard.

Yield: 2½ quarts

SIX THREES ICE CREAM

3 cups milk
3 cups heavy cream
3 cups sugar
Juice of 3 lemons (9
  tablespoons)

Juice of 3 oranges (1½ cups)
3 bananas, mashed

Combine milk, cream, and sugar. Freeze in ice cream freezer until mushy. Add remaining ingredients. Mix well and complete freezing.

Yield: 1 gallon

TEXAS PECAN BALLS

1 pint vanilla ice cream
1 cup toasted pecans, coarsely
   chopped

1 cup Karen Kelsey's Hot Fudge
   Sauce (below) *or*
   Butterscotch Sauce (below)

Form ice cream into balls. Roll in pecans, pushing pecans into ice cream with hands. Freeze on a pan lined with foil or wax paper. When ready to serve, cover each pecan ball with heated sauce.

Serves 2 to 4

KAREN KELSEY'S HOT FUDGE SAUCE

½ cup butter
4 ounces unsweetened chocolate
3 to 3¼ cups sugar

1 can (13 ounces) evaporated
   milk

Melt butter and chocolate in top of double boiler over hot water. Gradually add sugar and half the milk alternately, stirring well after each addition. Add remaining milk, stirring constantly. Cook till mixture is thick and sugar is dissolved, about 10 minutes. Store in glass jar in refrigerator.

Yield: Approximately 4 cups

BUTTERSCOTCH SAUCE

1 cup brown sugar
⅓ cup melted butter
⅓ cup heavy cream

In a saucepan, mix brown sugar, melted butter, and cream. Boil 5 minutes without stirring. Remove from heat and beat for 30 seconds. Serve warm.

Yield: Approximately 1 cup

BAVARIAN CRÈME

This is complicated but worth the effort.

Vegetable oil
2 envelopes unflavored gelatin
⅓ cup water
3 cups milk
1 vanilla bean
5 egg yolks

1½ cups sugar
3 cups heavy cream
Crème Anglaise (below)
Chocolate-covered almonds or
    candied violets for garnish

Brush inside of a 2½-quart mold, or 2 smaller molds, with oil. Wipe excess with paper towel. Soften gelatin in water and dissolve over simmering water. In a 3-quart saucepan, over moderate heat, bring to a boil milk with vanilla bean in it. Cover and set aside to cool. Beat egg yolks in a large mixing bowl until lemon-colored. Stir in sugar, and beat until mixture forms ribbons. Remove vanilla bean from milk and reserve. While whisking constantly, pour the milk into the egg mixture in a slow, thin stream. When thoroughly blended, put into double boiler and cook until custard thickens enough to coat a wooden spoon. Add dissolved gelatin and stir with whisk until completely absorbed (1 to 2 minutes). If lumps form, strain custard through a fine sieve. Pour custard into a large bowl. Whip cream in a large chilled bowl to form almost stiff peaks. Set bowl of custard in a larger bowl filled with ice cubes and stir until barely cool. Do not let it chill enough to become lumpy. Remove from ice and stir in ¼ of the whipped cream. Using a rubber spatula, fold in remaining whipped cream. Pour mixture into oiled molds and smooth the top. Cover with plastic and refrigerate overnight. To serve, run knife around top edge of mold and dip mold into a bowl of warm water. Dry outside of mold and invert on plate. Spoon Crème Anglaise around the base of Bavarian and decorate, if desired, with piped chocolate and chocolate-covered almonds.

Serves 16 to 20

CRÈME ANGLAISE

2 cups milk
1 vanilla bean (may use previous
    one)
4 egg yolks

½ cup sugar
4 teaspoons cornstarch
¼ cup almonds, toasted and
    chopped

Combine milk and vanilla bean in saucepan. Bring to a boil, remove from heat, cover, and set aside. Beat egg yolks and sugar until mixture forms a ribbon. Remove vanilla bean from milk. Mix a small amount of milk with cornstarch to dissolve. Pour remaining milk gradually into yolks, whisking vigorously. Add dissolved cornstarch, whisking until thoroughly blended. Return mixture to saucepan and stir over low heat until it thickens slightly. Strain into a bowl. Stir in chopped almonds and cool to room temperature. Cover tightly and refrigerate until ready to use.

Yield: 2½ cups

CHOCOLATE MOUSSE CAKE

1 package (8 ounces) semi-sweet chocolate
6 eggs, separated, room temperature
2 teaspoons vanilla
2 tablespoons orange juice
2 tablespoons Grand Marnier
1 package (8½ ounces) chocolate wafers
½ cup whipping cream, whipped

Melt 7 chocolate squares in double boiler over hot water. Remove from heat. Using a rubber spatula, stir egg yolks into chocolate until well blended. Add vanilla. Beat egg whites until stiff. Gently fold egg whites into chocolate mixture and set aside. Combine orange juice and Grand Marnier. Layer bottom of springform pan with chocolate wafers. Brush wafers with orange-juice mixture until moist. Spoon half the chocolate mixture into pan. Add another layer of wafers, moisten with juice, and top with remaining chocolate mixture. Cover pan with foil and refrigerate for at least 5 hours or until set. When ready to serve, loosen cake from sides of pan with spatula dipped in warm water. Remove sides of pan very carefully. Coarsely grate remaining chocolate square and press onto sides of cake. Serve with whipped cream. Use pastry bag to make whipped-cream rosettes.

Serves 10 to 12

CHOCOLATE INTEMPERANCE

BATTER:

1 package (23 ounces) brownie
    mix
2 tablespoons water
3 eggs

1 teaspoon vanilla
Filling (below)
Chocolate Glaze (below)

FILLING:

1½ pounds semi-sweet chocolate
½ cup strong prepared coffee
3 eggs, separated

½ cup Kahlua
⅓ cup sugar
½ cup whipping cream, whipped

CHOCOLATE GLAZE:

½ pound semi-sweet chocolate
⅓ cup water

BATTER: Preheat oven to 350 degrees F. Using a paper towel, lightly oil an 11 × 15-inch jelly-roll pan and line it with wax paper. Lightly oil and flour wax paper. Shake off excess flour. Blend brownie mix, water, eggs, and vanilla on medium speed of electric mixer until batter is smooth. Spread batter evenly in pan and bake 10 minutes. Turn cake onto wire rack to cool, and peel off wax paper. Lightly oil an 8-inch springform pan and line with the cooled cake. (Optional: Cut rounds of cake to fit top and bottom of mold. Cut strip for sides. Place one round at bottom of mold. Place strips around inside of mold, pressing sides if necessary to cover completely.) Spoon filling into mold. Fit larger round of cake on top (or cover top of mold with cake). Chill for three or four hours until firm. Unmold, and cover top of cake with Chocolate Glaze. Allow Glaze to drizzle down sides. Chill, and serve in thin slices.

FILLING: Melt chocolate with coffee on top of double boiler and remove from heat. Beat egg yolks until pale yellow and stir into chocolate. Gradually stir in Kahlua. Allow to cool. In a separate bowl, beat egg whites, gradually adding sugar, until stiff. Gently fold whipped cream into cooled chocolate mixture. Fold in egg whites.

CHOCOLATE GLAZE: Melt chocolate with water in double boiler over simmering water, and stir until smooth.

Serves 12 to 14

CHOCOLATE CHARLOTTE RUSSE

2 packages ladyfingers
4 squares unsweetened chocolate
¾ cup sugar
⅓ cup milk
6 eggs, separated
1½ cups unsalted butter

1½ cups powdered sugar
1½ teaspoons vanilla
⅛ teaspoon salt
1 cup whipping cream, whipped
Shaved unsweetened chocolate

Line sides and bottom of a 9-inch springform pan with ladyfingers. If necessary, trim one end so the scalloped end just reaches top of pan. Melt chocolate in double boiler over hot, not boiling, water. Combine sugar, milk, and egg yolks, and add to chocolate. Cook over medium heat, stirring constantly, until mixture is smooth and thick. Cool. Cream butter with ¾ cup of the powdered sugar. Stir into chocolate mixture and beat well. Add vanilla. Beat egg whites and salt until stiff. Gradually beat in remaining powdered sugar. Fold gently into chocolate mixture. Spoon into prepared pan and chill. Remove sides of pan and garnish with dollops of whipped cream and shaved chocolate before serving. This dessert can be frozen before adding the whipped cream.

Serves 12

EGGNOG CAKE

3 dozen ladyfingers
1 cup butter
1 box (1 pound) powdered sugar
5 eggs, separated

5 tablespoons bourbon
1 cup chopped pecans
½ pint whipping cream,
    whipped

Line bottom and sides of springform pan with ladyfingers. Cream butter and sugar. Beat egg yolks and add to sugar mixture. Add bourbon and mix well. Beat egg whites until stiff but not dry. Gently fold egg whites into mixture. Fold in pecans. Carefully turn mixture into prepared pan and refrigerate overnight. To serve, remove sides of pan and ice cake with whipped cream.

Serves 10 to 12

SUMMERHOUSE FANTASTIC FUDGE PUDDING

This is a chocolate lover's fantasy.

4 cups sugar
1 cup all-purpose flour
1 cup cocoa
8 large eggs

2 cups butter, melted
4 teaspoons vanilla
2 cups chopped pecans

Preheat oven to 300 degrees F. Sift together sugar, flour, and cocoa. Beat eggs in large mixing bowl. Add dry ingredients, butter, and vanilla. Mix well. Stir in pecans and pour into 3-quart Pyrex dish. Place in water bath and bake on oven shelf at lowest level for 1 hour and 20 minutes. *Do not overbake.* Remove from water bath and cool completely on wire rack. Top becomes crusty as pudding cools. For a delicious rich treat, top with coffee ice cream.

Serves 16

CHOCOLATE SUPER SPEEDER

1 pint heavy cream
1¼ cups Hershey's chocolate
  syrup

3 tablespoons rum
Walnuts and grated bitter
  chocolate for garnish

Whip cream. Fold in chocolate syrup and rum. Freeze. Top with walnuts and grated bitter chocolate.

Serves 8

FROSTY GREEN GRAPES

This is delicious with almost any fresh fruit.

3 cups seedless or Tokay grapes
Crème de cacao

½ cup sour cream
Brown sugar

Wash, halve, and thoroughly drain grapes. Several hours before serving, pour crème de cacao over grapes and refrigerate until very cold. Just before serving, drain grapes and reserve liqueur. Combine grapes and sour cream and spoon into dessert dishes. Sprinkle with brown sugar. Pour a little reserved liqueur over each serving, if desired.

Serves 4 to 6

L'ORANGE DE MENTHE

6 navel oranges	4 cloves
½ cup sugar	2 tablespoons white crème de
½ cup water	menthe
1½ cups dry white wine	2 tablespoons cognac
4 thin slices lemon	Fresh mint for garnish
1 cinnamon stick (3 inches)	

Peel and cut oranges into clean slices, eliminating all membranes. Place in a shallow bowl. In a saucepan, heat sugar and water until sugar dissolves. Add wine, lemon slices, cinnamon stick, and cloves. Bring to a boil and simmer for 15 minutes. Remove from heat and mix in crème de menthe and cognac. Pour over orange slices. Cover and chill for at least 3 hours. Serve in individual dishes and garnish with a sprig of mint.

Serves 6 to 8

MACAROON DESSERT

2 dozen almond macaroons, crumbled	6 tablespoons rum, preferably dark
1 package (3 to 4 ounces) chopped almonds, lightly toasted	½ gallon best quality vanilla ice cream, softened

Combine all ingredients and spoon into individual ramekins or serving dishes. Freeze.

Serves 12 to 14

DANCY'S GRAND MARNIER SAUCE

For fresh fruit

1 cup milk
½ teaspoon vanilla
4 eggs
½ cup sugar

¾ cup whipping cream
⅓ teaspoon salt
3 tablespoons Grand Marnier

Scald milk with vanilla; set aside. Beat eggs till light, then gradually add sugar and cream. Continue beating, gradually adding salt and slightly cooled milk. Transfer sauce to top of double boiler, and cook, stirring constantly, until thick enough to coat a spoon. Remove from heat and stir in Grand Marnier. Chill for 24 hours, then serve over fresh fruit. Keeps one week in refrigerator. Outstanding on fresh blueberries.

Yield: 2 to 2½ cups

PEARS IN CHOCOLATE SABAYON

PEARS:
4 to 6 Bartlett or large pears
3 cups water
1 cup sugar

1 piece lemon peel
1 stick cinnamon (2 inches)

CHOCOLATE SABAYON SAUCE:
3 ounces semi-sweet chocolate
¾ cup prepared coffee
4 tablespoons sugar

8 egg yolks
2 tablespoons cognac

BRANDY WHIPPED CREAM:
1 cup cream, whipped
2 tablespoons very fine sugar
2 tablespoons brandy

PEARS: Peel pears, leaving 1 inch of stem. In wide saucepan, combine and heat water, sugar, lemon peel, and cinnamon stick. When sugar dissolves, add pears, and poach over low heat until tender. Remove from heat and allow pears to cool in syrup. Refrigerate until serving time.
CHOCOLATE SABAYON SAUCE: Combine chocolate and 2 tablespoons of the

coffee in saucepan. Cook over low heat until smooth. In top of double boiler, combine sugar and egg yolks. Add remaining coffee, and whisk until creamy and thick. Do not let sauce come to a boil or it will curdle. Add chocolate mixture. Remove from heat and stir in cognac. Drain pears and place in serving dish. Pour warm sauce over cool pears.

BRANDY WHIPPED CREAM: Beat cream with sugar, and add brandy. Refrigerate until ready to use.

Serves 4 to 6

Variation: Fold Brandy Whipped Cream into chilled Chocolate Sabayon Sauce, or substitute Crème Anglaise (see Index) for the Chocolate Sabayon Sauce, and top pears before serving. When served this way, sauce may be prepared well in advance.

PEACHES AND CREAM DESSERT SOUP

4 to 5 fresh Freestone peaches	Water
½ cup sugar	½ to 1 pint vanilla ice cream or
5 gratings whole nutmeg or ¼	heavy cream, whipped and
teaspoon ground nutmeg	sweetened to taste
Juice of ½ lemon	Fresh mint for garnish

Peel peaches, remove pits, and slice. Place peaches, sugar, nutmeg, and lemon juice in saucepan. Barely cover with water. Bring to a boil and simmer until peaches are tender, about 10 to 15 minutes. Set aside and cool. Purée peaches and about half the liquid in blender. Chill for several hours. Meanwhile, melt vanilla ice cream in refrigerator until it pours easily. Divide peach purée into 6 sherbet or parfait glasses. Pour melted ice cream on top and garnish with sprigs of fresh mint. Serve with crisp thin cookies.

Serves 6

AMARETTO MOUSSE

4 egg whites	2 cups whipping cream
Pinch of salt	½ cup Amaretto
12 tablespoons sugar	Sliced almonds, toasted

Combine egg whites and salt. Beat egg whites. Gradually add 8 tablespoons of the sugar, beating until egg whites are stiff and shiny. Whip cream until stiff. Add remaining 4 tablespoons sugar. Blend in Amaretto. Fold in egg whites and freeze. Top each serving with almonds. This can be frozen in individual cups or ramekins.

Serves 10

EASY COFFEE MOUSSE

1 cup strong coffee (2 teaspoons
    instant coffee in 1 cup boiling
    water)
48 large marshmallows

1 pint heavy cream, whipped
Extra whipped cream and
    toasted slivered almonds *or*
    grated chocolate for garnish

In large saucepan, simmer coffee and marshmallows, stirring constantly, until marshmallows melt. This happens quickly. Cool thoroughly and stir. Fold in whipped cream. Pour into 5-cup ring mold. Chill. Unmold, fill center with additional whipped cream and sprinkle with toasted almonds or grated chocolate.

Serves 8

AMARETTO PIE

1 pound Hershey's Milk Chocolate
    with Almonds Bars
1½ to 3 ounces Amaretto
2½ cups heavy cream, whipped

8-inch graham-cracker or
    chocolate-cookie crust
Chocolate sprinkles for garnish

Melt chocolate in a double boiler. Remove from heat. Pour in Amaretto, and mix. Add ¾ of the whipped cream. Mix well and pour into crust. Chill at least 1 hour. Top with remaining whipped cream and chocolate sprinkles. Serve immediately.

Serves 8 to 9

ANGEL PIE

MERINGUE SHELL:

2 egg whites
⅛ teaspoon salt
⅛ teaspoon cream of tartar

½ cup sugar
½ cup chopped pecans
½ teaspoon vanilla

FILLING:

2 ounces German's sweet
 chocolate *or* 4 ounces Godiva
 chocolate

3 tablespoons water
1 teaspoon vanilla
1 cup whipping cream

SHELL: Preheat oven to 300 degrees F. Combine egg whites, salt, and cream of tartar; beat until foamy. Add sugar 2 tablespoons at a time, beating after each addition. Continue beating until peaks form. Fold in nuts and vanilla. Spoon mixture into a lightly greased 8-inch pie pan. Form into a shell and bake for 50 to 55 minutes. Cool.

FILLING: Melt chocolate in water over low heat, stirring constantly. Cool until mixture thickens. Add vanilla. Whip cream and fold into chocolate. Pour into cooled shell. Chill well before serving.

Serves 6

APPLE CRUMB PIE

6 large tart apples, peeled and
 sliced
9-inch unbaked pie crust
1 cup sugar

1 teaspoon cinnamon
¾ cup flour
⅓ cup butter

Preheat oven to 425 degrees F. Arrange apples in pie crust. Mix ½ cup of the sugar with cinnamon, and sprinkle over apples. Sift remaining ½ cup sugar with flour. Cut in butter until crumbly. Sprinkle over apples. Bake for 10 minutes. Reduce oven temperature to 350 degrees F. and bake for 30 to 40 minutes more.

Serves 6 to 8

CARIBBEAN FUDGE PIE

CRUST:
9-inch unbaked pie crust *or*
    chocolate wafer crust

CHOCOLATE WAFER CRUST:
24 chocolate wafers
¼ cup butter, at room
    temperature
¼ teaspoon cinnamon

FILLING:
¼ cup butter
12 ounces semi-sweet chocolate
¼ cup rum
¾ cup firmly packed brown
    sugar
2 teaspoons instant coffee
    (crystals)

3 eggs
¼ cup flour
1 cup coarsely chopped walnuts
Walnut halves (optional)
Whipped cream for garnish

CRUST: Preheat oven to 375 degrees F. In a blender or food processor, pulverize wafers into fine crumbs. Mix the crumbs, butter, and cinnamon. Press mixture into an ungreased 9-inch pie plate.

FILLING: Combine butter and chocolate in a small saucepan and let them melt together over very low heat. Stir in rum, brown sugar, coffee, eggs, and flour, in that order. The mixture should be smooth. Stir in walnuts. Pour into crust. If desired, decorate the top with walnut halves. Bake for about 25 minutes or until filling is puffed and pastry edge is lightly browned. Cool thoroughly before serving. Serve at room temperature topped with whipped cream.

Serves 6 to 8

CHEESECAKE FATHER SARDUCCI

1 pound ricotta cheese
2 cups sour cream
16 ounces cream cheese
1½ cups sugar
½ cup butter, melted

3 extra-large eggs
3 tablespoons flour
3 tablespoons cornstarch
5 teaspoons vanilla
5 teaspoons fresh lemon juice

Preheat oven to 350 degrees F. Combine ricotta cheese and sour cream in a mixing bowl. Beating slowly, add cream cheese, sugar, and butter. Increase speed to medium and add eggs, flour, cornstarch, vanilla, and lemon juice. Beat on highest speed possible without splattering for 5 more minutes. Pour mixture into a 10-inch springform pan. Bake for 1 hour. Turn heat off and leave in oven with door closed for one more hour. Cool on rack.

Serves 24

EASY CHOCOLATE PIE

½ cup milk
¼ cup butter
1¼ cups sugar
¼ cup cocoa
1 tablespoon flour

Pinch of salt
1 teaspoon vanilla extract
2 eggs
9-inch unbaked pie shell
Whipped cream for garnish

Preheat oven to 350 degrees F. Heat milk and butter together until butter is melted. Mix with sugar, cocoa, flour, salt, and vanilla extract. Then mix in eggs. Pour into pie shell and bake until filling is set, approximately 50 to 60 minutes. Top with whipped cream or vanilla ice cream.

Serves 6 to 8

EILEEN'S BUTTERMILK-COCONUT CREAM PIE

¾ cup soft butter or margarine
1 cup sugar
2 eggs
1 tablespoon flour
1 tablespoon vanilla

1 cup buttermilk
½ cup flaked coconut
9-inch unbaked pie crust, rolled
⅛ inch thick

Preheat oven to 450 degrees F. Cream butter until fluffy. Gradually beat in sugar. Beat in eggs and flour. Add remaining ingredients except pastry, and mix well. Mixture will be curdled. Pour into pie crust and bake for 10 minutes. Reduce heat to 300 degrees F. and bake for 30 minutes longer or until firm. Serve slightly warm or cold.

Serves 6 to 8

DIVINE LIME PIE

MERINGUE SHELL:

4 egg whites
¼ teaspoon cream of tartar
1 cup sugar

FILLING:

4 egg yolks
¼ teaspoon salt
½ cup sugar
⅓ cup fresh lime juice (2 to 3 limes)

1 cup chilled whipping cream
1 tablespoon grated fresh lime peel
Whipped cream and lime peel for garnish

MERINGUE: Preheat oven to 275 degrees F. Generously butter a 9-inch pie plate. In a small mixing bowl, beat egg whites and cream of tartar until foamy. Beat in sugar *very* slowly, 1 tablespoon at a time, until stiff and glossy, about 10 minutes. Pile into pie pan, pushing up around the sides. Bake for 1 hour. Turn off oven, leaving pie in the oven with the door closed for 1 hour. Remove from oven and let cool.

FILLING: Beat egg yolks until light and lemon-colored. Stir in salt, sugar, and lime juice. Cook over medium heat, stirring constantly, until mixture thickens, about 5 minutes. Cool completely. In a chilled bowl, beat cream until stiff. Fold in filling mixture and grated peel. Pile into meringue shell and chill at least 4 hours. Garnish with whipped cream and lime peel twists.

Serves 8

DREAMY HIGH PUMPKIN PIE

1 cup sugar
1 envelope unflavored gelatin
1 teaspoon ground cinnamon
½ teaspoon salt
¼ teaspoon ground nutmeg
3 egg yolks, slightly beaten
¾ cup milk

1 cup cooked or canned pumpkin
3 egg whites
9-inch graham-cracker crust
½ cup whipping cream
½ cup flaked coconut, toasted, for garnish

In a large saucepan, combine ⅔ cup sugar, gelatin, cinnamon, salt, and nutmeg. Combine egg yolks with milk and add to gelatin mixture. Cook, stirring constantly, till mixture thickens slightly. Stir in pumpkin. Chill, stirring often, till mixture mounds slightly. Beat egg whites till soft peaks form. Gradually add remaining sugar, beating to stiff peaks. Fold chilled pumpkin mixture into egg whites. Pile into prepared graham-cracker crust. Chill till firm. To serve, whip cream and spoon dollops in center of pie. Sprinkle with toasted coconut.

Serves 6 to 8

FRESH BLUEBERRY PIE

CRUST:
1½ cups ground graham
   crackers or vanilla wafers
2 tablespoons melted butter

FILLING:
2 pints fresh blueberries
1 jar (8 ounces) currant jelly
2 cups sour cream

Preheat oven to 350 degrees F. Mix together crumbs and butter. Press into a 9-inch pie plate and bake for 8 minutes. Cool. Place berries in pie crust, reserving a few large ones for garnish. Melt jelly and pour over berries. Top with sour cream and garnish with a few large berries. Chill.

Serves 6 to 8

FRESH STRAWBERRY PIE

1 cup sugar
3 tablespoons cornstarch
1 quart fresh strawberries
½ cup water

2 teaspoons lemon juice
9-inch baked pie shell
Whipped cream

Mix sugar, cornstarch, ½ cup of the strawberries, crushed, water, and lemon juice in a saucepan. Cook until thickened, and chill. Fill cooled pie shell with remaining strawberries, halved, and cover with cooked mixture. Top with whipped cream. Chill.

Serves 6 to 8

FROZEN BRANDY ALEXANDER PIE

1 can (14 ounces) sweetened
    condensed milk
1 cup whipping cream, whipped
2 tablespoons crème de cacao

2 tablespoons brandy
9-inch graham cracker crumb
    crust
Shaved chocolate for garnish

In a large bowl, combine sweetened condensed milk, whipped cream, crème de cacao, and brandy. Pour into crust. Freeze for at least 6 to 8 hours. Garnish with shaved chocolate. Serve on a chilled plate. Keep the leftovers in the freezer.

Serves 8

FROZEN RASPBERRY-ALMOMD TORTE

ALMOND PASTRY:
¼ cup unsalted butter
¼ teaspoon salt
2 tablespoons sugar

1 egg yolk
¾ cup sifted flour
¼ cup finely chopped almonds

RASPBERRY FILLING:
10 ounces frozen raspberries
1 cup sugar
2 egg whites, at room
    temperature
1 tablespoon lemon juice

Dash of salt
1 cup heavy cream, whipped
½ teaspoon almond extract
Fresh mint for garnish

PASTRY: Preheat oven to 400 degrees F. Cream butter, salt, and sugar until light and fluffy. Add egg yolk and beat. Stir in flour and almonds to make firm dough. Press into buttered 9-inch springform pan and chill for 30 minutes. Bake for 10 to 15 minutes. Cool.

FILLING: Thaw raspberries. Set aside a few for garnish. Combine remaining raspberries, sugar, egg whites, lemon juice, and salt. Beat for 15 minutes or until stiff. Fold in whipped cream and almond extract. Mound on top of almond pastry and freeze until firm. Garnish with raspberries and a sprig of mint. Remove from freezer 10 minutes before serving.

Serves 12

NO-FAIL PIE CRUST

2 cups flour
1½ teaspoons salt

1 cup Crisco
4 tablespoons ice water

Preheat oven to 425 degrees F. Stir flour and salt together. Blend in Crisco with hands. Mix ice water in well with a pastry blender or fork, remembering that too much handling from this point on can toughen the pastry. If the dough is sticky, chill for a few minutes. Divide dough into 2 balls. Roll out on wax paper or pastry sheet. Pat it out a little to begin the flattening. Roll into a thin crust, flouring the rolling pin often. Press into two 9-inch pie tins. Bake for about 30 minutes or fill with your favorite filling and bake according to pie directions.

Yield: Two 9-inch pie crusts

PECAN TARTS

PASTRY:

1 cup butter or margarine
2 packages (3 ounces each) cream cheese

2½ cups unsifted flour
½ teaspoon salt

FILLING:

1½ cups chopped pecans
1 cup brown sugar, firmly packed
½ cup light corn syrup

2 eggs, slightly beaten
2 tablespoons butter, melted
¼ teaspoon salt
½ teaspoon vanilla

PASTRY: Soften butter and cream cheese and blend with flour and salt. Shape into a 2- or 2½-inch-diameter roll, wrap in wax paper, and chill overnight. Preheat oven to 350 degrees F. Cut pastry dough into slices and press into 2-inch muffin cups. Do not make rims. If using tiny muffin tins, double amount of pastry.

FILLING: Place half the nuts in lined tins. Using a beater, gradually combine sugar and syrup with eggs. Add butter, salt, and vanilla. Pour into shells. Sprinkle remaining nuts on top. Bake for 20 minutes. Cool.

Yield: Approximately 36 average tarts

PECAN PIE

3 eggs
1 cup white sugar
1 cup white Karo syrup
2 tablespoons melted butter

⅛ teaspoon salt
1 teaspoon vanilla
9-inch pie crust, uncooked
1 cup pecans

Preheat oven to 400 degrees F. Barely beat eggs by hand. Blend in with fork: sugar, Karo syrup, butter, salt, and vanilla. Pour into pie crust. Sprinkle pecans over top. Bake for 15 minutes, then reduce temperature to 350 degrees F. and bake 30 to 35 minutes more.

Serves 6 to 8

RASPBERRY CHEESE PIE

CRUST:
1 box (6¾ ounces) graham
   crackers

⅔ cup sugar
½ cup butter, softened

FILLING:
12 ounces cream cheese, softened
2 eggs
½ cup sugar
½ teaspoon vanilla extract

Dash of cinnamon
2 cups raspberries or 2 packages
   (10 ounces each) frozen
   raspberries, thawed

TOPPING:
2 cups sour cream
3 tablespoons sugar
1 teaspoon vanilla extract

CRUST: Roll graham crackers into fine crumbs. Blend together with sugar and butter. Press mixture firmly and evenly against sides and bottom of a 9-inch pie plate. Refrigerate for at least 1 hour.

FILLING: Preheat oven to 375 degrees F. In a blender, mix cream cheese, eggs, ½ cup sugar, ½ teaspoon vanilla, and a dash of cinnamon. Drain juice from raspberries and fold berries gently into cream-cheese mixture. (Juice may be strained and frozen to reserve for future use as a sauce.) Pour into crust. Bake for 20 to 25 minutes. Cool.

TOPPING: Blend sour cream with sugar and vanilla extract and spread over cooled pie. Return to oven for 5 minutes. This may be made a day in advance and refrigerated. Strawberries or blueberries may be substituted for raspberries.

Serves 6 to 8

PRALINE CHEESECAKE

1 heaping cup graham-cracker crumbs
½ cup butter, melted
¼ cup sugar
3 packages (8 ounces each) cream cheese, at room temperature

1 ¼ cups brown sugar
2 tablespoons flour
3 eggs
1 ½ teaspoons vanilla
½ cup grated pecans

Preheat oven to 350 degrees F. Combine graham-cracker crumbs, butter, and sugar. Press into 8- or 9-inch springform pan. Bake for 10 minutes. Remove crust, and reduce oven temperature to 300 degrees. In a large bowl, beat together cream cheese and brown sugar. Add flour. Add eggs, one at a time, beating after each addition. Add vanilla. Pour into crust and top with pecans. Bake for 45 minutes. Turn off oven and allow cheesecake to remain in oven with door closed for 30 minutes. Cool and refrigerate for 2 hours before serving.

Serves 10 to 12

RENE'S CHESS PIE

1 ¼ cups sugar
½ cup butter, melted
3 well-beaten eggs

1 tablespoon white vinegar
1 teaspoon vanilla
1 unbaked pie shell

Preheat oven to 400 degrees F. Mix all ingredients together and beat well. Pour into uncooked pie shell. Bake for 10 minutes; then reduce temperature to 325 degrees F. Bake about 45 minutes more or until set.

Serves 6 to 8

SOUR CREAM LEMON PIE

1½ cups sugar
¼ cup lemon juice
Finely grated rind of 1 lemon
3 tablespoons cornstarch

1 cup milk
3 eggs, separated
1 cup sour cream
1 baked cooled pie crust

Preheat oven to 350 degrees F. Combine 1 cup of the sugar, lemon juice, grated rind, cornstarch, milk, and egg yolks. Cook over medium heat, stirring constantly, until thick. Let mixture cool completely. When cold, fold in sour cream and pour into cool pie shell. Beat egg whites with remaining ½ cup sugar until they form stiff peaks. Spread over filling and bake for 10 minutes or until top browns.

Serves 6 to 8

COLD KAHLUA SOUFFLÉ

¾ cup sugar
1 cup water
½ cup Kahlua
1 teaspoon instant coffee crystals
2 tablespoons lemon juice
1 envelope plus 2 teaspoons
   gelatin

7 eggs, separated
¾ cup diced, toasted almonds
2 cups whipping cream
½ teaspoon salt
Praline Powder (below)
Chocolate Sauce (below)

In heavy saucepan or double boiler, combine ½ cup of the sugar, water, Kahlua, coffee crystals, lemon juice, gelatin, and egg yolks. Cook over low heat, stirring constantly, until mixture coats a spoon. When thickened, transfer to large dish, cover, and refrigerate. When custard is about the consistency of unbeaten egg whites, stir in almonds. Whip cream and fold into custard. Beat egg whites with remaining sugar and salt until they form straight peaks. Fold into mixture. Prepare 6-cup soufflé dish by fitting with a wax-paper collar that extends 3 inches above rim. Pour in soufflé mixture and smooth top. Refrigerate overnight. Next day, remove collar and gently sprinkle Praline Powder on top and press into sides of soufflé. Serve with Chocolate Sauce.

Serves 12

PRALINE POWDER

1⅓ cups sugar
½ cup water
2 cups unblanched toasted
    almonds

Combine sugar and water, and cook over medium-high heat. Shake pan; do not stir with spoon. When mixture is clear, cover, and raise heat. Boil several minutes. Uncover and continue boiling, swirling pan constantly until mixture turns medium brown. Add almonds and stir until coated. Pour onto greased marble slab or cookie sheet. Set aside for 20 minutes. Break up and grind in food processor or blender.

Yield: 3 cups

CHOCOLATE SAUCE

¾ cup sugar
1 can (5⅓ ounces) evaporated
    milk
2 tablespoons water

3 tablespoons cocoa
¼ teaspoon salt
2 tablespoons butter
1 teaspoon vanilla

Combine all ingredients except butter and vanilla in heavy saucepan. Bring to a boil and continue boiling, stirring constantly, for 4 to 5 minutes. Remove from heat and stir in butter and vanilla. Serve at room temperature.

Yield: 1½ cups

FROZEN CARAMEL SOUFFLÉ

1 bag (9 ounces) small Heath
    bars
24 to 28 caramels
⅓ cup Amaretto or dark rum

½ cup sour cream
8 ounces heavy cream
Powdered sweetened cocoa for
    garnish

Crumble Heath bars in food processor. Line buttered 1½-quart soufflé dish with candy crumbs, reserving some for topping. In a saucepan, heat caramels with Amaretto or rum until melted. Cool to room temperature. Stir in sour cream and heavy cream. Whip until thick. Pour into soufflé dish and freeze. Top with reserved candy crumbs and cocoa and serve.

Serves 6 to 8

THE JUNIOR LEAGUE OF HOUSTON
RECIPE DONORS

Abercrombie, Virginia T.
Adams, Arvin
Adams, Barbara Elliott
Adams, Carol Nash
Adkins, Cynthia Johnson
Aldrich, Elaine Duke
Allen, Melinda Lynnette
Allen, Valerie White
Allison, Julia Dudley
Amonett, Judy Kemp
Anderson, Betsy Johnson
Anderson, Carol Ann Casseb
Arnold, Lucy Gray
Athon, Chris Garrett
Attwell, Toni Cannon
Atwood, Margaret Bachtel

Baber, Dorothy
Bailey, Allison Arnspiger
Bailey, Eleanor Bering
Bainum, Elizabeth Sloan
Baker, Ann McAshan
Bakke, Mary Lee Cottingham
Baldwin, Elizabeth Marsh
Baldwin, Patty Williams
Ballard, Marcia Radke
Barnes, Georganna Allen
Bates, Barbara
Bazelides, Susan Heuer
Beck, Mary Jo Smith
Beck, Nancy Scott
Bell, Elizabeth Chesnut
Bell, Sue Ledbetter
Benner, Karen Diehl
Bergner, Sarah Billups
Bertin, Nancy Sellingsloh
Biehl, Eveline Copley
Biehl, Margaret
Black, Joanie McConnell
Blackbird, Barbara Underwood
Blades, Sarah Gaye
Bocell, Cathy Long
Bonner, Leigh Flowers
Bowman, Margaret McMullen
Boyles, Jane Marie Park
Box, Suzy LaMaster
Braden, Jane White

Braden, Suzanne Schmidt
Bradley, Jenny Dickson
Brelsford, Virginia Gregg
Britt, Barbara Ledbetter
Britt, Robin Burke
Brown, Bonner Sewell
Brown, Cam Glauser
Brown, Diane Stephen
Brown, Donna Temple
Brown, Kathleen Gordon
Brown, Phoebe Reading
Brown, Ruth Kelley
Brown, Sidney Walsh
Brown, Susan Judd
Brown, Virginia Lee
Browning, Patsy Read
Bruns, Catherine Cage
Bryant, Sylvia Smith
Buck, Sharrie Farrar
Burger, Bonny Curry
Burrow, Nancy Allen
Burrow, Patsy McCafferty
Bushong, Shirley Patton

Cahill, Betty Scott
Callery, Caroline Staub
Camp, Margie Greer
Campbell, Beverly Melone
Campbell, Verlyn Miller
Cannon, Maurie Ankenman
Capps, Paula Morgan
Carlson, Joan Pancoast
Carruth, Ethel Greasley
Carter, Catey Van Der Naillen
Cartwright, Janet Carroll
Cassin, Jo Anne Sharman
Cauble, Barbara Bowen
Caudill, Claire Peterson
Chesnut, Susan
Chilton, Barbara Long
Christy, Gloria Parker
Christy, Kathy Clewis
Coates, Nancy Wright
Cobb, Nancy Hale
Cochran, Betty Lea Walker
Collie, Barbara Miller

Connely, Margaret Deuel
Conner, Sarah Gaye Blades
Corbet, June Mings
Covens, Marilee Winerich
Craig, Alice Picton
Crain, Jenny Adams
Crittenden, Betty Lou Lamaster
Crosswell, Emily Attwell
Crowe, Leigh
Cullinan, Claire Alexander
Cunningham, Georganne Rose
Currie, Dorothy Peek
Cutherell, Suzanne Sailer

Dabney, Elizabeth
Dalton, Terry Park
Daniel, Cecille Carnes
Darby, Charlotte Williams
Davis, Barbara Sterrett
Davis, Elizabeth Brown
Davis, Janet Houston
Davis, Renee Shockley
DeFoy, Susan Bann
Dehan, Carol Lovelady
Dennis, Miriam McGaw
Detering, Phyllis Childs
DiBona, Ina Fleishel
Dilg, Susie Gregg
Dilworth, Susan Strake
Doherty, Betty Finnegan
Doherty, Chrissy Knight
Doherty, Jan Fosdick
Doland, Cheryl Grimm
Duncan, M. Christine Ivers
Dundas, Barbara Bering
Dunn, Ione Vega

Earl, Sally Barnes
Eastland, Anne Stacy
Edwards, Karen Kimball
Ellingson, Louise Pincoffs
Elliott, Elizabeth Safford
Emerson, Ann Craddock
Emerson, Martha Vinson
Erwin, Louise Ewing
Estes, Gay Gooch
Etheridge, Carolyn Smith
Evans, Nancy Campbell
Ewing, Charlotte Kelty

Faubion, Dorothea Varisco
Fay, Homoiselle Haden
Fay, Sidney Hawkins
Ferguson, Charlotte Barkley
Ferguson, Dorothy Smith
Ferguson, Mitzi Riddle

Finch, Betty Grey
Fitzpatrick, Cathy Fosdick
Floyd, Lucy Saunders
Ford, Jane Stroud
Fox, Anne B.
Frost, Lucy Goodrich

Gillean, Prissy Rogers
Gillette, Virginia "Delph" Anderson
Gillman, Linda Bowman
Golemon, Elizabeth Perkins
Goodloe, Jan Davenport
Goodman, Ann Catlett
Gordon, Diane Asbury
Greenlee, Lucinda Arnold
Greer, Jan Havens
Gregg, Edwina Breihan
Gregg, Judy Anderson
Gregg, Katharine Parker
Gregg, Marilyn Morris
Grella, Kathy Riggs
Grima, Chlotille Cole
Grinstead, Linda Rowe
Gross, Bonita Blankenburg
Guerriero, Margaret White
Gunn, Ann Marie Johnson
Gunter, deSha Norwood
Gustafson, Barbara Birdsey

Hadlock, Lana Lowry
Hagerty, Veronica Henahan
Hale, Patricia Compton
Hall, Dorris Collie
Hall, Mary Lou Watkins
Hamilton, Carolyn Burton
Hancock, Julia Hartman
Hancock, Mary Wood
Hannah, Catherine Coburn
Hannah, Kenzie Ganchan
Harper, Nancy Nash
Harrington, Anne Lawhon
Harris, Julie Dunbar St Paul
Harrison, Georga Finley
Harrison, Sally Ann Judd
Harrison, Sylvia Norsworthy
Hart, Lois Young
Hawkins, Elizabeth Bixby
Hayes, Lib Young
Hedges, Kay Sealy
Heiskell, Linda Yadon
Henderson, Elizabeth Keenan
Henderson, Minifred Smith
Henry, Janis Frank
Heyne, Marie Flack
Heywood, Jennifer Wynn
Higley, Laura Carter
Hilliard, Lydia Caffery

Hochner, Carroll Robertson
Hodges, Julia Burnam
Hogan, Mary Burke
Hohl, Carolyn Knapp
Holcomb, Mary Carol Crump
Holland, Antha Adkins
Holland, Nancy Stroup
Holmes, Carolyn Russell
Holmes, Dianne Dwyer
Holstead, Marilyn Morris
Horton, Charlotte Wood
Hoy, Gail Cole
Huge, Martha Anderson
Hughes, Jane Broome
Hughs, Edith Leavens
Hunt, Cathy Swengel
Hurgeton, Virginia Williams
Hurt, Patty Parrish
Hutmacher, Rietta Adkins

Ingraham, Jeanne Bel

Jackson, Sarah Faulkner
Jarrard, Isabel Mackenzie
Jenkins, Margie Wilmore
Johnson, Jane Perrin
Jones, Audrey Thompson
Jones, Molly Milligan
Josey, Elizabeth Traylor
Josey, Susan Fowler
Judd, Sallie Matthews
Justice, Sandra Dunnam

Kahle, Cynthia Vietor
Keeland, Margie Scott
Keenan, Carolyn Frost
Keenan, Virginia Meek
Kelsey, Mary Margaret Wier
Kempner, Sharon Miller
Kerr, Mimi Hackney
Kerth, Judy Delay
Ketchum, Ellen P.
Kiersted, Janet Tarbox
King, Ellen Carrington
Kirksey, Margaret M.
Kirk, Karol
Kirkland, Lois Cleveland
Kletke, Elizabeth Millice
Knolle, Marilyn Flaitz
Knox, Karen Hays
Kobb, Carol Settegast
Koelsch, Francita Stuart
Krusen, Jessie Thompson
Kyger, Mary K. Pederson

Lake, Fredrica Lanford
LaRoche, Katherine Cottingham
Laughlin, Fanelle Logue

Lawhon, Elaine Seewald
Lawhon, Susan Light
Lawhon, Virginia Vinson
Lawson, Virginia Cronin
Layton, Elsie Landram
Leaton, Nancy Eastland
Lee, Carter Kerr
Lehman, Sara Borroum
Leslie, Susan Moore
Lewis, Cornelia Fitzgerald
Liddell, Lise Putnam
Lidstrom, Judith Martin
Liedtke, Laura J.
Ligon, Mossy Pollok
Lindsey, Sara Houstoun
Lloyd, Robin Hill
Loeffler, Margo Meynier
Lombardo, Karen Elizabeth
Lord, Katharine Clark
Luckett, Evelyn Sanford
Lum, Patricia Perry
Luther, Pat Dayvault
Lybrand, Becky Bradley

McCament, Margaret Lester
McCann, Anne McCullough
McCarty, Mary Powers
McClung, Jeanne Sable
McCollum, Sally Wall
McCorquodale, Robin Hunt
McCulloch, Ann Knickerbocker
McDonough, Nancy A.
McDougal, Janie Grant
McFall, Donna Binion
McFarland, Virginia Holt
McGlasson, Ellen Archer
McGurl, Mary Martin
McHenry, Molly Macon
McHenry, Sandra Lovin
McKay, Emily Ann Finch
McKeithan, Mary Ann Smith
McKnight, Ann Vaughan
McLaggan, Paula Lowery
McLeod, Donna Dwelle
McMurrey, Sue Henderson
McNearney, Sharon Parsley

Macharg, Laurie C.
Maddox, Donna Gray
Maddox, Donna Magill
Maer, Martha Bell
Mahoney, Rebecca Scott
Malone, Catherine Carter
Manuel, Christian Inkley
Markland, Elizabeth Bonnet
Marston, Graeme Meyers
Martin, Anne Layman

Martin, Helen Holmes
Masterson, Constant Taylor
Mayfield, Susan Ray
Meredith, Mary Wilkins
Meyer, Rosemary McKinney
Meyer, Susu Zimmerman
Meyers, Alice Jones
Miller, Dale Porter
Miller, Margaret T.
Mischer, Leila Winters
Monroe, Rhue McCullough
Monteith, Mary Frances Dorrance
Montgomery, Elizabeth Black
Moore, Betty Kyle Walker
Moore, Joan Lewis
Moreland, Jane Philp
Morgan, Nancy Bowne
Morrison, Linda Larkin
Morrison, Sandy Foster
Moses, Jeanne Wehmeyer
Mosle, Eleanor Thompson
Mount, Carol Shanks
Munger, Kathleen Dies
Murphy, Linda Lackey

Neath, Virginia Richards
Nelson, Marjorie Shepherd
Neuhaus, Lindy Wyatt-Brown
Niblack, Eleanor Allen

Oaks, Susan Gresham
O'Connell, Laurie Salvatori
Ogilvie, Beverly Means

Paddock, Carol Ann Weber
Paddock, Lenita Davis
Parker, Hilma Sandegard
Parsley, Louise Bayless
Parsley, Sarah Bertron
Patton, Anne Berry
Pengra, Francey Hawkins
Peterson, Nancy Cogburn
Pinckard, Jane Burton
Pitts, Allan Greenwood
Plumb, Susan Cooley
Phillips, Betsy Bowen
Pressler, Maxine Blalack
Price, Sue Harrington
Prim, Judy Rust
Protzmann, Sharon Laessig
Pruden, Nancy Paris
Purcell, Ann Herron

Quirke, Georgene Adams

Reading, Agnes Pearson
Redinbo, Gay Caffey
Reed, Valma Vernoy

Reese, Maggi Kenyon
Reeves, Ebby Davis
Register, Elizabeth Halsey
Reichert, Betsy Calhoun
Renaudin, Genie Atmar
Rice, Ann Townes
Ricker, Lori Ann
Ritch, Nancy Smith
Roach, Holly Goldenberg
Roady, Sarah Jones
Roberts, Lorraine Phillips
Robertson, Barbara Moses
Robinson, Ellen Atwood
Roe, Molly Donohue
Roe, Peggy Ratcliffe
Rogers, Rebecca Brown
Rogers, Sara Bell
Root, Sally Grumman
Rothermel, Jane Lynn
Russell, Lynn Fawcett
Russell, Ruth Arbuckle
Ryan, Margaret Borden "Dede"

Safford, Georgia Howard
Salmonsen, Margo Whitley
Sampson, Frances Bedford
Sanford, Marion Kiser
Santa Maria, Blake Ford
Sautter, Marie Peene
Schall, Belen Wagner
Schwall, Sallie Davis
Scott, Nita Bassett
Scranton, Mary Jane Campbell
Scruggs, Kathryn Trammell
Seal, Joan Mulligan
Searls, Eloise "Pinkie" Pollard
Sells, Sandra Stuart
Shearer, Betty McGee Andrews
Sherwood, Mildred Wood
Shockley, Shirley Doan
Short, Agnes May
Shuart, Elizabeth Chenoweth
Simpson, Betty Eastham
Singleton, Martha Francis
Singleton, Paula Fitzhugh
Sipes, Andrea Murphy
Skelton, Betty Boyd
Smith, Ann Shannon
Smith, Barbara Hartung
Smith, Mary Hannah
Smith, Sally Simmons
Soriero, Jan LaMaster
Spear, Cora Conner
Sponsel, Mary Jane Price
Stabell, Brenda Britt
Stanwood, Missy Turner

Startz, Anthony Long
Staub, Alice York
Stephanow, Margaret Lee Isaacks
Stephenson, Ruth Peters
Stewart, Jane Colhoun
Stewart, Jane Peden
Stotler, Nance Fruit
Strange, Ione Monroe
Strong, Elisabeth John
Stroud, Elayne Prados
Stugard, B Jo Oberklein
Sweet, Carol Monek
Sykes, Mary Stern

Taylor, Anne Finch
Taylor, Carol Jordan
Taylor, Marilyn Dubach
Taylor, Patricia Reckling
Taylor, Susan F.
Tellepsen, June Learned
Temple, Jody Boddy
Tenney, Joan Woodruff
Thomas, Julie Gragg
Thomas, Katherine Sloan
Thomas, Shelly Nowlin
Thompson, Katharine Park
Thomson, Ray Taggart
Thornton, Ramona Meyers
Thurman, Judy Ross
Thurmond, Julie Head
Tomlin, Kate Thornberry
Trammell, Ann Gordon
Trick, Jane Dean
Tucker, Anne Peden
Tucker, Susan

Umstattd, Catherine H.
Underwood, Lynda Knapp

Van Der Naillen, Victoria
Vandervoort, Carolyn Eddleman
Vandiver, Bettie Ebaugh
Vaughan, Blake Campbell
Vaughan, Helen McFarland
Vaughn, Susan Westbrook

Walker, Kathryn Kerr
Walker, Madeline Linn
Wallace, Julia Picton
Wallace, Pat Smith
Walne, Laura Margaret
Walsh, Eloise Steele
Walton, Mary Jane
Watson, Priscilla Hess
Wells, Page Thomson
Wells, Sue Browne
Wheeler, Elma Landram
Wheless, Edith Allen
Wheless, Nancy Park
Whinery, Jane E.
White, Margy Hall
White, Sue Stiles
Wilby, Routh Trowbridge
Wilkens, Elizabeth Hartin
Williams, Betty Blalock
Williams, Bobbie Ruth Richardson
Williams, Merle Hendershot
Williams, Nan Luckett
Willingham, Delby Geeseman
Willoughby, Jan
Wilson, Aline Dearing
Wilson, Ruthe Meyer
Winter, Diane Schmidt
Winterman, Eula Goss
Witherspoon, Jan
Witt, Ann Lipscomb
Woodard, Shelby Skidmore
Wooten, Evelyn Wilkey
Worth, Jane Smith
Wozencraft, Shirley Ann Cooper
Wright, Renee Paris
Wyatt-Brown, Mary Shephard Quintard
Wynne, Paula Gay Edwards

Yeakle, Suzanne
Yeoman, Alma Jean Vance
Young, Carolyn Josey
Young, French Anne Pruitt
Yount, Dale Dawson

INDEX